ACTING

AND HOW TO SURVIVE IT

PETER FEENEY

ACTING
AND HOW TO SURVIVE IT

Everything you wanted to know about acting but were too afraid to ask...

PETER FEENEY

TINDER BOX
- PRESS -

PRAISE FOR THIS BOOK

'Acting and How to Survive It' is exactly what Kiwi (and Aussie) actors need as they try to make their way in Show Business. I am going to recommend that all actors, anywhere, read it. It comes from somebody who is a very experienced practitioner, but Peter is also a terrific writer…

Jam packed with all sorts of good advice – stories, anecdotes, tips – it's got everything. After you've read it you've got no excuses in understanding what a demanding and challenging business it is to work in, but you will also come out feeling inspired and full of enthusiasm for the craft of acting. The way Peter attacks things is incredibly useful. There's an enormous amount of common sense and useful suggestions in the book. I think it's one of the most important books written about acting, anywhere.
Peter Hambleton, Actor, on Radio NZ National, 14/12/20

For actors, teachers and directors alike I believe this collection - this wonderful organisation of what you believe is worth working with - is going to be very useful as a checklist of what we might do, should try, or should go back to doing. Your instincts for how to speak to us, how to share your ideas, totally unpretentiously, flow right out of your keyboard, word by word, idea by idea, onto the page.

Many practitioners will be encouraged and just plain grateful to be introduced to, or reminded of, these tried and tested performance ideas, all presented in such a warm, human, truly empathetic voice. You know some shit: those who pick this book up will be better off for it. I am 'buzzing from the wonderfulness,' to quote Stephen Fry.
Alex Murphy, Head of Acting, Mulholland Academy, Amsterdam

PRAISE FOR PETER FEENEY

AS AN ACTOR…

Peter Feeney delivers a colorfully nasty lead villain… a certified Kiwi answer to Bruce Campbell.
Scott Weinberg, EfilmCritic

A wonderfully layered performance by Peter Feeney.
NZ Listener

Peter your passion for your craft and your desire to engage with audiences of all ages is inspiring.
Hilary Beaton, CEO, Downstage Theatre

Peter Feeney's finely judged performance as the klutzy protagonist elicits considerable sympathy… his encounters provide an instructive journey of self-discovery.
NZ Herald

Performing as both an actor and director, Feeney succeeds admirably as the proud mentor, stalwart friend and the disappointed colleague… extremely personable, his character strikes a remarkably genuine note.
Theatreview

WRITER...

He's turned his childhood into an amazingly funny novel - one that will appeal to members of his own generation, as well of those of us who grew up in the fifties and sixties, or even earlier.
Evening Standard

A triumphant debut. It is hilarious from the outset: *Blind Bitter Happiness* became known as the giggle book in my household within a matter of two pages.
NZ Listener

You don't get any better or funnier than this delightful tale ... one of this year's most hilarious novels. I can't wait for a sequel.
Sunday News

AND A TEACHER OF ACTING

Peter is a very gifted actor who will always be genuinely interested in exploring his work and finding new approaches to it, and opening this out to his fellow actors.
Cicely Berry, OBE, Voice Director, Royal Shakespeare Company.

A gifted man with much to contribute to his profession.
Dean Carey, Director, Actors Centre Australia

Peter brings fresh vision to his work coupled with professional wisdom and his inimitable energy.
Miranda Harcourt, Actor, Director, Acting Coach

I so appreciated working with you. You bring a fantastic combination of experience, optimism, hard work and pragmatism to it all, and you're so very good with your fellow actors. Thank you!
Vincent Ward, Film Director

Peter is a gifted teacher and industry professional. I trust him implicitly with our actors for all areas of developing and maintaining their craft. He is extremely accessible, sensitive and caring.
Kathryn Rawlings, Kathryn Rawlings & Associates Agency

Peter gave me not only invaluable tools in terms of theory and practice, but also a professional approach to acting that proved essential when trying to break into Hollywood, plus an ongoing support that I truly appreciate.
Julie Collis

I started attending Peter's classes at a time that I was uninspired and, from day dot, Peter reinvigorated my imagination and confidence through consistent creative technique all packaged in an extortionate amount of knowledge and wit. After a year of classes I had a renewed sense of excitement and commitment and was accepted into *NIDA*. Peter teaches with a depth of patience and intelligence paired with a precise perception of what the individual in front of him needs. I am forever grateful for our time together and continued association.
Olivia Mortimer-Eade

It was Peter who showed me the real essence of what acting is. Not the power of the words you speak, but the space inbetween. The space for reacting and expressing emotion when words just don't cut it. His influence on my acting is what put me on the road to my role in the TV series *Mystic*, and his wisdom opened my eyes to listening not just with my ears, but with my heart.
Antonia Robinson

Published by Tinderbox Press.
New Zealand.
First Edition 2020
Expanded and revised First edition 2021

Copyright © 2020 by Peter Feeney.

All rights reserved.

Peter Feeney asserts the moral right to be identified as the author of this work.

National Library of New Zealand

Softcover ISBN 978-0-473-52511-8

Acting and How to Survive It

by Peter Feeney.

Cover and book design by Nicola Feeney.

Cover photo by Lawrence Smith.

Photo permission Fairfax NZ.

All rights reserved. No part of this publication may be reproduced, stored in a retrieval system or transmitted in any form or by any means, electronic, mechanical, photocopying, recording or otherwise, without the prior written consent of Peter Feeney.

Printed in New Zealand by Benefitz.co.nz.

This book has been printed using sustainably managed stock.

actorslab.co.nz
actorslabstudio@gmail.com

Teaching has forced me to scrutinise the craft of acting far more intensely than I would otherwise just as an actor. Writing this book has meant I've had to dig deeper still, as I've sought a way to understand what makes acting great without deadening the explanation in dogma. Now, as I reach the end of that journey, I understand the debt I owe to my students of the last 20 years or so. Therefore, I dedicate this book to you, those who have capered inside experimental hamster-wheels of my cruel design, suffered my ignorance and misjudgments, leapt unhesitatingly through flaming hoops of artistic fancy and suffered, mostly without complaint, for the benefit of learning. Without watching you perform and figuring out what worked, and what didn't, and why, I could never have written this book.

Thank you.

I salute you.

CONTENTS

INTRODUCTION — 1

PART ONE: CRAFT — 3

CHAPTER 1: The investigative process — 4
CHAPTER 2: Character: the nuts and bolts — 7
CHAPTER 3: Acting boot camp 1: The basic tools — 23
CHAPTER 4: Baring your soul — 47
CHAPTER 5: Acting boot camp 2: Script analysis, the rest — 54
CHAPTER 6: Character: further explorations — 73
CHAPTER 7: Screen acting — 83
CHAPTER 8: Theatre acting — 90
CHAPTER 9: Killer concepts — 94
CHAPTER 10: Technique summary — 105

PART TWO: WORK	**111**
CHAPTER 11: Auditions	112
CHAPTER 12: Self-tests	125
CHAPTER 13: On the job	133
CHAPTER 14: Preparing for a role: actors speak	146
PART THREE: THE HEAD GAME	**167**
CHAPTER 15: Learning and the long game	168
CHAPTER 16: Excitement. Nerves. Doubt. Dread.	179
CHAPTER 17: Failure & the Mighty 1B4	193
PART FOUR: LIVING	**205**
CHAPTER 18: Telling tales	206
CHAPTER 19: A life in acting	213
CHAPTER 20: Exercises, games & group work	234
Appendix 1: On fame – two poems	264
Appendix 2: Scene Group guidelines	265
Appendix 3: Scenes	268
Recommendations for further learning	282
Useful books and resources	283

INTRODUCTION

Creativity in its DNA is riven with chaos and doubt. When you act, you'll probably be great. But you can never know for sure. There's no way to permanently silence our inner critic. There's no foolproof non-narcotic cure for nerves. There's no 'right' way to play each scene or role.

Instead, acting happens in an unkind and wicked environment. There are so many variables that mutate job to job that, no matter how much we yearn for it, no single infallible system can guarantee perfect acting results every time. All actors attack the job differently, and their approach alters job to job too. There are no guarantees in any career and no final destination. There's a reason it's called the *greasy* pole: if you're just holding on, you're already on your way down.

The one constant in acting, as in life, is learning. Whether welcomed or not, the learning never stops. Or at least it shouldn't, because actors are like sharks – if they're not moving, they're in trouble.

Because acting is such a slippery fish I've avoided here the peddling of a one-size-fits-all approach. Rather than trying to peg down a tent in a hurricane, I've gone for flying some beautiful kites. If you're just starting, or mid-career, here's your one-stop-shop: an acting book that aims to be useful rather than straining to be original. You'll find here not a set of commandments, but a helpful guide along every step of your personal learning journey.

This book is made up of four main parts: *Craft*, *Work*, *The Head Game*, and *Living*.

The purpose of the *Craft* section is twofold. If you're building your personal technique, it will impart everything you need to know about the nuts and bolts of acting. I've also included insights to inspire more experienced actors – who will also benefit from revisiting first principles that have been precisely described.

The chapters of the *Craft* section bring together approaches from my own experience and different schools of acting, all under one roof. As I make no claims to exclusive truth I've not had to omit any technique based on attachment to another competing system – or worse, bend it out of shape and rebrand it so it looks new. Instead, I've been a Weka, unashamedly borrowing and adapting shiny acting morsels wherever I could find them.

The *Work* section gives you the insights to make the most of your career opportunities, starting with self-tests and auditions. I share not only my own experience on the job but the know-how of other actors as well.

The Head Game and *Living* sections aim to impart the virtual wisdom needed to survive and thrive in this vocation over the long run. A life as an actor invites a cluster of challenges. These include not just getting but creating work, finding the stamina to stay in the game, building a supportive creative family, marketing yourself and maintaining your faith. Recent research has shone new light on how our operating human software works. In these last two parts of the book you'll find these fresh ideas, alongside my own insights, beaten into a sense that will enlighten and empower you.

The Head Game is about bringing winning psychology to the pressures of performance, with advice on nerves, overcoming your fear of failure, and owning your learning.

You may have the greatest skill in the world, but at some point you have to connect to an audience to have a career. The *Living* section covers the intersection of your art with commerce: understanding who you are and how to best promote your talent, as well as how to manage the setbacks and opportunities you will encounter.

As we go to print the planet is still reeling from the impacts of the Covid-19 pandemic, and New Zealand is emerging tentatively from a lockdown which, ironically, gave me time to finish this book. The full impacts of the pandemic, good and bad, have yet to be revealed. But it's an event that once again throws into sharp relief why we need our story-tellers: to help make sense of our ever-changing world, and remind us of our shared humanity. There's never been a more important time to be an actor.

* Performers, male and female both, are called actors here and, rather than using a male or female third person 'voice' throughout, I've opted for jumping from 'he' to 'she' randomly – and, I hope, about equally.

PART 1

CRAFT

Talents are best nurtured in solitude; character is best formed in the stormy billows of the world.
Johann Wolfgang von Goethe

CHAPTER ONE
THE INVESTIGATIVE PROCESS

Private study is the backbone of any fine actor or actress.
Peter O'Toole

I once read that the great Renaissance artist Michelangelo, before he even picked up hammer and chisel, could already see his subject, the embryonic sculpture, trapped within the marble. All he had to do was release it. But then I subsequently learnt that, in fact, for his every masterpiece there were ten misshapen failures, the bastard children of his genius, hidden away from the starry-eyed patrons who visited his studio. We actors don't have that luxury. We can't hide our unloved performances. Our average films, the terrible opening nights, the TV guest roles we'd rather forget: all are paraded for eternity for the public to see.

It's no wonder then that so many acting books promise the warm assurance of a winning formula. Such a fiction is particularly attractive to actors starting out. The truth is rather less comforting. You can prepare diligently and still fall flat on your face. We crave certainty but it is an illusion. Performing under pressure alongside self-consciousness and difficult feelings *is* the gig.

Yours then is a fresh voyage of discovery into every new role. What you prepare at home is what you bring to the party. New Zealand actor Joel Tobeck said in one of his visits to my Acting Studio: 'Come in with something – anything – and believe in it. Don't worry about getting it right. Commit to it and drive it home.' Your talent lies in your choices; how you have decided to approach this role. You still cannot be entirely sure if it's worth the price of a Netflix subscription or a theatre ticket. But at least you have a basis to begin work. You're now a contributor, ready for as much collaboration, input and direction as time and budget allow.

And, contrary to what you may think, bringing a strong offer makes you *more* directable, not less. It's far easier to move from something tangible to anything else, than from nothing. This is because if you have a tangible

The Investigative Process

choice in hand, it follows that from the process of finding it you considered the many other possibilities that also exist in the script. Said cartoonist Scott Adams: 'Creativity is allowing yourself to make mistakes. Art is knowing which ones to keep.' Your offer is what's left after winnowing out the chaff. It's not a narrowing of possibility. It's the spine of an idea you'll hang your acting on, making your full personality available.

I seem to get an acting lobotomy served alongside my audition sides and this is a not uncommon experience. Broadway director and Emmy award-winning producer Bob Benedetti told me that acting is at its heart anxiety making because it's the actor's job to make order out of the chaos of every new scene and role. We always seem to be starting at ground zero with every fresh script. You're not of course, because you've won a technique: your unique approach, your 'way in.'

But there are many ways 'in' actor to actor – read Chapter 14, *Preparing for a Role*, for proof of that. And any seasoned actor knows that there are no guarantees of outcome. It's why we're such a superstitious lot. Each night before the first day of a new acting job Cate Blanchett has what she calls her '3am moment.' She turns on the light, wakes her husband, and asks him with utter sincerity: 'how do I act again!?'[1]

Sometimes our anxiety can draw us into a ritualistic process when we prepare. We may unimaginatively plonk layer upon layer of work onto the words, methodically applying actions or objectives and given circumstances, trying to insulate ourselves against disaster by striving to 'get it right' in our prep so that in the room we can present some finished masterpiece. But of course, there is no 'right' way to do a scene. It's never 'finished.' There's always another take, more collaboration.[2] That's why we often dislike seeing our work at a premiere or on TV - we can no longer improve on it. Our prep should be like making a cake without a recipe. Our kit bag of acting tools holds all the ingredients we might need. We just don't know what the combination will be until it's baked.

Working actors aren't just talented. Some great actors will insist they're not talented at all. 'I'm a skilled professional actor,' asserts Sir Michael Caine. 'Whether I've any talent is beside the point.' Actors like Caine are driven by the need to learn as much as they can in the time available about their role. They ask the hard questions – of themselves, of their imagination, of

---

[1] Revealed in an interview with Sir Ian McKellen: 'Actors on Actors: Cate Blanchett and Ian McKellen,' Youtube.
[2] If it's not green and growing it's ripe and rotting, my acting teacher Dean Carey used to say.

the director, of their collaborators. They want to go into a scene knowing precisely what they are doing because they know then they can be open to being surprised.

Talent can't be relied upon. Work can - but only the right kind of work, that asks the right kind of questions.

The way our brains make connections and burrow into the characters we play is not logical or predictable. But any meaningful investigation of a role takes time. Honour your work by making the time and space to prepare. Nature abhors a vacuum. Do the work and create the time to do so and inspiration will follow.

We should enjoy acting, otherwise what's the point? On occasion a job can be a real white knuckle ride: your co-star a complete nightmare, everyone screaming while the show goes off the tracks and hurtles towards a cliff. But we owe it to ourselves to find the fun where we can, and we can always do that in our prep; our 'private study,' as Peter O'Toole said in the quote that began this chapter. Research shows that most workers can't manage more than eight hours of quality work in a single day. But for creative jobs, the figure can be just six. Our brains like variety so mix up your prep: do some script work, some online research, watch other actors tackling similar roles on Youtube, do a bit of character work, then accent drills, learn some lines - and so on. Once you've prepared you need to trust it. Acting is not the execution of a minutely detailed plan. It's playing with the energy of the other actor, living in the moment, reacting to what's happening. Better a live sparrow than a stuffed eagle.

You know more than you think. You know how to act. Your instincts are all you have. You just need to know the right questions to ask to bring them to life. Let's get started on that.

CHAPTER TWO
CHARACTER – THE NUTS AND BOLTS

The Lists; Base Character; Status; Imaginative Explorations; Physical Explorations; Research; Getting into Character; Empathetic Imagination

> *An actor's only job is to enter the lives of people who are different from us and let you feel what that feels like.*
> **Meryl Streep**

IS CHARACTER WORK FOR YOU?

It's nerve-wracking to be watched. It shouldn't be. But it is. It's always you up there. But every role you play has not been written specifically for you. The audience doesn't see you. They see your character. Understanding that can free you from self-consciousness and free your acting.

Imagine that here *you* are but over *there*, on the other side of the room, stands your character: an imaginary person. She has your body shape but much else is different. She's wired differently: she thinks, feels, talks - even walks - differently. If you stepped inside her body and wired yourself up to all the neurons in her brain, and the nerve endings in her extremities, how would that feel? What would the world look like through her eyes?

If you can get involved with that made up person as a separate entity, if you can think about what might make them tick, figure out what you have in common with them, empathise with what they're doing - *then* you'll be on your way to creating a character. Creating a character is moving from where you are to where she is, sliding inside her skin and breathing life into her, creating something unique as you do so.

This chapter is full of suggestions about how you might make that journey. Just know that everyone approaches character differently. Some actors kind of haunt their characters until they inhabit them. For his role as 'Bud' White in *LA Confidential* actor Russell Crowe spent weeks dressed in too tight clothing, living in a small apartment to embody Bud's hulking strength. To prepare for what ended up being his swansong role, 'The Joker' in Chris Nolan's *Batman,* the late actor Heath Ledger lived like a hermit for weeks. In his journals, there are pictures of hyenas, clowns and comic strips of Malcolm McDowell's character 'Alex' in Stanley Kubrick's *A Clockwork Orange*. Said Heath of the process: 'I sat around in a hotel room in London for about a month, locked myself away, formed a little diary and experimented with voices – it was important to try to find a somewhat iconic voice and laugh.'[3]

It's also true that 'character work' isn't for everyone. Often we are cast simply because of who we are; because we're similar in some way to the role as written. Great contemporary performers who we may see as 'character' actors, the likes of William H Macy or Bill Nighy, actually disavow character work. David Mamet, the American playwright and director, also argues that there is no such thing as a character. Audiences, he believes, just construct character in their minds out of story, costumes and sets, without the actors having to do anything, except act.

But of course there are also many self-confessed character actors, true chameleons like Brenda Blethyn and Gary Oldman. Today, as pay-TV takes on film, and the star system erodes, we may even be evolving into a new age of the character actor. More than ever before the ability to inhabit different personalities, to play different aspects of ourselves, grows our versatility, and our employability. What sort of career would Matthew McConaughey have enjoyed if he hadn't stepped out of the leading man box in his middle years and embraced character roles?

Studies have shown that actors display different brain activity when in character.[4] But we can be unaware of the character work we do, and therefore unappreciative of it. The truth is that when we act we are *always* in character. The likes of Macy and Nighy, our two prominent character deniers, just remind us not to make too much of it. Once, during an unscripted improvisation, I reacted off the cuff to the question: 'how is the divorce going?' I'm usually pretty relaxed when asked a personal question myself. But on this occasion my character responded very tartly. I hadn't felt that I was deeply in character at all, but there 'he' was. The lesson from this is that it can be a mistake to hold out for a towering transformation of yourself with character work. It's often a small shift from where you live in your head, but a meaningful one.

Start by accepting that, like it or not, you are always in character. Just don't

---

[3] In *Empire* Magazine, November 2007.
[4] Nicola Davis, 'Actors show different brain activity when in character, study finds.' *The Guardian,* Wednesday 13 Mar 2019.

Character – The Nuts And Bolts

hold out for some grand arrival: it's always a work in progress.

There are definite pluses to including character work in your process. As an actor you're going to work occasionally on average material. But when you craft a character, you can always bring a creation of genuine artistry, all of your own. When constructing your character, your choices will be bounded not by the range of your own experiences but by the wider world of your imagination. When performing you instinctively know how to react because you understand how your character would behave in almost any circumstance. You know your character better than anyone in the world.

Unlike Mamet, British theatre director Mike Leigh, who uses character at the heart of his work, considers that the actor's job is *only* character. They should leave everything else to the director and not burden themselves with the weight of the whole story. Certainly, it won't feel so personal if it's your *creation*, not you, being criticised. Direction becomes a delightful opportunity to explore yet another facet of your character.

For all these reasons introducing character to your process can be deeply satisfying. 'The further you get away from yourself,' says Benedict Cumberbatch, 'the more challenging it is. Not to be in your comfort zone is great fun.' Our ability to become someone else is one of the essential functions of story-telling, inspiring audiences by giving them a sense that in their lives transformation is also possible.

The techniques outlined in this chapter are not a 'to do' list; they are just different doors to open. Not all will work for you. And there usually won't be time to do them all. But a little character work is better than none.

THE LISTS

The lists are how you collect the writer's ideas about your character. Writing them out is a labour, no question. As with line actions (we'll get to them in the next chapter), the lists aren't for everyone. But as for all the tools I offer in this book, persevere. Once you have mastered the lists, you can then decide if they are for you. Like panning for acting gold, the lists shake the text through a sieve that reveals shiny details not immediately visible on a first read. They allow us to absorb the writer's full contribution before we add our invention.

Typically, along with your Character Diary (see 'On the Job'), the lists are work you'd do once you are cast. But even for an audition where you don't have the full script, a version of the lists can still be helpful.

The lists are gleaned from multiple readings of the script. Try and write just one list per reading.

You'll be surprised at what you discover. Multiple reads are a tremendous benefit just on their own. We should read and re-read our scripts regularly, even when filming or doing a run of a play. There's much our brains miss, or forget, and more still to discover when we think we know the script inside out. Here are the lists as British theatre director Mike Alfreds describes them:

1. Facts about your character

These are the incontrovertible facts. Write them down as you go along. They'll include physical descriptions, behaviour patterns, biographical details and things your character does e.g. join the army, marry a princess, have nightmares about death. Pay attention to big print (the scene directions) for any relevant information. Your list may be short: accuracy is the key.

2. What your character says about him or herself.
3. What your character says about others.
4. What other people say about your character (and do record who it is that says it).

Write the lines verbatim; don't paraphrase. But do choose the relevant sentences – don't copy out whole speeches if they are full of irrelevant chunks. Include what characters say both to others face to face, and behind their backs. Sometimes the same text may be written down in more than one list. That's fine. Don't interpret or make choices at this stage.

For the lists 3 & 4, you can collate them either in character blocks or chronologically.

A fifth (optional) list is of imagery used by your character. This is a list you need usually only for heightened text where imagery is important, for writers such as Edward Bond, Lorca or Shakespeare. The images that your character employs can give you insight into the character's psychology. For example, in his 'serpents egg' speech, Brutus is describing Julius Caesar. But the pictures he paints with his words tell us more about the dark place he lives at this moment in his head, than Julius Caesar himself.

And so the lists are completed. At the very least you've had the benefit of reading the script numerous times. But you've also likely started to make connections in your head that will have escaped you just from a single read.[5]

FLESHING OUT THE LISTS

If working in a group, read your lists and get feedback from others. An outsider can often see things you might have missed. Let it all stew in your

---

5 There's a great example of how completed lists look in Mike Alfreds' *Different Every Night*, where he does the lists for Masha in Anton Chekhov's *The Seagull*.

subconscious, then write a fast first impression of your character. This might start with something like: 'He's easy-going, likeable, with a mischievous sense of humour. He's young but feels like he's from an older time. He's sensitive to others' opinions…' Avoid value judgements like 'she's a real bitch.' It's hard to play someone you don't like (more on that in Chapter 6).

You now have a starting point: all the information the writer gave you about this character. For guest roles in episodic TV, or for a small role in a play or film, you'll find your lists rather short because the information given is skimpy. This will often be the same for some auditions and tests, at least until the whole script is provided. In any case the next step is to flesh out the facts and information the writer has given you with your imagination.

A spur to your imagination can be to now ask a list of specific questions about your character. This is a bit like doing a solo effort of 'Interviewing the Character' (more on that in Chapter 6 too). Ask any of these questions of your character, built on the bones of Lajos Egri's suggestions in his book 'The Art of Dramatic Writing.'[6] Add more of your own. The answers can be as long, or as brief as you like.

The Physical Facts
1. Fitness/ Health
2. Posture – how does your character stand? Sit? Carry themselves?
3. Appearance – what does your character wear for work? Play? Home?
4. Defects – physical faults, birthmarks, things unseen

Social aspects
1. Class – Upper, middle, lower. Class origin of parents
2. Occupation – the type of work, hours, conditions
3. Education – last level completed
4. Home life as a child – parents and what they did? Description of upbringing. Number of siblings? Position in the family? Their feelings toward parents and siblings. What did their childhood home/s look like?
5. Home life as an adult – does your character have a spouse, partner, children? Relationship to/ feelings about them. Where do they live now?
6. Religion/ race and nationality
7. Place in the community – leader, follower, engaged, reclusive
8. Political affiliations and beliefs – are these similar or different to your character's parents/ peers?
9. Amusements/ hobbies – what does your character do for pleasure or fun?

---

[6] As the title suggests, a (provocative and useful) book for writers published in 1949, and which you'll find to be refreshingly free of formulas.

Psychology

1. *Sex life* – moral standards, fantasy, romance, history, current/ past frequency
2. *Personal motto* – the assumption your character lives by
3. *Personal ambition.* This is similar to super-objective, except more grounded, and your character is consciously aware of it.
4. *Frustrations, regrets, disappointments*
5. *Attitude toward life* – positive, fatalistic, resigned
6. *OCEAN* – what is your character's personality? How do they rate by the following measures: Open/ closed; Conscientiousness; Extrovert/ Introvert – or a bit of both? - Agreeableness; Neuroticism
Note: More on the OCEAN personality test in Chapter 18.
7. *Abilities* – languages, music, other learned skills.
8. *Qualities* – imagination, judgement, poise/ composure
9. *IQ* – street smarts, book smarts, people smarts

If you're time poor (as in, the audition is tomorrow!) or you just prefer to work that way, you can do this work verbally.

A BASE CHARACTER

By this point in your investigation your character may be starting to put you in mind of someone you know. Or you can think of a person who fits *some* of your character's attributes. This person can become a base character. Sometimes it's helpful if this is someone you don't know well: sometimes such intimacy can prevent objectivity. Alternatively, you could take a leaf out of Ian McKellen's acting playbook: he likes to think of a public figure who is like the character he is playing in some way. This reassures him that people like his character do exist. As real-life types like John McEnroe or Donald Trump demonstrate, truth is sometimes stranger than fiction.

Thinking of a real person like this gives you something solid; a justification for their behaviour. Of course, you can just steal some interesting aspect/s of any real person and pull that into your character.[7]

STATUS

The work opportunities we get are often based on how we look. But how we come across depends on how we feel. We may look magisterial in our headshot but walk into the audition room feeling small and nervous. Playing status physically allows us to bridge that gap, making us both look *and* feel

---

[7] I was walking to an audition once and spotted someone on the street whose looping gait was perfect for my character: I copied it immediately.

as the role demands.

Amy Cuddy is a Harvard Business School social psychologist who studies non-verbal behaviour. She has found that if body language reveals where you are at emotionally at any given moment, the opposite can also be true. What we *do* physically can affect how we *feel* and come across.[8] As part of your prep always ask yourself if your character is low or high status, and adjust your physicality to match. Your mindset will follow.

If we are scared and nervous we'll take up as little space as possible, crossing our legs, and slumping, as if we are trying to hide. By contrast, if we feel confident we'll take up more space. But Cuddy's research has also shown that if we behave high status in physical ways, we'll start to *feel* more confident. She has a power pose – arms outstretched, legs apart, taking up as much space as possible – which really does make you feel more confident (try it now). Cuddy's power pose can be helpful, ahead of auditions and performances, to crank up our confidence. But adapting our posture and manner in other ways can also help us play characters who are either more or less confident than how we might feel.

Let's say your character is described as 'self-assured.' However, right now, you may be feeling nervous. If you try and act 'self-assured' while you feel like that, people will see acting: someone who is pretending to look one way while feeling another. We should never underestimate our audience. They can read a lie. On the other hand, if our character is feeling confident they will *also* physically be high-status. And THAT is something we can play. 'High-status people move slowly and talk slowly,' said Michael Caine, in his autobiography, 'because they have no fear of being cut off before they are finished.' In contrast, low-status people talk and move quickly.

The key features of a ***high-status person***, according to Professor Ken Rea, an acting teacher at Guild Hall in the UK, are *economy* and *relaxation*.[9]
The physical traits are as follows:
- Their body is open (not closed) and relaxed, they will take up more space than a low-status person;
- Their head is fairly still and they make eye contact with others;
- They stand with their feet planted firmly, and not too close;
- Their gestures are economical (not cluttered).
- As per Amy Cuddy's work, we can expect that after spending some time playing high status we will not only look confident but will start feeling

---
8 See Cuddy's TED talk *Your Body Language Shapes Who You Are.*
9 His book is called *The Outstanding Actor.*

confident; our thoughts and sentences will be continuous and clear.

The key features of a *low-status person*, Rea tells us, are *clutter* and *tension*. **The physical traits are as follows:**

- Their body is closed, a low-status person will take up less space than a high-status person;
- The head is moved around a fair bit and they blink more often, as well as lose eye contact with others;
- If standing their feet may be shuffling;
- Their gestures are fast and fidgety (not economical).
- In low status, we will start to FEEL less confident, and our sentences will be broken up. It can be difficult to think clearly in low status.

When playing status remember that it is not fixed. It changes depending on who your character is with or the situation they find themselves in. Think of how your own confidence and behaviour alters from an audition room to relaxing with friends, or meeting your boss.

So, even when playing characters who are recognisably low or high status, don't play them as always the *same* status. Status should be played *relationally*. This has the advantage that it tunes you into the other actor/character, enhancing connection. Before the scene decide if you are *higher* or *lower* status. If for example, you have decided that you are higher status than the other character, and they are already high status, you'll have to be even stiller, even more focused, than them.

There's no emotional component to status as such. You can be sad and very much in control of the room, or happy to be low status and not in control of the room at all. A confident person may in certain situations be content with looking small and not being noticed. And status may well change for your character throughout a play, film, episode or series. For example, your character may be a high-status character at work, but lower status with her husband. She may be the same status with her lover.

These status changes can be great signifiers that help you shape a character. Sam Neill plays with status as Inspector Campbell in the TV series *Peaky Blinders*. He's high status with everyone except his boss, Winston Churchill, where he's subservient, almost obsequious. This wonderful choice hints at something rotten at Campbell's core. Another example is Samuel L Jackson in Quentin Tarantino's film *Django Unchained*. He plays Stephen, the butler, a twisted house slave and second in command to the slave plantation owner played by Leonardo DiCaprio. Jackson plays Stephen so low status - bent over, shuffling and cowed – that we can barely recognise the actor when he

Character – The Nuts And Bolts

first appears. But when you see Stephen alone with his slave owner for the first time, the difference is profound. Playing the same status as DiCaprio's character, Jackson is suddenly sleek, still, economical: HUGELY higher status. We realise that Stephen is an equal partner to his owner. His OTT public grovelling is just for show. It is a chilling revelation, and one of the most satisfying artistic moments of the film.

Finally, sometimes the text as written can give you clues to the status of your character. If you see a lot of these *within* their dialogue: – '...' - then the character is interrupting themselves a lot. Their thoughts are broken up. It's a clue to you about their inner state. Read any Woody Allen script – these ellipses are peppered through them. If that's how a character often talks, it tells you something about who they are as a person.

IMAGINATIVE EXPLORATIONS

Here are some explorations to consider while you dig deeper into character. They may well lead to some illuminating and unexpected discoveries.

Your character's profession

Think about your character's job. How might it influence them, or give clues to their personality? If they're a newsreader, watch newsreaders to get a sense of how they behave. If she's a politician, pick one and watch footage of them. If you've seen a performance where you remember an actor nailing a profession in a particular role, look it up and see what you can steal. Think about what your character did earlier in their life that might still have an ongoing effect on them. If he spent a lifetime in the army, would that affect his posture? How would 20 years as a cop or prison guard affect her mindset?

Don't forget that your nurse or builder was a human being long before they had that job. Figure out what their home life is like, what drives them, and what their dreams are. They will be *more* than just what they do for a job.

Your character may enjoy their job. Or not. Harrison Ford, in the original *Bladerunner* movie, decided his character was 'a cop who was good at his job but hated it.' In a nice counter-intuitive choice, New Zealand actor Craig Hall, in Taika Waititi's movie *Boy*, decided that this character, a teacher, wasn't very good at his job. Your character – be she a doctor, a musician, or a gardener - might be the worst or the best in her field. If the latter, think about what you are expert in: what have you mastered?

Look, Music, Era

Some actors are image-based and their starting point is the 'look' of the character and their world. If that's you then find pictures of what your character might wear, what their home might look like, and so on. A search on Google or Pinterest can be helpful. Or you can make a paper collage with your character surrounded by things they own, wear, and obsess about.

Think about how your character would dress, how they do their hair, how much make-up they wear, if they like jewellery, or have tattoos, whether they would wear a hat, and so on. If you've been cast think about all this before your costume and make-up calls so you can make a meaningful contribution.

Similarly, listen to the kind of music your character might like. Give your character a theme song! If the show is contemporary ask yourself: what's my character's favourite tune or rock anthem? What do they listen to when they're sad? What song has a happy memory for them? Why? Have a dance to it. How does it make you feel? If the period is historic also listen to the music of the era. Does it glean any insights into the thinking of people at the time? Baroque composers such as Handel and Bach reassure listeners of the continuity of the existing way of things. The symphonies of later composers such as Mozart and Beethoven open windows to the world, with all the exhilaration and uncertainty that comes with that.

How might the era, country or culture of the character's world be relevant? What were the prevailing opinions, prejudices and beliefs of the time? Would your character have shared them, or swum against the tide?

Running conditions

Running conditions are circumstances of mind or body, permanent or temporary, affecting or afflicting the character: something like an itching leg from an old wound, a haze of depression, or a pain in one part of the body (don't forget how debilitating pain can be, and the dark places it can take a person in their head). If these are mentioned in the script, take them on board. If not, invent a running condition if it helps your characterisation.

Character traits

Character traits are ingrained personality characteristics, such as inordinate shyness or a trigger temper. These can be given to your character by the writer without any great back story or justification. This was the case, for example, with Timothy Olyphant's character in the TV series *Deadwood:* Sheriff Seth Bullock. At the start of Season one creator David Milch told Olyphant that Bullock was angry – but gave no reason as to why. In this circumstance, it might work just to accept the trait as genetic. Or you can work out how to manifest a personality trait physically. A shy person may avoid eye contact, shuffle their feet, and so on.

Which brings us to...

Character – The Nuts And Bolts

PHYSICAL EXPLORATIONS

Manifesting a trait physically works because once we *do* things we start to *feel* things too. Working from the outside in, exploring your character's physicality, behaving and doing as they do, allows us to experience how it feels to *be* them. Here are some physical based options to explore.

Do what your character does

Do what your character does. If they play a sport, or spend time in nature, or listen to heavy metal music – do these things. If your character has a job, then go and do that job, or observe others doing it.

How does your character express their feelings?

What your character feels may well be written into the script. But *how* people express their feelings differs, person to person. A shy, unconfident person may get flushed and raise their voice when angry; a confident person will plain let rip; a smug person may come across as self-righteous. It's the same emotion, but there is scope for a different expression of it, character to character.

What actor and teacher Michael Chekhov called the *Psychological Gesture* allows you to gain an insight into your character's inner emotional world, and therefore how they express feeling. To find the Psychological Gesture think about what your character wants in their life. It might be 'to dominate everyone and everything,' or 'to be loved,' or 'to be protected from hurt and pain.' This is your character's 'Super-objective.'[10] Once you've settled on it, try different physical shapes and movements, all the while whispering your character's super-objective to yourself. You're seeking a whole-body movement that sums up the driving obsession, and with it the inner emotional life, of your character. Once found, doing the movement with commitment lets you feel where your character lives emotionally, opening a window into how they might express feeling.

Body Centre

Like Psychological Gesture, Body Centre is only an idea, but it can be a useful and freeing one. Your character's physical centre, the focus of their energy, could be anywhere: in their hands say, if they are a labourer, or in their head if they are a more cerebral type. It will be lower possibly if they seem to have a heavy energy. Or the centre could be high and light in your body. It could even live within another person your character is obsessed with.

Ask yourself if there is any particular quality to the body centre, in terms of shape, size, weight, colour, temperature and so on. Then, take your character

---

[10] We cover objectives, in all their wonderful forms, in the next chapter.

for a walk, playing with different body centres and types, and see how that changes them. Explore their gait and how they stand with this body centre. It's likely a distinctive walk will emerge from this exercise, so ask yourself: are your character's toes pointed in or out? Is their stride long or short? Fast or slow? Watch how other people walk and carry themselves. Guess what their body centre might be. Try their walk out - and see how weird that makes you feel!

Animal & Mask Work
Animal and mask work are catalysts to freedom, getting us over the resistance of our inhibitions so we can listen to our instincts.

Mask work in acting goes back at least to the days of Classical Greek theatre, but using them for learning is relatively new. In 1913 French theatre director Jacques Copeau first employed them as a way for actors to overcome their self-consciousness and focus on telling the story.

How do masks help us? Well, putting on a mask is an act of concealment. When you do, then look in a mirror, you see a completely different person. The value of mask work is experiencing how free one can be when you truly feel that it's not you up there, but a character at one remove from you.

When actors perform in mask my instruction is to go big or go home. There's plenty of subtlety in mask work, but it can only be found with full commitment. The results are then sometimes extraordinary. The actor's range and with it their sense of freedom and transformational possibility expands. Tellingly, the actor's voice comes to life because in mask they are fully living the scene: bringing the full vitality of their body and spirit to the work. This is our job, after all: to pretend to be someone else, to wear their clothes, walk in their shoes – and feel free.

Not everyone has a set of masks, but they are readily obtainable online, and I would encourage anyone to study further if they were intrigued with them (as I am). In my classes we have a range of masks we use for skill development (we use half masks so the voice is not impaired). Some are traditional Commedia Dell'Arte masks, such as Grottesco, or Strega. Others are of animals – a mouse, or a bird - and others are character types, such as an angry old man, or a happy one.

When you put a mask on, think about who this person is and what experiences may have made them look the way they do. Explore their walk, their mannerisms, and last of all, their voice - all the while returning to watch yourself in the mirror, reinforcing the idea that this really isn't you. Give this character a name if you like and, if others are present, chat to the group in character. Tell us a bit about yourself. Sing us a song! When you come to text, a scene or monologue, imagine that it is *this* person saying the words - not you, but this *other* person, very different from you, whose persona you are inhabiting.

Freeing too is spending time experimenting with different animal types until you settle on one that feels right for your character. In my studio we once had several visits from a trained Bhutoh dancer, Peipei Zhu. We learnt from her the importance of discovering what the *attitude* of your animal is in the wild. It's different, animal to animal. Then, she asked us to imagine what animal the *other* character in the scene might be. When a powerful creature like a lion meets an elephant, another commanding animal, that's going to be a different encounter from when the lion meets dinner (say, an antelope). Creating this parallel animal relationship helps our understanding of the relationship we have with the other characters in the scene and helps with our emotional connection with ourselves and the other characters.

Peipei also taught us the power and focus that comes when that entire animal attitude is conveyed just through the eyes.

Internal Rhythm

When I walk with my wife, she's always a few steps in front. When we go out she's always ready before me. She's a rabbit. I'm a tortoise. I'll relinquish my natural languid energy, but only when I have to - for example, when I sprint for a bus. But of course, not every character I play will have my slow inner pulse. It will be the same for you. We all have a natural rhythm of our own. It may be slow or fast, or somewhere in between. Sometimes your character will have a different energy from you. Simply adjusting the inner speed of your character is sometimes all that's needed to make the dialogue sing.

So ask yourself: is your character's internal rhythm fast and restless, or slow and unhurried? What's their tempo: a slow waltz, or a head-bashing metal anthem? What show are you in? Is it frenetic, like an English farce, or Pinteresque, full of moody pauses? If you're going to play a character from a Noel Coward play, and your own energy is slow, you're going to get notes from the director to 'pace it up.' You could speak faster, but a more authentic way in will be to give your character a racier inner pulse than your own.

Laban

I don't cover Laban in this book because I'm not trained in it. But I do recommend you study it if the opportunity arises. The various 'efforts' and movements can be helpful in finding how your character moves through space, and where they live emotionally in their bodies.

RESEARCH

Research is fundamental, and for some roles it's all you need to do. I spent hours practising knots preparing for the role of sailor John Glennie, in the telemovie *Abandoned*; I coiled and threw a rope into the sea, again and again, to toughen up my skin. I wasn't the greatest sailor when we got on the water by any means, but I felt, and looked, like a competent one.

Research pays off in unexpected ways. Marianne Jean-Baptiste, who played Hortense in the Mike Leigh film *Secrets and Lies*, spent months working at an Optometrist's office. Even though her character is never seen at work, the research helped Jean-Baptiste in a scene where her character meets her birth mother for the first time. It's a highly emotional scene and Hortense falls back on a familiar, robotic question and answer structure, as if her mother was a client – a familiar place her character naturally goes under stress. Watching this, the audience doesn't know exactly what's going on. But they know they are looking at specific and truthful human behaviour.

Ask yourself if there are any abilities, activities or 'business' appropriate to your character that you might usefully study. Some skills - such as handling a weapon, if playing a soldier or a police officer - may be required. Shakespeare's Othello has been a soldier all his life; when he sheaths his sword in Act 1, as scripted, he must do so instinctively, without even glancing at his scabbard – the ingrained and unconscious habit of decades of battle.

But even if not specifically written, skills' mastery may allow you to pick up a mannerism, some kind of clue, which might come in handy. You'd certainly want to practice writing on a blackboard if your character is a teacher from the 1980s. That might be a skill you end up using. You might decide that your teacher is also expert at tossing and catching chalk. All this practice with chalk may glean further insights. These might include how it 'feels' to do this job, to work with your hands, or rub chalk dust on to your pants.

GETTING INTO CHARACTER

It's possible to prep for an audition, get cast, turn up on set and hear 'action!' - having only ever spent an hour as that character; while you were practising the scene. Any additional time you can give to experiencing the world as that other person can only make you more familiar and more comfortable in their skin, and therefore more free in performance. Don't wait until your character work is 'complete' before you allow yourself to do this. In this business you'll never be ready. There's never enough time. So, anytime, say to yourself, 'I'm in character!' And bang, you're there. Or, start walking, as yourself, in a space.

Character – The Nuts And Bolts

Snap your fingers: you are now in character. Pace up your walk slightly when you transition, as if your character was in a bit of a hurry. This helps differentiate *you* from the character. Stand, or sit still, in character. Listen. How does your character respond to what they hear and see?

YOU VS YOUR CHARACTER

Near the end of your character investigation consider two things.

First, how are you *like* the character? There will be a string of facts of course, like race, social class and age, to compare, as well as psychology, behaviour, and personality. You'll have some beliefs and experiences that are just right for this role. It's important to find the commonalities between you and the character you are playing, especially if they are repugnant in some way. You can't play distaste at their behaviour; you need a way in. Ask yourself what you have in common with your character even if, at first glance, you appear different in every respect. 'Acting,' says Meryl Streep, 'is not about being someone different. It's finding the similarity in what is apparently different, then finding myself in there.'

That done, second, consider all the ways you are *different* from your character. Here you may have to do a bit of research and use your imagination to stretch out into some foreign territory. If you haven't been a heroin user for example, but in a scene your character 'shoots up,' then you'll want to find out what need that satisfies, and how it feels. How can you draw a line from such behaviour to something you can relate to?

These sorts of reflections require self-honesty. Plato was credited with saying that 'an unexamined life is not worth living.' Self-knowledge may have to be painfully acquired, but it is hard to imagine being an actor without it. We are all infected to some extent with feelings of disquiet for those who are different from us, what Albert Camus called 'the other:' other races, cultures, choices, lifestyles, or ways of living. Our job as an actor is not to judge but to empathise with every aspect of alien-ness that we find in our character. How else are we to fall in with love them and understand their struggles?

How, for example, could you play a racist, if racial hatred is something you feel entirely foreign to you? Perhaps by digging down to a deeper truth. I've always considered myself free of anti-Semitism. Yet reading New Zealand author Diana Witchel's *Road to Treblinka* I realised that growing up in Auckland in the 1970s my cultural milieu undoubtedly encompassed an unconscious bias against Jews. As a child, if someone was tight with money, it wasn't unusual to hear it said that 'they're being Jewish.' This is something I myself was probably guilty of saying at some point. While nothing to be proud of, recognising the potential for such a casual racism in oneself, might prove the start of a fruitful exploration to its dark heart. If you are rigorous with yourself, if you are honest, you'll find acting gold within yourself.

EMPATHETIC IMAGINATION
'Imagining what it is like to be someone else other than yourself is at the core of our humanity,' says British writer Ian McEwan. 'It is the essence of compassion and it is the beginning of morality.' Taking on a role written for someone who isn't you, who may see the world very differently, forces you to find what it is you have in common with this person. Over time these efforts inevitably grow your powers of empathy. It's one of the greatest incidental benefits I can think of from being an actor.

In our character study, empathetic imagination can allow you to take a leap based on a 'hunch' and turn even just a few scraps of observed knowledge into an understanding of a complex character. Sir Ian McKellen by his own admission very quickly intuited the character of Gandalf in *The Lord of the Rings*. After several days of costume and makeup tests he looked in the mirror, to see Gandalf staring back at him – voice, posture, attitude: all. British actor David Harewood was told by director Jake Mahaffy, that his character in the movie *Free in Deed* wasn't working. 'I did study the real Ray Hemphill…' Harewood later recollected. 'But we had to throw that out and start again.' Harewood had about 30 minutes to come up with a new character. He walked through the wardrobe bus, grabbed a new outfit, shaved his moustache – and he had it. He and the film went on to win awards.[11]

SUMMING UP
Any character work you do will take you down rabbit holes and dead ends. But asking the hard questions has power. Getting it 'wrong' opens doors to seemingly random discoveries later. Time in character, where there's no pressure to be interesting or get things right, is time well spent. When you come to act, the scenes feel less like a stodgy main course, and more like a tasty appetiser: another intriguing opportunity to live in the character's skin.

---

11 'Ask the Filmmakers: Free in Deed star David Harewood and writer-director Jake Mahaffy.' Susannah Bragg McCullough, *Screenprism,* March 14, 2016.

CHAPTER THREE
ACTING BOOT CAMP I – THE BASIC TOOLS

Job Description; Lines; Objectives; Keywording; Scene Actions;
Line Actions

*Life beats down and crushes the soul and
art reminds you that you have one.*
Stella Adler

ACTING: A JOB DESCRIPTION

Homo Sapiens are storytellers. It almost defines us as a species. Stories are entertainment, but we also need them to live good lives. They justify our actions and interpret our lives as a meaningful progress. We listen to stories in all their cultural forms, from water cooler conversations to grand opera to social media gossip, to help us comprehend the world we live in. All stories deal with how the central character manages change, the one constant in our existence. So, they give us virtual experience, a store of wisdom for the lean, mean times which, if they are not upon us now, soon could be in this ever-mutating world.

We actors are also storytellers. Only they're not usually our stories. We serve the ideas of the writer. Their stories pass to the intended recipient, the audience, through us. All those humans scrutinising us are Zen experts in believable behaviour. This is the result of them watching other humans all their lives. Our acting must fool these experts that what they are watching is real. Of course they know what we're doing is made up, but such is our cultural adherence to the importance of story that an audience will willingly suspend disbelief to hear a good one. It's as if they say: 'we'll go along with this dress-up so long as you don't remind us it's not true with bad acting.'

But it's also not enough, whether performing in a Shakespeare play or an ad for McDonald's, to be *just* truthful. We have to also be *intriguing*. We can hardly serve the writer's ideas, be it to hold a ruthless mirror up to nature or sell a burger, if the audience gets bored, leaves the theatre, or flicks to a different channel.

I use the word *intriguing* because I think we can easily feel pressured to be *interesting*. That burden can result in us trying too hard. A good acting technique gets us interested in the other actor, and then we become interesting by default. By contrast, doing too much means leaving no room for the audience to do some work. *And they want to do some work.* They complete the story in the space between you living it and them filling in the blanks: that's when they lean forward in their seats or gasp in recognition. They are finding your work not just truthful - but a little magical.

Our job description then is to honour the ideas of the writer, interpreting their words in a truthful and intriguing manner for the good of our tribe – the audience. If we try too hard to be interesting, if we pile obligation onto ourselves and over-act, we kick the audience out of belief. But we can't play it safe either: that's boring and predictable. We must follow our instincts and embrace the uncertainty that comes with that or our behaviour may appear contrived. We are here to serve, but we must not be servile. We have an important contribution to make.

How are we to be intriguing *and* truthful? That's the purpose of this section. Good acting looks easy *not* because there's no craft in it, but because the craft is invisible. It's your technique that makes acting look easy.

LEARNING THE LINES

Know your damn lines. Know your lines inside and out, to the point at which they become second-hand...
Leonardo DiCaprio[12]

It was only when I began teaching that I understood not only how important fluency with lines is but also, that *how* we learn them is important.

First, we should own up to the fact that forgetting lines is a common anxiety for all actors. One day in Sydney in 1998 I shared a cast camper with the legendary Australian actor Bill Hunter during the filming of *A Difficult Woman*. As we waited he knocked back a beer and told me how he *never* had trouble with his lines. He was then called to set - and fluffed line after line. This is the stuff of all our nightmares. When Bryan Cranston turned up for the first day of rehearsal for a play, post-*Breaking Bad*, he'd prepped exhaustively for his character (American President Lyndon B Johnson). But

---
12 From the *Back Stage* website.

Acting Boot Camp I

he didn't know his lines. Three weeks of sheer horror followed. Cranston learnt the hard way. He'll never turn up to a theatre rehearsal 'on book' again.[13]

The problem, if we are struggling to remember our words, is that they then become *all* that matters, and we are not available to do our job. The work shrinks from the lofty possibilities of art into a ghastly memory test. If we're on set the takes mount. We can feel the crew's patience melting away. We thought we'd learnt them but in the pressure of performance discover that actually our lines are not 'in.' Or at least not sufficiently. When something unexpected occurs we are thrown, lose our line, and can't find our way back. But of course something unexpected is *exactly* what we want to happen. We want our acting to have that spontaneous quality. Director Jordan Windsor, on a visit to my Studio, confessed a common and contradictory desire: that actors know their lines really well, but also be able to sometimes lose them, not drop out, and find their way back into the scene. When things go wrong acting instantly gets interesting. There's a magic in us being lost, in that uncertainty, that mimics life. The actor may be in hell, but their struggle is fascinating to watch.

Writers work from the inside out – they create an entire world before they start to think about dialogue. Actors work from the outside in. Our work has to start with the words because they're all we've got. They hold our clues to character, psychology and motivation. But once we've used the written dialogue to understand and interpret the scene, *we must cast the words aside*. In performance it's the connection between the characters that's interesting; how they're responding to and dealing with each other.

Not only that, we must cast aside the punctuation, the page breaks, all the wrapping that came with the writer's gift, but can creep into the performance in unwanted ways. So, a full stop may command a pause, when in fact we must discover for ourselves where our character's thoughts begin and end. It's possible to even visualise a page break or big print in your head as you act, which can lead to you playing an acting beat there - when there is none.

To do our job – to be able to cast aside the words and the punctuation and take flight – we must be fluent in our lines. Some actors will do next to no prep, turn up to work and run 100% on instinct. But no actor does not learn their lines. It's the most basic and yet the most important work you'll ever do.

How to learn your lines: active recall

Dialogue will sink in as a by-product of your preparation, as you study and

---

[13] You should always have your lines learnt before rehearsal starts. Read the full horror story in Cranston's autobiography *A Life in Parts*.

nut out the script and your character. But often, say for fast turnaround TV or an audition, time is short. You need to get line learning straight away.

For some actors line memorisation leads their learning, providing a structure for them to interpret the scene and the role. The French call rehearsals 'repetition' because they appreciate the value of just getting up and doing it – again and again. Anthony Hopkins goes over his lines 250 times until he's bored with them.[14] Fellow British actor Bill Nighy is another slogger, repeating a line 20 times, then moving to the next, and repeating that 20 times, and going back to the start if he makes a mistake. He takes one to two weeks, six hours a day, to learn a theatre role, depending on its size.

Recent research suggests that more effective than learning by rote, as these actors do, is to instead use *active recall.* Instead of cramming them in, focus on getting the lines out via early testing. So, try this 'closed book' method: read a scene or a page once, then put it down immediately. Recall as many lines as you can, mistakes and all. Go back, re-read, and repeat. You'll get a lot wrong, but you'll also be surprised how many stick. Each time you'll remember more, and you won't be putting time into memorising lines you already know. Instead you can circle the few that are eluding you and focus on them.

Leave longer and longer intervals between testing – a minute, then five, then an hour, a day, and so on. If you can, run the lines alongside a randomised physical activity, something that doesn't have a fixed pattern, but that continually surprises you, like drying and putting away dishes. Then the lines are learnt in your body: by heart, not by head. In the heat of the moment, when you are surprised in performance, you'll be less likely to forget them.

Active recall works so well because the harder your brain has to work to recall something, the better and faster it is retained. The method also makes you search for the words from the get-go, which mirrors how it should be on the day. Your dialogue will be more likely to have an improvisational quality. You'll be less likely to get hung up on getting the lines 'right.'

Another advantage of active recall is that it puts your brain 'off guard,' activating your instincts, dipping you into the power of the unconscious. So, when using active recall, you're more likely to make creative connections within the material than when rote learning.

If audio is your jam, record all the lines in the scene (not just your own, but

---

14 Although it has to be said: this need to repeat may also be a legacy of his dyslexia. 'Interview with Anthony Hopkins: Most of this is nonsense, most of this is a lie,' by Miranda Sawyer, Sat 26 May 2018, *The Guardian.*

do your own without intonation), and listen back, repeating them, hitting the pause button as needed. Listening has the advantage that you can learn your lines any time – walking the dog, sitting on the bus, going for a jog. And by listening to all the lines you are not only learning your dialogue but your cues as well. Your performance needs to come out of the other actor, and it can be helpful to listen to their lines for this reason. Some actors record only their character's lines so that in performance the other actor has to interrupt them. This can aid spontaneity in performance.

You can download an App or use the voice recorder on your phone. Some Apps (for example Script Rehearser) can take your script (if a PDF) and automatically playback the other characters lines to you.

For an audition learn your lines early. Once learnt, if you can, spend a day running the words in your head, no script in sight. Then leave them alone. Don't run them for the day or two before the audition date. Sleep is how they sink in. Spend your time working on the scene if you wish. Then the afternoon before the audition look again at the lines. You'll be surprised to discover: you know them. *You've got this.*

It seems for almost every scene we get to play there's one line that just won't 'go in.' Ask yourself what is the intention, expectation or action behind the line? Rather than obsessing over words look at the function of them as a way to trigger your memory. Then, if you do happen to forget the line you'll still remember what you're doing, and improvise something appropriate.

On the day, whether you've run them twenty or two hundred times, trust that you know the lines. Let go of getting them exactly right and get on with playing the scene. If you get the odd word wrong don't let that throw you. Think of this sports analogy. Let's say you play rugby. The practices are training. When you're playing the actual game you're not thinking about your training. That just got you ready to play the game. Line learning is training. In performance the words are the least important thing. It's you, teetering on the precipice of doing something intriguing that the audience cares about.

Patterning

Now on to a common actor trap: learning the lines in a set intonation, rhythm or pattern. If we do this we can then find it hard to change our performance. We can't play off the other actor, suddenly run with a hunch, or change with direction. We're acting in our own bubble and nothing the other actor does can change it. That isn't as interesting to watch as something that's spontaneous and so has the potential to be unpredictable.

To avoid saying his lines in a set pattern Dustin Hoffman writes them out again and again to learn them: the first time he ever says them aloud is on set. Actor and teacher Michael Chekhov would tell his students to read the script silently as many times as possible, allowing their unconscious the freedom to explore the possibilities within the role. Once they started to add emotion he would caution them to only whisper the lines, not say them.

My early acting mentor Kevin J Wilson would run his lines a dozen different ways, with contrasting intentions or points of concentration. That way he was ready for any kind of accident, or direction. Or, you can learn the lines to a set beat, as if to a metronome, without inflection. Then again - *vive la différence* - Michael Caine recited his lines with feeling every time. He believes that if you run them robotically you may end up performing them like that.[15] If that works for you, and you can avoid falling into a pattern, all good! Learning lines via *active recall* will also help avoid the patterning trap.

It'll take some trial and error, but you'll find your way. Just remember during your prep not to focus on *how* you'll deliver the lines. This must be discovered on the day. And be sure that, however you drill them, you don't get stuck in a pattern that then can't be changed.

Exercises for Patterning

Here are some ways to help avoid getting stuck in a vocal pattern:

- Run the lines while doing some domestic activity. Let the rhythm of that activity affect how the words come out.
- Speak loud, like you were trying to be heard by someone in the next room. This will stop you saying your lines with a particular intonation, but also help you discover some of your character's inner thought processes. Pause and imagine responses being shouted back.
- Read your lines as if dictating a letter. This keeps the words spontaneous – you're thinking of them as you say them, committing to each moment while not knowing what you're going to say next.
- Jump up and down repeating the lines to a set rhythm.
- Sing the lines as in grand opera.
- Move around the room as you drill your lines, making random changes in direction. This can break up any pattern you might risk falling in to. It also helps get the lines in your body.
- Run the lines in an exaggerated foreign accent (one that doesn't stick!)
- Figuring out your LINE ACTIONS (explained later in the chapter) can help you avoid getting stuck in one way of saying any particular line.

---

[15] See his wonderful masterclass for these and other insights of his I have peppered through the book: *Michael Caine Teaches Acting In Film* (1987), https://www.youtube.com/watch?v=bZPLVDwEr7Y.

Acting Boot Camp I

TO ENGAGE YOUR INTUITION: OBJECTIVES
In life most people do not know what they want. But the actor must always know what the character wants.
Michael Chekhov

An objective is the change your character wishes to make *in the other character's eyes*. You can also call an objective an intention, want or need; no one will shoot you. Objectives live in the engine room of drama. In a typical dramatic scene two characters with opposing wants meet and clash. There is a moment of crisis or decision when one character caves in and the other overcomes. This event is the change that moves the story forward. Objectives drive this change and the unfolding of the story.

Objectives are worded thus: 'I want you to [insert here desired outcome – love me/ leave me/ commit to me etc...]' Straight off, therefore, your objective reminds you that you are pretending to be an imaginary person wanting some change in another made-up person. When you repeat your objective just before you go into a scene you are buying into the make-believe of the scene and getting into character *without even knowing it.*

Objectives place importance on the other actor. Our focus becomes on them because we are seeking to influence them. This connection gives us something to concentrate on outside of our self-consciousness. Objectives also help with a big problem for the actor: knowing what happens next.

In our daily lives we don't get the benefit of a rehearsal before a conversation. Ahead of any conversation someone may know roughly what they want to communicate. But they'll have no certainty what will be said, or what the other person might do, or what the outcome might be. We actors have read the script and so, unlike life, we know all that in advance. So, we have to act like we don't know what's going to happen next, and be surprised when it does. Instead, the first thing that can go out the window when we act can be the spontaneous quality of real life. We recite the lines rather than discover them. The words emerge lifeless; dead on arrival. Without knowing it, we play what we know will happen *from the beginning of the scene...*

In class I once worked on a scene from the 1994 film *When a Man Loves a Woman* (you can read the scene in Appendix 3). The actors know the scene ends in their characters breaking up. As well the words are pretty confrontational. So, there's a risk the actors may play the whole scene as an argumentative break-up, sucking up any nuance, and airbrushing out any possible alternative outcome, such as their character wanting to save the relationship. But if the scene is played this way nothing *happens:* from the first utterance of each character *the audience already know* how the scene is going to end. The gig is up. To the audience everything we say will, from the get-go, be thoroughly predictable.

If our goal is to be watchable story-tellers, this approach is a fail. Instead, we want to act *as if* we don't know what will happen next. Then our acting will have the quality of *scripted improvisation*. To achieve this we have to be imaginatively alive to the outcomes in the scene that are unwritten; that might have been or could have happened – but didn't. Objectives do this by allowing you to go after a want or need in the same way, as if you honestly believed you could change the scripted outcome of the scene. It's not enough just to have an objective – you have to imagine its actual realisation for the scene to have life and unpredictability.

Your character's chosen objective is not necessarily the scripted outcome. It might be, IF she gets what she wants. In that case remember: perhaps your character didn't *expect* to get what she wanted. Or, maybe, she was going for something else and failed utterly. In either case you can play around with objectives and expectations in your prep. Did your character get what she wanted, or not? Was this the expected outcome for your character?

Check out the scene from *Memento*, also in Appendix 3. If you are playing Natalie, how can you, the actor, best craft your choices? Think about what the writer has intended and what spin you can make on that. Let's say Natalie's objective is to provoke Leonard to hit her. Does she expect to achieve her objective at the start of the scene? Or to fail? So is she surprised by the outcome at the end, or not?

In the moment all you can ever remember is a single, simply worded, objective. So, find just one objective for each scene. Coming up with a single objective that works for every line you have in the scene forces you to think. That's good because it's our job to ask the hard questions. And in truth, in the heat of the moment, one objective is the most we can consciously remember.

The exception to the single objective rule is if you're working on a play where the acts or sections are very long. You may need to break them down into smaller scenes. As a general rule when a character arrives or leaves, or you have a change of location, you have a new scene.

Make the scene objective fun and exciting, even a bit scary. Make it a spur to action, something that makes you want to jump in and *change* someone. Avoid what the celebrated Broadway casting director and teacher Michael Shurtleff called 'comfort' goals – pallid verbs to describe what you are fighting

Acting Boot Camp I

for like 'I want to be understood,' or 'I want to be liked.' The wording should be active: say 'I want to earn your respect,' not 'I want you to respect me.' Objectives should be simple. If you are trying to get $200 off a person in a scene, that may just be the scene objective. What can ratchet up the drama is the WHY: your character's motivation. This gives you the stakes and hence the *importance*. Give your character something to lose if they DON'T get what they want. The greater the stakes the more important the other actor becomes, which ultimately helps *your* acting.

Take a scene from Spielberg's *Munich* (see Appendix 3). In it, Carl, one of the assassins in the Israeli death squad, wants to convince his colleagues to STOP THE RANDOM KILLING.[16] He specifically wants to limit the deaths to just the targets (scene objective). Why? Because he has seen too much death, including of his son (motivation). Indeed, as the dialogue of the other character's suggests, he may be losing heart in their mission altogether.

Finally, once you've decided on your objective - *commit to it*. After a run, if it doesn't feel right, maybe that's because your chosen objective is the wrong one. Or, maybe, the problem was your commitment to it. Ask yourself, did you only go to 5 or 6 on it? Do you need that to be at a 7 or 8? Don't ever back off from the conflict inherent in any scene. There is always competition: your character wants to win their *objective*. Commit to strong choices and don't be scared to fight your character's corner. The heart of drama is conflict after all, and the clash of objectives highlights the element of competition in the scene. FIGHT for your objective.

Go in to win it.

How to figure out your Scene Objective

The most dependable way of figuring out the objective is to ask 'if my character were writing the scene what would they have the other character say and do at the end?' Whatever that is: that's your objective; the outcome your character wants. It must be measurable in the other actor: what it is you want the other actor to say or do, the look you want to see on their face, the change you want to make *in their eyes*. The change you want must be *to them*. Otherwise the objective fails in that major function, to make the other actor important and reinforce connection. The interesting space in any performance is not in you: it is the connection between you and the other actor.

Read the scene and think. Don't agonise; if you've got a workable objective, jump up and do it. It may well be a mess, but the run will likely reveal

---

16 In a multiple character scene choosing one person you are trying to convince can work better as it is more specific.

something - most likely a better objective! If you're stuck, just start with one you know is wrong. Run the scene with it, and chances are you'll be closer to figuring out what you're actually going for. As director Jonathan Brough once told me - a wrong objective is more helpful than none at all.

If you're unsure, read the scene and look at your character's emotional journey. Remember that you don't always achieve your objective. Broadly, if your character gets what she wants, she may well feel better at the end of the scene; if she doesn't, she'll likely feel worse. The exception to this is if there is a significant cost to your character getting what they want. But, generally, looking at the emotional shift in the scene will help you figure out what it is your character is going for. This reflection can also help you justify the emotional change you have to play.

The totem pole of Objectives

There is a hierarchy of objectives. Reading about these now may get you a bit stuck in your head. Bear with. One of the aims of this book is to make you aware of a conscious technique. This gives you the ability to not just act well but also name your choices, have a degree of control over them and be able to collaborate more effectively.

At the top of the totem pole is the *super-objective*. This is the character's central aim in life; their obsession. It exists before and after the time scale of the play or film. For example, your character might want to dominate others, or hide from the world, or be loved. Defining character, the super-objective psychologically motivates the *overall-objective* for your character for the whole film/ play. This is plot-driven; it's what your character wants. The overall objective is also sometimes called the *through-line*.

Your *counter-objective* exists on the same plane as the *super-objective* but is in opposition to it, creating a conflict within the character. Almost as strong as the *super-objective*, it is also character-driven.

Finally, there is your *scene-objective*. This is what the character wants from scene to scene. Each will further her *overall-objective*.

The interplay of your *super and counter-objectives* can set up some interesting dynamics. In the words of the Rolling Stones: 'you can't always get what you want, sometimes you just might find, you get what you need.' So the *counter-objective* can be understood as how your character is sabotaging herself, if the *counter-objective* is what she *really* needs (the *counter-objective* is often unconscious, or unknown to them).

Sometimes the *super-objective* is counter-intuitive. Let's say that the character needs love (*super-objective*) even though they're pushing people away. This may be because of a character trait, which can be expressed as a *counter-objective*, to 'stay safe,' in a world the character perceives to be a dangerous place.

As your *super-objective* conflicts with your overall or *counter-objective* then if your character gets what she wants that may cost her something. As the concept of *opposites* tells us, the same logic should apply in every scene you play. (Opposites are discussed in Chapter Five). There's usually something in opposition to what you want, that you want almost as much, so that every change, even positive ones, costs us something. That's human, isn't it? It's also interesting to watch.

Let's look at an example of this interplay. If you can, read the screen-play *The Limey*, made into a film starring Terence Stamp. The overall objective of the lead character, Wilson (played by Stamp) is to avenge the death of his daughter, Jenny. His *Super-objective* might be something like 'to right the wrongs in the world,' because directly after dealing with the 'Jenny' business he's off to wreak revenge on those responsible for his recent nine years in the slammer.

Anywho. In the climactic scene (included in Appendix 3) Wilson is about to dispatch the bad guy. This is Valentine, his daughter's ex, played by Peter Fonda. But just then Wilson learns something important. By this point we already know that Jenny abhorred her father's criminal lifestyle. When Wilson was contemplating his last 'job' she'd told him she would never want to see him again if he did it. And now Wilson discovers that Valentine murdered Jenny because she had said the same thing to him: she'd asked Valentine to choose between her, or the 'deal.'

In that moment of the scene something shifts for Wilson. He doesn't kill Valentine as we expect. He flips to his *counter-objective*, something like, 'to make meaning of my daughter's tragic death.' When this becomes his motive, it overrides the object of killing Valentine and avenging Jenny's death. To kill Valentine was a simpler choice, but there's a powerful resonance for the audience as his hand is forced and he accepts the harder truth of his *counter-objective*. Not killing Valentine costs Wilson something: he has to accept the part he himself played in his daughter's death.

This may strike you as an overly complicated unpacking of the scene. Terence Stamp, playing the role of Wilson, may well not have comprehended the scene this way. It's clear in the writing that there's a shift, but what tools and terms an actor chooses to interpret that is their business.

In this scene Wilson fails, because of the unexpected moment of revelation, to win his scene objective, which is to kill Valentine. But note that while your character may 'lose' the scene and not get what they want, they never just 'give up.' Wilson's desire to kill Valentine should still be alive right to the end of the scene and beyond. It doesn't go away, it's just superseded by events.

So, if you are scripted to 'lose' a scene but then read through to the end of the script you may well see that your character DID affect a story change in some way. The change may come later, but it does come. In any case, your character darn well didn't give up on wanting to affect a change. It's far more interesting if you keep an objective alive to the end of the scene. Otherwise you risk playing a victim.

EXERCISES FOR OBJECTIVES
For highlighting competition
Actors can sometimes step back from the competition, the clash of objectives, that is at the heart of drama. These exercises remind actors of the importance of conflict in a scene.

Tick To Win
Cicely Berry, the Royal Shakespeare Voice coach, taught me this exercise. It's a wonderful leap out of naturalistic acting and for this reason actors can find it challenging. But they also love what it brings, namely an exorcism of niceness that highlights the cruelty of the characters. This is often needed in comedy, where characters tend to be tough, and for the dialogue to work, the actors must be unafraid to be nasty – think of the delicious robustness of characters in Noel Coward and Oscar Wilde plays. As well as highlighting the competitiveness in the scene, a sense of play is drawn into the acting.

Throw out the blocking (the physical moves) and just place the actors behind a table with a piece of paper and pen. Then run the scene, but with the following instructions:

At any time, either character should give themselves a tick under their character's name if they feel that they have won a point. They have to work their hardest to extract any advantage they can; not just on their own lines but with their reactions - even if their brave attempt ends in dismal failure. *Your character must want and try to win* all the time with every atom of their body in every beat of the scene.

As well, your character must want to win the audience over to their side. At all times I ask the actors to acknowledge us, the crowd: the fourth wall is gone. Every time their character wins a point I want them to celebrate this with the crowd, much like a tennis champion might. Equally, if the other character 'wins' a tick and they 'lose' a point I want them to feel the shame from the watching audience and express this truthfully. Each tick has to mean something, either way. I also encourage watching actors to be vocal in their support or barracking.

The actors should not be too generous with scoring themselves points – they must earn them. They mustn't be too miserly either, or nothing happens.

At the end of the scene we tally up the ticks. If both actors have done their best the tally will often tell us who is intended to win the scene as written.

Again, as with all text-based exercises, afterwards it's a good idea to run the scene one more time to bed in the work.

I'm right, you're wrong

This is a simple brain switch you can do on your own. Michael Shurtleff says actors should imbue every scene they play with two ideas: (1) I am right and you are wrong, and I'm going to prove you wrong; and (2) You should change from being the way you are to be what I think you should be. So: figure out what it is your character is going for, what they are right about, then run the scene for this. Again it will highlight the competition. Sometimes just *playing* that your character is *right* about everything they say and do can be powerful.

Change the ending

If the actors are playing the end of the scene from the get-go – in other words, predictably - change the written outcome. So, for a run, if your character as written DID achieve their objective, re-write the ending to make it that they DON'T; and vice versa. When you rewrite you'll need to identify the moment of decision/ winning/ losing and get the relevant actor to make their alternative choice in that moment. In the scene we discussed earlier – *When a man loves a Woman* – this moment will be around when Michael announces he's going to pack his bags. Instead he might decide to stay.

When the actors come back to play the scene as written, the work will have been injected with a degree of spontaneity as they have lived its alternate outcome.

Play the wrong objective

This exercise gives a hint at the power of playing *opposites*, which we'll get to soon. Run the scene working hard to win an objective which is the opposite of what you want in the scene.

When actors do this they get a feel for how changing the objective changes the playing. On the odd occasion we even discover, to our surprise, that the opposite works better than our original choice of objective.

Once actors in my classes change the objective around like this a few times they realise what a useful tool objectives can be: the choices they make do make a difference. They also lose their preciousness about getting the objective exactly right.

KEYWORDING FOR UNDERSTANDING
Less is more; content dictates form; God is in the details; clarity is everything.
Stephen Sondheim, Broadway Musicals master[17]

At the simplest level of the scene, we need to understand what our character is saying and why. A way into this is a technique called Keywording. Circle one word in every line or phrase of your dialogue, the word that strikes you as the most important. You can't emphasise every word you say. You have to choose. Which word you choose alters meaning.

If it's not obvious which word in the sentence is the most important, sound out every word, emphasising it and trying to make sense of the sentence as you do. The best interpretation of the line becomes clear. Another way is to say the sentence over and over, removing a different word each time. The reading that makes the *least* sense will tell you that the word you have omitted is the most important.

Sometimes when I'm listening to a scene or monologue in class the words seem predictable; somehow dead on arrival. This is reportage; the actor telling us something they already know rather than discovering their thoughts through the act of speaking. Sometimes stiffening up the objective will work this away. Keywording can also help make the words fresh, like the character was figuring them out in the moment, not reciting them. So too does 'The game of arrows' (see below).

When you come to perform you don't have to stress the words that you have highlighted. The exercise is for your understanding. But if you want to view a performance where the actor concerned uses this technique and does stress the keywords, watch Rosemary Harris as May Parker in the 2002 film *Spiderman*. She stresses a particular word every phrase and it works, giving her character a dogged, emphatic, everyday quality.

KEYWORDING, REACTING & THE GAME OF ARROWS
Listening is not merely hearing, it is receiving the message that is being sent to you.

---

17 'If the audience understands it, and they don't like it, fine. But if they don't understand it, you have no chance of making them like it.' *Still cutting it at 80: Stephen Sondheim interview*, by Mick Brown in *The Telegraph*, 27 Sep 2010.

Acting Boot Camp I

Listening is reacting. Listening is being affected by what you hear. Listening is letting it land before you react. Listening is letting your reaction make a difference. Listening is active.
Michael Shurtleff

Listening when we're acting is such a gift to us. It's almost all the work we need to do: not to act but to truly listen to the other character and respond to that. When we do we are taking that risk of being in the moment; of our acting being unplanned. But to truly listen you have to know what you are listening for. Listening in acting isn't only reacting just before you speak. Active listening is having responses triggered in us and wanting to interrupt, but having to wait. It's silently stepping on the other character's toes all the time.

Now let's approach keywording from the other end: what words the other character/s in the scene are saying that are the most important to our character, that elicit our responses and reactions, spoken and unspoken. *Understand that you are not an actor. You are a reactor.* Our character only says or does something because we are forced to respond by the other character/s. To do that we need to figure out where our impulse to speak came from – whereabouts in the script it is that the other character does or says something that kicks off our reaction. 'The words should always cost you something,' was a favourite adage of Cicely Berry. And the words will always cost you something if you are *forced* to speak.

Working with New Zealand actor Jennifer Ward-Lealand on the film *Vermilion* she spoke of the places in our scene where her reactions and thoughts originated as 'lightbulb' moments. These moments weren't at all passive. Once the lightbulb went off, she immediately went to speak. In one scene our dialogue became particularly messy. I'd see her urge to speak, and speed up my delivery because I wanted to get my bit out before she interrupted. Each of us sought to communicate our thoughts in the face of the other's desire to speak – just like in real life.

Figure out where each of your scripted lines or actions originates from. To do this go through each scene and circle the words or actions of the *other* character/s that have forced you to respond. If you like you can do this at the same time you are keywording your own character's lines. These circled words or actions are your character's 'lightbulb' moments; the place where what the other character has said kicks off a thought in your character's head (that may or may not end in an actual spoken response). Then draw a line in your script from there, the place where your character's thought is initiated, down to the line of yours that is the response: a game of arrows.[18]

A lightbulb moment leading to a line of your dialogue may have come from something that has just been said. But it might also be from another line two pages before, or sometimes even a scene or two before. Your character might have felt impelled to speak then, but had to wait. Then, just before they went to speak, the other character said something else which kicked your character into *another*, immediate, knee jerk response. If you can identify all your character's lightbulb moments in this way you'll mimic natural human behaviour. The 'game of arrows' allows you to genuinely react, not act, all through your performance. Good writers know how humans think, and the game of arrows allows you to tap into this wisdom and perform with watchable spontaneity. Dialogue is not a test set up so we can fail. Trust the writing.

When we're listening, each lightbulb moment elicits a response in our heads, much of which will end up unspoken. This unspoken dialogue is everything our character is thinking and feeling, but chooses not to say. If you wish you can also scribble these unspoken responses down at the appropriate points when you prepare – the note might be as simple as 'what the f&*k!' or 'this isn't right!!' The name we give to these particular scribbles is Sub-text or Inner Monologue, which we'll cover in Chapter 5.

SCENE ACTIONS, PERSONALISATION & THE BASIC SITUATION

I'm looking for the truth. The audience don't come to see you. They come to see themselves.
Julianne Moore

As well as figuring out a good playable objective, figure out the basic *situation* your character is in and what they're doing (the *Scene action*).

When you study any role you want to find your way in and make it your own. You' want to truly experience any scene because you have found an emotional connection to it. You can achieve this by relating the events of the scene to something in your own life. This gives your acting roots in your own lived truth. In the same way you'll want to find some similarities in your character's behaviour to your own. Sure, you may not be obsessed with killing low life criminals, as Clint Eastwood's character in *Dirty Harry* is, but you

---

[18] I first heard the term 'game of arrows' in Kevin Spacey's (now withdrawn) online masterclass. Michael Caine uses a similar technique.

may have a powerful drive to tidy any disgusting mess you find, which may be your way into playing a character like that.

So when we have nutted out what the scene is about - the basic human situation – then we can relate it in simple terms to our own personal equivalent. That is something we know and it's something we can truthfully live. We may not have ever killed someone, or robbed a bank, or even broken someone's heart – but we only need to *look* like we are doing those things.

It's worth stressing again that as actors we don't have to believe, or pretend to believe, in everything we're saying and doing. It's true that some actors, such as Claire Danes, work in this way. David Suchet, the great interpreter of Agatha Christie's iconic Hercule Periot character, has to do an exercise after each theatre performance to wrench himself out of character. He can get stuck in there.[19] You can immerse yourself totally in character if it works for you, no question, but if that's not your jam, that's also fine. Most actors come up with a parallel story that they play so that it *looks* like we are in that situation. The audience can't tell the difference.

Scene actions are taught at the Chicago Theatre school of David Mamet and William H Macey, with *A Practical Handbook for the Actor* by Melissa Bruder being their bible. There's a good example in the book of how personalisation works. In Act 1, Scene 1 of *Hamlet*, Horatio stands with the guards of Elsinore Castle. He has been asked by them to witness the ghost of Hamlet's dad, the late king. They already saw the old (dead) King grumpily striding the battlements the night before and decided that Horatio, fresh from Uni, would be just the chap to figure out what he was up to.

Playing this scene, the trap for beginners is to put their energy into trying to pretend, when the ghost duly appears, that they really are seeing a ghost (I've played the role of Horatio myself and was guilty of just that). But if the idea is to ask what Horatio is *doing* you realise that he's trying to solve a mystery. This is something you have probably had to do, or you can imagine a circumstance where you might. You can play that scene action. But I doubt most of you have ever seen a ghost.

Let's look more closely at a particular scene. Our example is from *In Between Lives*, a US TV pilot filmed in 2018 (See Appendix 3). Our analysis will be from TOM'S point of view. Here are the steps:

After you've read your scene, *put the script away*. Don't refer to it. Think objectively about what is happening. Ask yourself what is the *general situation*,

---

19 He does this by repeating mundane personal facts like his own phone number. 'David Suchet - Hercule Poirot, and more,' *Radio NZ National,* 11 August 2019.

the recognisable human event at play here, at its most basic level?

Then ask: 'in this kind of situation, what are the SORT of things people like Tom's character might be wanting to achieve?' Write these possibilities down, without worrying too much about the scene as written. Then you'll have a list of possible, playable objectives, for this situation.

It's easy to gloss over what the general situation is that we are playing. But knowing this is 'a break up' or 'woman gets fired' or a 'make up' scene gets us grounded in a simple and playable reality from the start.[20]

Tom has just come back from work as a police officer where he has seen a grisly murder victim. At home is Brian, who has just thrown his dinner at a nurse, and doesn't recognise Tom. Because of the age gap we may initially think Brian is Tom's father. Over the course of the scene we figure out that Brian and Tom are actually partners, and that Brian is suffering some form of dementia. For this scene you could decide that the basic situation is that a man comes home from a tough day at work to hang out with his partner, who is unwell, and seeks connection. In this sort of situation the kind of things your character (Tom) might want are: to relax and unburden, to cheer Brian up, or experience again their feelings of love for each other. Probably all of these things may be alive at some point in the scene.

Now select the scene objective for your character. This may be from one of the possibilities you wrote out, or inspired by them, or just from first principles. So, you might decide that if Tom was to rewrite the dialogue to suit him, that would mean that Brian in some measure recognised him. You could go for: *I want to fire a spark of recognition in my partner.*

Now you can figure out your character's *Scene action*: what are they *doing* to get what they want? Write down a bunch of possibilities and play around with them until you settle on one you like. Let's go for this for Tom: *I'm forcing Brian to own up to something - that he does know and recognise me.*

To ground the work and make it real for you, you can now personalise the scene. This can be from either your actual experience - when have I been in a situation where I have needed to force someone to own up to something? Or you can take an imaginative leap - when *might* I be in a situation where I would be doing that? This last step grounds the scene in your own truth.

Your personal scenario must come from the objective or scene action, not directly from the *actual situation*. Chances are you've never been in the exact

---

[20] In a similar way, back in ye olde early days of NZ Cinema Geoff Murphy used to ask his actors to write 'NAR,' for 'no acting required,' next to many of the lines in the script. For theatre trained actors unused to film acting it was like saying 'keep it real.'

situation of this scene. You're far more likely to have lived something close to the *scene action*. You've certainly at least once in your life wanted to force someone's hand, or can imagine a time when you might have to. I'm sure you've come home from a terrible day at work just wanting a hug and instead walked into some kind of domestic hellfire. If you can't find an exact personal parallel, no matter. Use your imagination. Or use a bit of both. Why not?

The big idea of scene actions is that rather than putting your energy into pretending to believe in the fiction of the script, you can put it into *doing* something you can personally relate to, that is close enough to the situation that it looks to the audience like the truth. Using scene actions helps you avoid being overly dramatic in heightened situations. It's seeing life - not cliché, and certainly not overacting - that engages audiences.

You sometimes have to find a way to enjoy playing unsavoury characters and personalisation can also help with that. If the scene or character is dark or heavy you can come up with an imaginative situation that's irreverent or quirky; something that's fun to play. I once played the villain of the week in the US cable series *Legend of the Seeker*. In the climactic crowd scene, where I was trying to scare the townsfolk into giving up a fugitive, I came up with the action (mad as it sounds…) of 'I'm spanking this town!' It was a variation of the Emperor Nero's purported wish that the Roman mob had just one neck. It worked well, first of all because that's how my character felt – I did want to punish the whole village - but second because it was fun to play. Giving some light to the scene helped me go dark when I had to.

Finding a good playable objective and scene action, and a useful made up or actual scenario, can be tough tests of our imagination. Always remember that once we've asked the difficult questions we don't have to figure out the answers straight away. In fact sometimes we never do. Our sub-conscious is like compost; we need to aerate it with the hard questions, but sometimes leave it so the answers can bubble up later. These instinctual discoveries are delicious. It can feel like we are remembering something about the role, rather than inventing it.

EMOTION & SCENE ACTIONS

Emotions aren't doable. Actions are doable, and if you do them correctly, they prompt the feelings.
Stella Adler, American actor and teacher

When we DO something, our emotional state shifts. This is why finding a scene action can be so helpful. It's a process of reverse engineering that helps us discover our character's feelings.

In real life, if you start *doing* something, say, defending yourself against an accusation, pretty soon you'll start to *feel* defensive. We are wired up this way. If you beg for forgiveness, you'll begin to feel a bit sorry. Good acting, acting that tells the story, is *doing* something behaviourally, and letting the emotions follow. In turn, the playing of authentic emotion in the scene by you DOES something to the other actor, so long as they are open. And they then return the favour – there's an emotional flow between you now. The actor's job is to get out of the way of that flow of feeling and trust that how they are feeling will work for their character in the scene, *even if it's not what they planned*. As a general rule actors should focus on what they are doing, not emotion.

Here's an example of how *doing* something behaviourally can create *feeling* in a performance. In the 1987 film *No Way Out*, directed by New Zealander Roger Donaldson, Navy Lieutenant Tom Farrell (Kevin Costner) meets a woman, Susan Atwell (Sean Young), and they share a passionate affair. Farrell then finds out that his superior, Defense Secretary David Brice (Gene Hackman), is also romantically involved with Atwell. When Farrell unexpectedly learns of Atwell's death he's in the presence of Brice, and so is not able to betray his feelings. He asks to be excused and once he's shut a bathroom door he can allow himself to grieve – silently though, as Brice is in the next room. In that scenario many actors would be thinking: 'okay, I have to cry, so what I'm going to do is think of a time when I was really sad,' and so on… But Costner imagined that as soon as he shut the door someone punched him in the guts. He bent over physically as if struck, and slumped to the floor, gasping for air. It was a wonderful choice; surprising but authentic.

As I've said, the words should cost you something and the audience loves to see this. 'In order to bring feeling into their work,' says director-trainer Judith Weston, 'writers, directors, and actors must be honest about the emotional cost of the characters' *actions*.'[21] By owning the action of every scene you do, you can go to its emotional heart, and then calibrate the emotional intensity - what Australian actor Ben Mendelsohn called, in a 2017 interview, 'adjusting the volume up or down'. Joel Tobeck has spoken about how he gave himself early on in his career permission to take intensity 'as far as it could go.' It became his hallmark and has helped him have a busy

---

21 From her book *The Film Director's Intuition*.

career. But unless we have first discovered the heart of the situation we are in, so that we can *do* something, namely play a scene action that is personalised and real to us, we're just spinning the wheels. We're burning the smoke of generalised emotion rather than living an emotional truth.

Being able to acknowledge our human pain sometimes means going to some pretty difficult places and it isn't always fun. At times we don't have a choice, and there is a personal cost. But our courage in going to our dark places also enables us to go anywhere emotionally in our acting, including the joyful and playful places. It can be an enormously satisfying way to work, as well as to watch.

LINE ACTIONS

As well as Scene Actions, some actors like to figure out an action *for every line* of their dialogue.[22] Doing this can ground you in the moment to moment detail of what you are 'doing/ playing,' rather than 'saying/ feeling.' *Doing* something with every line takes the focus away from the dialogue onto affecting the other actor with behaviour. Line actions thereby tether a scene without locking in the 'how' of every line's delivery. So, line actions, like scene actions, but in more precise detail, can help actors get out of the traps of chunking (playing just one or only a few different actions over a scene) or colouring (playing one emotional note over the whole scene).

Doing line actions for a time renews your respect for beats, moments and detail – the minutiae of acting, which we can glide over in our work. Sometimes it's useful to be reminded that we are animals who developed speech only relatively recently. We *do* things, not say things, to achieve our objective. Actions also reveal character: we are what we do, not say, after all. Figuring out what your character *does*, then physicalising their line actions, is another way, via doing, to get you feeling who they are in your body.

How to action lines

For every sentence of yours in the scene, write down an action that describes what your character is *doing* with that line. The sentence may be short, or long; it's one thought, and ends when your character has a new thought. If the thought changes, there's a new action.

Verbs are *doing* words, so express each action as a verb, and relate it to the other character. Test the action with 'I' and 'you.' Actions are not a 'note

---

[22] Constantin Stanislavski, the Russian director and actor who has had a huge influence on our modern acting tradition, initially devised actioning as an approach. It later came to be called 'the 'method of physical actions.'

to self' on how to play a line, so 'I scream at you' is better replaced with 'I denigrate you,' if that is a more precise description of what you character is doing with that line. Actions may be either physical or psychological, so make them about moving or affecting the other character, as well as describing what you are doing. Physical actions might be: 'I push you' (to sell the farm); 'I embrace you;' or 'I spurn your advances.' Psychological actions might be: 'I fight your contention' (that our son is useless); 'I declare my love for you;' 'I contradict your claim' (that we have no future together); or 'I warn you' (that your abuse must stop).

The words in brackets are important, especially if you physicalise the actions as part of your prep (see below). They help you incorporate the given circumstances of the scene into the wording.

If you are asking: 'How are you?' with your dialogue, 'I greet you,' is probably a good action. But if your character knows that the other person is sick, a line action of 'I express concern for your health' would be a more precise description of what you are doing.[23] You should play the action of the big print as well as the lines: you might turn the stage note 'John sits down' into 'I collapse onto the sofa.' Try not to repeat actions, except perhaps once in a scene: using the same action repeatedly risks the playing being repetitious.

There is no right or wrong way to action for any particular line, but there are better or worse actions. Make your actions more literal than interpretive: simple is good. Avoid guesses – what the character is doing with any line is usually pretty clear. Also, avoid emotional choices in an action (such as 'I hate you'). It may predetermine your emotional state and therefore the playing. Finally, stay away from lazy actions like 'I tell you' or 'I say to you.' These actions could be true for almost all lines of dialogue and are therefore meaningless.

Actions shouldn't box your performance in. Any action can be expressed in a multitude of ways. Actions should give you a sense of being grounded in the scene while still being open to how each line is played, depending on where your instincts take you and what the other actor is doing. Don't be a slave to actions in the playing. Do them so you can then be open to the moment. Actions help you avoid getting stuck in one way of saying a line. 'Finding a way to say a line of text is NOT the ultimate purpose...' says line actions proponent Mike Alfreds. 'Planning or working out how to say a line is deadly. Using a line in order to pursue an objective is lively. The HOW should happen instinctively in the moment.'[24]

---

23 Remember Sondheim, on page 36: 'god is in the detail.'
24 From his book *Different Every Night*.

Acting Boot Camp I

To bed actions in, write all your actions down, then run the scene, saying aloud, after every line, the action for that line. So, for example, say, 'there's no future for us' - the dialogue - then 'I push you away', (the action). Physicalise the action when you say it, making some physical gesture with your body that sums up the meaning of the line for you. If working with a scene partner, physicalise with them as much as possible. This all helps lock the actions into your muscles (a better store of memory than just your head). It also illuminates what your character is feeling in the scene. Physicalising actions such as, 'I berate you' or 'I challenge you' will certainly make you feel different than running actions like 'I placate you' or 'I pacify you.'

Next, do a run where you just say the actions, physicalising as you go. Now you are exploring the bones of the scene using pure animal intention.

Once you come to do the scene trust your muscle memory. The physical moves that accompanied your actions will be read as impulses and urges to physicalise, even if you don't follow through.

A final word on line actions…

Line actioning might not be something you'll do for the rest of your acting life. Some actors swear by them. Others find they just get them 'stuck in their heads.' Part of the problem may be that just finding good, playable actions takes a lot of head work and some actors don't enjoy such an intellectual approach. Those actors can get stuck at the first stage of just *choosing* actions. If you're like that, feel free to just use noises, gestures or nouns to convey actions. Or, to help you find actions you can download the App (or buy the book) – *Actions: The Actors' Thesaurus,* by FirstyWork.[25]

Line actions can be a great tool for actors to move through at least for a time. When you have developed an inherent awareness of pitch, spontaneity and variation in your choices, you can drop them. In future you'll find those nuances more unconsciously. If need be you can always go back to actions for a tune-up.

If you want to get into more detail about actions, read the relevant chapters in Mike Alfreds' book, *Different Every Night*. It also has exercises to use in class or rehearsal situations to understand better how actions practically affect the playing.

---

[25] Line actions guru Mike Alfreds does caution that not all the actions listed in this book are playable. But I think it's fairly obvious which ones aren't going to work. And there are many wonderful actions listed. There's a lot of useful information about actioning in there too, for instance for actioning a soliloquy, a voice over, and actioning of sample scenes.

CHAPTER FOUR
BARING YOUR SOUL; EMOTION AND INSTINCT IN YOUR ACTING

If you have the emotion, it infects you and the audience. If you don't have it don't bother; just say your lines as truthfully as you are capable of doing. You can't fake emotion.
Sanford Meisner

THE EMOTION TRAP

Emotion can be a trap for actors. Sometimes we worry if we have the right emotion for the part: too much, or not enough. We may fear that if we are not feeling *something* then we are not *doing* enough – even, somehow, that *we* are not enough.

But only actors try to manufacture emotions. Human beings try to keep a lid on them. If an actor wants to feel grief in a scene, a person in that actual situation probably wants NOT to. No one LIKES to cry. Most of the time people act out their feelings with *behaviour*. Figuring out how your character thinks and feels about something, then choosing to hide it in a chosen behaviour, so using their feelings as obstacles, is highly watchable because it's more typical of what people actually do.

When we read a script for the first time and are moved at a certain point we can assume that we need to play that part with that same emotion. In fact, our initial response is the 'audience effect.' This is how the writer intended the audience to *respond* to the performance at that point, not an instruction to us as to *how* to play it. If we laugh reading something it will almost certainly be the wrong choice to laugh while playing it. It can be the same if we cry reading a scene. It's the story – dry ink on a page plus our imagination – that produced an emotional reaction. To make the audience cry we may not have to cry at all. Our character's courage in choosing *not* to cry may be an even stronger choice. Feel less, and sometimes you allow the audience to feel more. When we, as audience members, watch an actor crying in a performance, we are as likely to feel empathy for that character, rather than to be upset ourselves. We may even be 'put off' if the emotion seems 'put on.' Our job as actors is to figure out what it is the writer intended. Understand also that it doesn't matter *how* you feel: what matters is how what you are doing *looks*. And it may look rather different from how you feel.

American actor and comedian Billy Crystal likens acting to being consciously aware of the hidden emotions inside Riley's brain in the animated film *Inside out* – all of them arguing and pulling on levers and pressing buttons. For him the buzz in acting is not from emoting but from feeling fully alive; sensorially activated as our conscious and creative selves whir away, intersecting and firing off each other. As you perform, you are discovering insights and seeing moments unveil themselves in ways miraculously in line with the requirements of the scene. 'I've got to hit this mark,' you are saying to yourself, at the same time as your character is feeling cross. You shuffle imperceptibly to the left to stay in your key light while simultaneously remembering you have to look surprised on the next line.

This is all immense fun. Actors who get hooked on emoting for its own sake are not only missing out on this creative buzz, they may also be so caught up in their feeling that they have forgotten that their principle function is storytelling. This is because when we go for emotion first and foremost in a scene it can create what's known as an *emotional wash* or a *generalised feeling*. This is like when a red hanky in your white wash makes everything come out looking one shade of pink.

This can happen when the actor has a certain note that they tend to lean into when they act. It might be a default note of 'sad' that they unconsciously go to in every role they play. This doesn't necessarily mean they are sad themselves; it's just the place they go to emotionally when they act. Now, this personal acting note may well match that of their character. But if it doesn't, those actors need to ask themselves 'what is my character's note? Is it different from my default acting note?'

When you're colouring everything with the one emotional hue, your playing of generalised, unspecific emotion risks overwhelming story. If it does we are not watching a character in a scene going for something (the Intention/ Objective), or doing something recognisably human (the Scene Action). Bill Nighy has said that he doesn't feel *anything* when he's working – he's too busy. You too have a job to do, and you should just get on with it. When you first read the script you were moved by story, not performance. If the story is somehow not being told in your playing, then the audience may be unaffected, no matter what emotional gymnastics you are performing.

Emoting in performance can also make the audience feel as if the actor were somehow instructing them how they should be feeling – by crying, so we know it's a 'sad' scene, or yelling, so we know it's an 'angry' scene - rather than letting us discover the feeling for ourselves. This leaves us, the audience, with little to do. But our performances must always leave space for the audience to meet us. There's a scene from Polish-French director Roman Polanski's *Rosemary's Baby* in which Minnie Castevet (played by Ruth Gordon) makes a telephone call. To represent the POV of Rosemary, who is eavesdropping on the call, Director of Photography (DOP) William Fraker initially framed the shot on Gordon through a doorway, seated on the edge of the bed in full view. But Polanski insisted the audience see only a glimpse of Gordon, and not the phone at all. 'I didn't get it,' says Fraker, 'until we were in dailies and I saw everyone leaning in their seats, trying to look around the edge of the door frame to see what was happening.'[26] Let the audience do some of the work for you. If we go to 100% on the emotion we show them all we've got. There's no mystery left. Trust yourself. You are enough.

THE 'FLOW' OF FEELING

Only actors feel in chunks – sad for a bit, then angry for a minute, then joyful. Humans do not play 'sad' or 'happy' scenes in their lives. Emotions are not singular. They are multiple, contrasting and simultaneous. Feelings are a *flow*. Some actors have an easy command of their flow of emotion. Bryan Cranston is a good example. In his autobiography he explains with great self-honesty how his early life unintentionally equipped him with this helpful acting asset. An 'unhappy' childhood can be an actor's greatest boon.

However some actors find emotion difficult to conjure up. For them, American acting teacher Eric Morris found that difficulties with expressing emotion often actually had to do with blockages in the *flow* of feeling.[27] Some actors try and produce an emotion, but if it doesn't come easily to them they end up playing that *generalised* feeling we've talked about. While they're straining to attain the ONE feeling they think they need, they disallow all other emotions the character may also be experiencing in the scene. But this flow of feeling they are squashing could, if let alone, get them to where they need to go emotionally. And it brings life to the performance as it does.

---

26 *Beyond The Frame: Rosemary's Baby,* American Cinematographer, March 29, 2017 David E. Williams.
27 Eric Morris became in the 1980's the 'go to' teacher for actor 'refugees' from Lee Strasberg's Acting Studio. Strasberg's 'emotional recall' exercise seemed to work for actors able to produce emotion easily anyway. For some it felt like a test, seemingly set up for them to fail, that disqualified them from acting.

By contrast, for Morris, an emotional flow means we are free to follow our instincts wherever they take us, *even if that's not where we envisaged the scene might go*. We are open to the other actor, reacting off what they give us and letting ourselves feel whatever comes up. This is the same thing as being 'in the moment,' 'present' or 'spontaneous'.

The point here is that feeling, emotion, and being in our instincts *all live in the same place in our acting.*

In the end, emotion in acting, as in life, just happens. If we try to play a feeling we do not genuinely feel, suddenly the actor becomes visible. But if we live the feelings as they come up, the audience equates how the actor is feeling with how the character is feeling. Your feelings are the characters feelings – that's how it looks. So, in this sense your feelings can never be 'wrong.' Our job is not to feel, but to trust our instincts, letting the emotion go where it wants to.

That is, of course, easy to say. But it can be difficult for us to express feelings readily in our acting if we don't always permit ourselves to be expressive in our everyday lives. If we can't own how we are feeling we may be unable to access those feelings in our acting as we should. As a teacher I've seen many times the greatest talent initially carrying the greatest blocks; a burden of ancient feelings buried under a lifetime of socialisation. We may have been told that 'nice girls don't get angry.' Or shame has somehow become attached to particular feelings in more subtle ways. We can get habituated to censoring ourselves or denying our impulses and become unaware we are even doing this. But all the feelings and behaviours we are socialised out of are the very ones that make our acting interesting. They may constitute that uneasy sense of 'negative capability' that John Keats wrote about as defining creative greatness (more on negative capability in Chapter 9).[28]

If in our regular day to day life, an emotion pops up that feels somehow inappropriate, or even shameful, we may quickly repress it. It's possible that when we act, the same mechanism can operate. As we try and stay true to our feelings in the scene we can then butt up against self-judgment, doubt or personal taboos. We may not make this connection. 'My character wouldn't do/ feel this,' we might say to ourselves, without even knowing that we are censoring our feelings, just as we do in life.

Heather Timms, head of Acting at *Toi Whakaari*, the National Drama

---

28 True artistic character, Keats believed, 'has no self - it is everything and nothing - it has no character and enjoys light and shade; it lives in gusto, be it foul or fair, high or low, rich or poor, mean or elevated - it has as much delight in conceiving an Iago as an Imogen.' From 'A 19th-century poet's trick for cultivating a creative mindset,' by Leah Fessler, *Quartz* Online Magazine, March 23, 2017.

School of New Zealand, told me once that much of her first year of training was spent mitigating the effects of socialisation, just so the students could 'turn up' and work. The feelings that we are busy repressing are the organic responses we are having to the human being in front of us. We need them in our acting. We may want to be nice in our lives, but there is no place for 'niceness' in our acting. We want to be unafraid to be disagreeable, to be an asshole – to be anything.

Learning to trust our instincts and flow of feelings is scary at first, but it's liberating to discover that the bits of us that feel ugly or shameful are actually useful in our acting. How many jobs is that true for? When following your instincts brings the work alive, you know you're on the right track. If you shine a light into the nooks of your psyche you'll embrace your full humanity and become a character the audience will love to watch, even if they don't love the character. 'Your acting will not be good until it is only yours,' said the esteemed American acting teacher Sandy Meisner (whose quote began this chapter). 'That's true of music, acting, anything creative. You work until finally nobody is acting like you.'

PRODUCING EMOTION ON DEMAND

We actors live in the real world, but TV, film and theatre seldom deal with the everyday. The stories we are called on to bring to life are often about people under stress. Heightened emotion is often called for and sometimes scripted. We have to rise to that challenge. If you are reading your script and see the big print telling you 'Jane bursts into tears,' then you know that's something you have to do.

Here's how NOT to do it. In 2007 I was cast in a role in the feature *30 Days of Night*. My character was dealing with a pile of loss and suicide was on his mind. In one scene, where I'm discussing the killing of my sled dogs with the local sheriff (played by Josh Hartnett), my character became teary. So, when the day came to film it I spent the morning wandering around the set, checking in with my emotions. Every time I tried I cried. Then, when we came to shoot the scene, to my surprise: nothing. I couldn't squeeze out a single tear. The only moment it counted was the exact moment that I was unable to produce the required feeling on demand.

My take out from that experience was that emotion shouldn't be rehearsed. As Dean Carey, founder of the *Actors Centre Australia*, once told me: 'the way to do a difficult thing is to just do it.' Sometimes, when there is an expectation or a scripted obligation to produce emotion, you *can* adopt the

NIKE adage: 'just do it'. But you have to trust yourself. So, ahead of time prepare the conditions to feel *something*. Remind yourself why your character is emotional, what's at stake for them, and so on. But if the feeling comes in, *move away from it*. If you know you have an emotional scene coming up let your subconscious whirr away, doing the work for you.

The process of acting has been described by the useful mantra 'Want-Do-Feel.' The DO part of this equation is expressed in acting terms by figuring out and playing what our character is *doing* in the scene. That is their behaviour. Feeling follows the action/ doing/ behaviour because when we DO things it produces an emotion. For example, if our chosen scene action is begging for forgiveness and we commit to that, then a minute into the scene, sure enough, we will likely start to feel contrite, guilty, sorry, and other things – even though at the start we may not have felt much of these feelings at all. We're not focusing on the end feeling as such, but living truthfully. Our chosen behaviour disguises, betrays and expresses feeling.

So, as part of the 'just do it' approach to emotion, investigate the psychology of your character as far as you can. Investigation enables instinct. By asking the hard questions and not forcing the answers you are making the space for something to organically occur. On the day, trust that your subconscious has got this; whatever accidents that occur will be on point.

But then, the worst happens. You've read this book, you've tried the NIKE approach, but after all your work your instinct fails. Yet you still have to cry, and you have to cry now - and you can't!

Well, here's some insurance. For any emotional reaction you need think of a thing, person or situation that makes you feel that way. If you have to feel, say, scared, then take a minute before camera roll to think of something that terrifies you. If it's spiders, recreate what it would be like, using all your senses, for spiders to be crawling all over you: the touch and smell and sound of their sticky little feet. If it's disgust, what makes you feel disgusted? A puddle of vomit? A rotting carcass? What would that look and smell like?

Fill up with this feeling. Go to 10 on it. *Then trust you have it, focus back on your objective, and start the scene.*

I want to reiterate that it's important, once you possess the required emotion, to let it go and come back to your objective/ intention. You can't play an emotion – and the scene falls apart when you do. BUT you *can* play an objective or action, with an authentic emotion alongside it.

When you fill-up with the required feeling, you make changes in your physiology at a cellular level. You will feel something chemically in your body.

Trust this. Then focus back on intention. This brings you back into character. It can be tricky when start a scene, playing an imaginary character, whilst thinking of your chosen emotional rocket fuel. When, halfway through a scene, you suddenly populate your head with the recent death of a beloved pet. When you do that you break the fourth wall in your head: you jump out of the imaginary world you have created. A better way to produce emotion on demand may be to find the feeling, park it in your body, repeat your objective (or scene action, if that works for you) - and begin.

INCLUSION

Eric Morris argues that we should not block *any* emotion in a scene, no matter how inappropriate it feels, as it may be helping us get to the feeling we want. Morris wants the actor to be able to act without censoring the flow of feeling, or judging its appropriateness. He is the originator of the term *Irreverent Acting*, which means performing with no obligation to result: honouring the flow of feelings and impulses, rather than following some acting plan. When playing a character, Morris sees the actor's duty to own up to how they are feeling and start with that, no matter how heretical to the material it may feel.

Acting is being private in a public space. Yet most of us are private people: we don't talk about personal things except to our close friends. As we've seen, and even when we're in character, it's possible for our socialisation to suddenly make us trip over a conditioned taboo. You can then seize up and short circuit the flow of your instincts and feelings. 'Anything you feel uncomfortable about expressing,' says Morris, 'will create an interruption in the flow of your impulses... at this point most actors panic and begin to 'act' and impose life that seems right for the scene.'

So Morris came up with the idea of *inclusion*: meaning to *include* all the feelings that occur at the point of panic or interruption. Then, says Morris, 'they become a part of the total behaviour of the character as opposed to an unwanted interruption.' If you're performing and suddenly feel stiff and uncomfortable, 'isn't it possible,' says Morris, 'that the character could feel that way *exactly?*'[29]

We may be waiting in the wings and feel anything from nervous excitement to sheer naked terror. Yet, this may not be so inappropriate if our character is walking into a high stakes situation. Like Morris, playwright and David Mamet maintains that *whatever* we feel when we play a scene is probably

---

29 Quotes are from Morris' seminal text, *Irreverent Acting*.

right, and we shouldn't seek to replace it with an emotion we *think* is more appropriate. Thinking happens when we prepare, but when we act, we need to trust the prep and fly on instinct. There's no time to think. And going with our instinct means *inclusion*.

Morris believes that, creatively, there isn't any alternative to this way of working. If you elect to deny any reality in your acting you risk looking stagey, or stale, or wooden. What do you have to lose? Yes, there will be some stumbles. Yes, your judgement about HOW to play any instinctual choice will improve with time. But inclusion, alongside saying yes to every misstep and mistake that occurs, should become second nature.

EXERCISES TO ENCOURAGE IRREVERENCE

The first two exercises here are for use with text. The third is an irreverent warm-up.

Inclusion: monologue or scene

An Eric Morris exercise. In the first run of your monologue or scene allow everything you think and feel to express itself through the words of the text (and do stick to the words).

Forget the meaning of the piece the first time, then do it again, including the impulses while ALSO attempting to fulfil the obligations of the scene: the relationship and the objective.

The good result will see you looking more alive, with more of you engaged. You're learning to bring even more of you and your feelings to the work; giving yourself permission to keep it real.

Like line actions, doing this conscious work of *inclusion* may be just a phase you move through. Then it's in your acting DNA.

Gibberish with a choice

As above, but in place of the scripted dialogue, speak gibberish or an imaginary foreign language.

Strangely effective at helping the actor intuitively make sense of a text – by removing sense/ the words.

Intimate share – verbal – in a pair

This exercise, explained in the *Exercises, Games & Group Work* chapter, is a warm-up and work-out to free you up emotionally. Intimate share chips away at our fear of exposure if we reveal our true feelings. It's a way to explore those feelings we may find hard to express in our life, and perhaps therefore in our acting.

CHAPTER FIVE
ACTING BOOT CAMP II – SCRIPT ANALYSIS, THE REST

Sub-text; Moment before; Beats, Pausation, Cues, Pace & Interruptions; Opposites & Obstacles; Given Circumstances; The Repeat Game; Change/ Travel; Humour; Role Playing; Substitution; Activities; Story Function; Accents

One way we can enliven the imagination is to push it toward the illogical. We're not scientists. We don't always have to make the logical, reasonable leap.
Stella Adler

SUB-TEXT: THE DARK MATTER OF THE SCENE

The words are the clues scattered in our path by the writer that are the starting point of our investigation of any role. But in our performance we don't need to do the work of the words all over again. The writer did that when she wrote them. What can be missing in a scene that focusses just on delivery is *sub-text* (also known as inner monologue). This is the life that exists in all moments of the scene, not just the spoken bits. Like the dark matter that has mass and holds the universe together, sub-text is ever-present, invisible, but alive in every moment as our character's bottom line.

A well-written scene is rarely about what it seems at first glance. There's usually an inner life that contrasts with or even contradicts the words. What people say is not always what they are thinking. Sometimes we lie or hide our true feelings. Often we don't know what we think until we've said it. As human beings, our characters are processing what they are hearing or actively wanting to interrupt all the time.

Sub-text is this unscripted dialogue: it's everything your character is thinking and feeling, but doesn't say. It's the thoughts that precede our dialogue, or fill a pause, or are the unspoken responses of our character to what is being said.

Our sub-text may well be stuff that wouldn't help our scene objective – which may be why it's left unspoken. Figuring out your character's sub-text creates an inner life and often an *obstacle* for your character – in this case, the desire to speak something that would sabotage your character's objective. An obstacle, especially if it creates an inner conflict, is always interesting to watch. And writing out your sub-text through a scene – in and around both you and your scene partner's dialogue – can alert you to nuances for your character that you hadn't thought of.

Like listening, there's nothing passive about sub-text. Your imagined sub-textual responses should be sharp, leading to a yearning to interrupt or interject. Sub-text can be playful, irreverent, and fun. It hints at a hidden world. It's especially useful when you don't have much dialogue but are listening a lot in a scene.

To discover the sub-text you could do a run of the scene in character, solo or in a pair, and verbalise all your character's thoughts as you go. Or you can write down all the things your character is thinking and feeling, underneath or alongside the relevant lines – your own, and the other characters. Always say 'you' not 'he or she' – e.g. '*You* are *such* a dick' NOT '*He* is *such* a dick.' Don't be nice. Swear words and sexual references introduce an element of rawness. Remember too that this is not a scriptwriting exercise – keep your thoughts brief, sharp, at an instinctual, even primitive level (write 'GRRRR!' if it works for you). Nor is this a memorisation exercise – except that you'll likely remember in your body the gist of your thoughts and feelings afterwards. Be imaginative in your choices but keep your sub-text aligned with the given circumstances of the scene and personality of your character.

We actors want to be in the moment when we perform. But how often in our own lives are we NOT in the moment? Often we'll be preoccupied as someone is chatting to us, thinking of the shopping, or of something that is worrying us. Some actors (think of Jeremy Irons) have this preoccupied quality in their acting almost permanently. So, think about that – a subtext running through the scene, built on facts you know about the character, that has nothing to do with the scene in play at all…

EXERCISE TO BED IN SUB-TEXT

In a class or rehearsal situation write up your sub-text then do a run with your scene partner, script in hand, with both actors speaking their sub-text *along with* their scripted dialogue.

- If you have sub-text during the other actor's dialogue, say it. The actor should stop until you have finished, then carry on.
- Imagine in this run that your character is not hearing the other character's sub-text/ inner monologue. Of course you are, and it will affect you, but your responses are to their line delivery, rather than their sub-text delivery.
- Physicalise while you work – muscle memory aids subconscious memory of the discoveries from this run.

At the end of the run put the scripts down, do a run with the dialogue and no spoken sub-text: connect, forget the sub-text and pace it up. Discover what has stuck.

You can follow a similar process at home in your prep for audition or work. If writing sub-text down feels like a bit of a chore just jam a run verbally, making up your sub-text as you go, in character. Physicalise as you go.

MOMENT BEFORE/ EXITS-ENTRANCES

'Every scene you will ever act begins in the middle, and it is up to you, the actor, to provide what comes before,' said Michael Shurtleff. Most of the scenes we actors perform are cutting into the action, or out - before the scene 'starts' or 'finishes.' You need to start the scene warmed up. This is true even when you walk in, surprising someone, and the scene starts from the beginning of that interaction. Something must have preceded your entrance. You can't walk in with a blank slate. No scene starts 'cold.'

So, for every scene you do, ask yourself, what is your character's 'moment before'? How and why is your character there? What has just happened? What's on their mind? What has just been said? Where have they come from? What is their mood/ preoccupations/ agenda? Start any scene with some combination of expectation and hope – and often there'll be some trepidation wrapped around that.

When working on any scene you must, of course, tailor your moment before to what is scripted. When doing your scene prep, look at the last thing your character did, what he may have been up to since we've seen him last, and what he knows (and doesn't know) about the character he's with.

As you prepare, also ask yourself: do you enter/ exit at the head/ end of the scene? It's especially important to work this out for auditions. I've seen so many scenes where it is scripted that the character will leave at the end of the scene, and the actor is itching to go from the start. Find a reason to be there. Where is the pull to stay in the room? When you enter, you should be pulled in - part of you doesn't want to. And when you go, part of you should want to stay. These are subtle choices, but they bring an intriguing quality to your acting.

BEATS, PAUSATION, CUES, PACE, INTERRUPTIONS
An important part of our prep is to break each scene into smaller bite-sized chunks – or beats. Mike Alfreds defines them as 'the largest piece of text in which one event, pertinent to all the characters present, takes place.'[30] Beats are like acting paragraphs within each scene.

We need to be aware of when the beat changes. At that point, in theory anyway, where you are pitched vocally should change. Because this is a new idea, the audience wants to hear that at the time - not be figuring it out five lines down the track. Remember – we actors get to run a scene multiple times. For the audience, it's once. Our playing must always be clear.

So, when you're reading your scene, identify the beat changes and ask yourself what they could mean and what's going on inside the characters' heads.

There will often be pauses or silences written in the script. They're there for a reason. In their own way, they move the story forward, as to hesitate or not speak is in itself a choice - indeed a meaningful choice. Cicely Berry told me once that, 'when characters on stage speak, then we know they're alright.' Conversely, if they can't speak, it means something must be wrong. Pauses should be loud with meaning; packed with sub-text and the desire to speak. This is the origin of that hoary but true saying that 'pauses must be earned.'

Actors are often tempted to stop and drink deeply from a pause as a well of truth. But there has to be a compelling reason to do this. Otherwise we must proceed apace. Pace doesn't mean rushing or gabbling. It means being on cue: our dialogue starting the moment the other actor finishes – or even before. Contemporary scripts have more and more overlaps written in. This is because of improvements in the technology of sound recording and mixing, and also because writers understand that's how we humans roll – interrupting each other often.

Scenes are generally written to have an energy, a clashing of ideas, running up to a turning point. If you're on cue then you have no time to think before you speak. You are forced to rely on instinct. If you stop to question an impulse, you've broken the flow; the moment to moment energy of the scene. This is true too for the screen, where editing can tighten up the cues but not

---

[30] He actually calls beats 'units,' but let's not quibble.

energise the delivery.

I once saw a brilliant one-man show, *Tom Crean*, and boy, did that actor (Adrian Dooley) rattle through the dialogue, bewitching a huge audience in an acoustically unfriendly venue. I heard every word. It was a testament to his technical ability, but also a reminder that audiences think faster than we give them credit for. You too must be able to find truth in fast-paced delivery.

You cannot wait until the other actor stops speaking until you go to talk or there will be an unplanned pause and the build-up of tension or conflict or comedy will be lost.[31] You must draw breath while the other actor is still going. The best way to do this is to figure out what it is that you hear, while the other character is speaking, that forces you to speak (using the 'Game of Arrows;' see Chapter 3). From that moment you are wanting to interrupt. Then you can come in hard when they finish, because you're waiting to go. In real life people talk over each other all the time, and our acting must have that energy also.

All pauses are not created equal. Many, you might be better off calling a 'poise' – a pivot of meaning, rather than a great silence an articulated truck could slowly rumble through. To help you figure out what the pauses might mean, and to find your beats, try the following: as you read your scene - for both you AND other characters - look for the scripted pauses and beat changes and mark them as follows: one slash - / - for a *poise* for breath; two - // - for a *poise* for thought (slightly longer). These slashes indicate thinking and processing that can be dense but rapid and can also occur on the other actor's dialogue. Three slashes though - /// - really do indicate a beat change, an *actual* pause, where a significant choice is made in the scene (either by you or another character).

Check out the scene from Appendix 3 *When a man loves a woman*. You'll notice a lot of these: '…' This (and sometimes a '-' in the script) usually indicates an interruption. This could be the other character interrupting you, but if the '…' is *during* your dialogue it means your character has interrupted *their own thoughts*. Always work out what your character was intending to say in these moments. Keep talking if the other actor doesn't interrupt you. OR, when your character has interrupted themselves, work out what it was your they meant to say, before they changed their mind to say something else.

---

31 In his book *The Intent to Live,* Larry Moss recounts hearing an original Noel Coward and Gertrude Lawrence recording of the stage show *The Red Peppers*. He notes how the comic pay off from the scene can only come if it is delivered – almost breathlessly - on cue. Pace is especially important in comedy, where we must never underestimate the audience's ability to keep up.

Consider these possibilities (in square brackets) in the following exchange:

MICHAEL
OK. When's the next freight train coming through? Can I get a schedule? I could plan around these things so you could... smoke.

ALICE
Maybe... you shouldn't have to Michael. One of the women at my meeting is going to a halfway house because she's... she's not making it in her home environment.

You could imagine here the following interrupted thoughts:

MICHAEL
OK. When's the next freight train coming through? Can I get a schedule? I could plan around these things so you could [have a good old rant]... smoke.

ALICE
Maybe [that's not your business]... you shouldn't have to Michael. One of the women at my meeting is going to a halfway house because she's [in a really toxic environment]... she's not making it in her home environment.

OBSTACLES

Dean Carey, now head of *The Actors Centre Australia,* and past head of acting at both *WAAPA* and *NIDA,* was an early teacher of mine. I remember him telling us in a class that it's always interesting when a character has more than one thing going on. On its simplest level this can be achieved by playing an objective alongside its *opposite* (more on them shortly) OR an *obstacle*. An obstacle is anything that's frustrating you as you strive to achieve your objective. Obstacles add to the dramatic tension by giving you something to work/ fight against. Audiences love to see struggle – it's why good writers make life so hard for their characters.

The other character in any scene usually presents some obstacle to your character. So too can be a trait of your character ('I should tell the truth, I hate lying to this person') or their back story ('this is the same way my Dad used to talk to me, I hate this'). Some internal obstacles such as these will be written into the script. Others you can deduce from the given circumstances (the facts about your character you can find in the script).

Internal obstacles can be psychological and can create a highly watchable inner struggle; or they can be physical, like having a cold or being drunk.

External obstacles too affect how you play the scene, adding a realistic dimension. External obstacles might be physical (a locked door or a hot day) or historical/ cultural (e.g. socialisation dictating that women in past times should not be openly assertive).

If you're nervous, don't forget that your character might be too. This is because most scenes have stakes – something for your character to lose. Remember the *Inclusion* section in Chapter 4? If you trust that how you're feeling could well be right for your character in the scene, you can then incorporate that in the performance as an obstacle for them. And truth be told you don't have much choice. You should play the truth in your work because trying to deny your true feelings will usually be picked up by the audience. So, accept and own your nerves as an obstacle but then get into character and focus on winning the scene. 'Character is courage under fire,' Ernest Hemingway said. It's often pluck in the face of doubt that audiences find appealing and watchable.

OPPOSITES AS OBSTACLES

Look for the opposites. Whatever is true for your character in a scene, as a rule, the opposite will also be true, to a greater or lesser extent. Whatever your character wants, whatever your objective is, there will be a part of her that wants the opposite. This lesser want is an obstacle for your character, an alternate objective, the *other* tempting choice in the scene. If the opposite/obstacle is something your character wants almost as much as their objective, it follows that getting what they want in the scene would then cost them significantly. As we've seen in our work with Scene actions and Personalisation, audiences love to see the cost to the character of the story. Life is hardly ever black and white; it's riven with compromise and ambiguity. Life is change, and change brings choices, and with choices – always – comes a price to pay. The woman deciding to stay in the contented marriage for the sake of the children is sacrificing her yearning for adventure and fulfilment. Wanting two – or more - things at the same time is what makes us human.

The objective and the opposite exist in *every* beat and moment in the scene. Never mind what the words are saying, don't ever *chunk* opposites – that is, play one opposite for a chunk of dialogue, then the other, and so on. The opposites should be alive in the playing through the whole scene, beat by beat: objective-opposite. This creates a character at war with themselves.

Here's an example of how an opposite-obstacle might work. A scene from David Mamet's film *Glengarry Glen Ross* has actor Alec Baldwin's character ripping into the sales staff in his iconic 'Coffee is for Closers' speech.[32] Each of the employees wants to keep their job. But they'd also probably like to punch Baldwin's character in the face. The opposite of keeping your job is

---
32 It's lovely work by Baldwin; check it out on YouTube.

losing it in this case. Actor Al Pacino's character Richard Roma is absent from this scene and that might be because he would never put up with being talked to in this way. In his absence the sales team feels immense indignation at this unfair treatment (obstacle/ opposite) but submit (objective – to stay employed). If you were playing one of that sales team you'd get what you wanted at the end of the scene, namely keeping your job, but at a cost to your dignity. That ties into writer Mamet's overal theme – that this job, this environment, is inherently de-humanising.

Teacher Michael Shurtleff loved opposites. He impressed on his students to act not only what is said, but its opposite as well. The way to play the opposites, he maintained, was to say yes to every possibility in the scene. *Play the positives*, he would say: *the negatives are always written*. You don't need to play the words; let them do the work as written and play something else: *anything else*. This is the basis of preparing imaginatively. If you're playing, say, a break-up scene, like *When a Man Loves a Woman* (see Appendix 3), and the lines are angry, look for something contrasting to play *as well*. 'When your character's involved in an argument,' says LA director and teacher John Swanbeck, 'don't argue against the character with whom you have a relationship, argue for the relationship you have with the other character. The character that struggles to achieve something positive while they're engaged in a conflict scene is the character that makes the camera care about them, and the one that truly moves the audience.'[33]

To prepare literally means playing only what is said. Being literal could also mean *only* playing the objective. But there may be many opposites in the scene – too many to fully intellectualise. Play the moment and discover them.

EXERCISES FOR OPPOSITES

These exercises will help you appreciate the dimensions of playing that become available when we embrace opposites. Try them in a scene group or class situation.

The chairs

A great exercise from Cicely Berry: place two chairs a few feet apart, facing the class (if there is one). Each chair represents the two OPPOSITES that you have identified as inherent in the speech or scene. They must be contrasting themes. For example in *When a man loves a woman* for Alice one opposite could be 'I want you to talk me out of leaving you,' and another, 'I want you to let me go.' Abbreviate these down, if you like, to 'Stay,' and 'Go.'

---

33 From John Swanbeck's website: blueswanfilms.com.

They could be for Michael 'Hate' and 'Love': loving Alice but hating her addiction. Or indeed the reverse. As you run the scene, move between the two chairs. Only speak when behind a chair, embodying the opposite of that chair 100% – pushing hard on the meaning of that opposite while there.
- Don't dawdle between the chairs – otherwise you'll be adding pauses. Make quick decisive choices about which chair.
- Don't think the choice – it's not dependent on the line. Any line for either opposite will do – they exist for every line and beat in the scene. This is just an exploration of the layers of meaning that exist in the scene. While doing the run, your choices may seem arbitrary, but they may shine a light on the sense of a moment or line in unexpected ways for that reason.
- If doing a scene, the other actor can set up two chairs opposite yours and run the exercise as well.

Once you've done the run on opposites with the chairs, do a run of the scene as normal to 'bed in' the discoveries. You can continue to explore all the possibilities in the scene by pulling out more opposites to play with.

Exploring opposites in a character

If you're playing a character who's starting to feel somewhat two dimensional or black and white, go for an opposite choice for a time. Doing so may open a window into the character's past and shine a light on why she turned out the way she did. For example, as a villain, try being gentle and loving with everyone. Feelings of hatred may start to arise because, despite your character's new, opposite, loving choices, he or she is *still* overlooked or detested.

GIVEN CIRCUMSTANCES

Given circumstances are the facts we know from the script that may be relevant to the playing. They may include:
- Where you are – a crowded café, a bedroom, a battlefield.
- When you are – the time of day, period/ era, and with it culture, social structure, social mores, politics, religious attitudes;
- Who you are: character, relationships, upbringing, back story;
- Environment – weather, season, temperature;
- Previous happenings, imminent happenings;
- Profession and work history;
- Hobbies, obsessions;
- Race, class, family;
- An arrival or departure can be a given circumstance, if your character is affected by it.

Acting Boot Camp II

Some pertinent facts, conditions or events may not be specifically mentioned in the scene you are about to play, but may be important. For example, Shakespeare's *Macbeth* was written soon after James I, the King of England, had written an academic treatise about witchcraft, called *Daemonologie*. A belief in the occult was widespread at the time, and this must be appreciated to understand how the characters, and the audiences of the time, responded to supernatural elements in the play, such as the appearance of Banquo's ghost, and the witches – as fact, not fiction. Equally, important facts may be mentioned, but easily missed. Most of *Macbeth* occurs at night, which makes the characters even more susceptible to superstition or fear (not to mention the audience!)

Even when you have not much time you can explore given circumstances quickly and productively. Examine your scene for the following:

- WHERE you are (place) will radically affect the playing. Is the scene set in a crowded bar? Or a bedroom? Are you inside, or outside? What time of year is it?
- WHAT period does your character live in? How might this influence the playing? For example, earlier times in history were marked by far greater deference from the lower classes to their betters: first-class passengers got priority seating on the lifeboats on the Titanic. Until recently, violence in everyday human interaction was far more common: in the nineteenth century Royal Navy it was typical to accompany a simple command with a routine whack from a length of rope.
- WHEN are you? If it is the end of the day, is that a clue that your character might be tired? Or happy the day's work is done?
- WHO is your character? A father, son, wife, lover? Who are they with, and what role-playing does this infer?[34] What is the class, age and gender difference, the relative status and the back story? This all has a bearing to how you play against other characters in a scene.

One way to explore given circumstances on your feet, in rehearsal or class, is via point of concentration (POC) runs. Here you choose one fact or circumstance and run it, alongside your objective, as a point of focus right through the whole scene. Here are some guidelines:

- Do pursue your objective/ intention at the same time as your POC. It is the contrast between the two that shines a light on the layers in the scene.
- There are different ways to approach any single fact. If you are doing a

---

[34] See the section below for more on role playing.

run emphasising 'the family's poverty,' you might find yourself remembering a time when money was abundant and taken for granted. Don't choose what your approach will be in advance, just be open in the run to letting your imagination roam. The best discoveries are accidental.

- After doing one POC/ given circumstance run you can do another, but always focus only on one POC at a time. The discoveries from the previous POC run may bleed into this new run, and that's fine, but make your focus the new POC.
- The accumulation of learning from all the runs will alter your understanding and playing of a scene for future runs. You don't need to consciously change your playing – the experience is remembered in your body.

Sometimes objectives and given circumstances interchange. For part of the scene, the given circumstance takes over. Playing with this idea can help get around the problem actors have choosing one objective for a scene that seems to have two or more; it may be just that there are different elements at play, given circumstances and opposites, alongside the single objective.

HUMOUR

We actors can be a serious lot. We'd usually rather break hearts than make people laugh. As a consequence, we can be rather masterful at sucking the humour out of any scripted situation. But the more serious the scene the more likely levity will also be there. Humour is a coping strategy almost unique to our species. As well, all good writers use humour. They know it helps humans stay alive and keep marching in the face of life's unfairness, incomprehensibility, pettiness and tragedy. Not always, but often, our species is likely to use humour in precisely the kind of life events where actors leave it out – in intense, dramatic situations.

So always ask yourself: what is the sense of humour the characters use to keep sane and survive in this show? You're not looking necessarily for jokes. Jokes make the audience laugh, but humour is when the characters laugh. So, they may put themselves down, or others (or both). Or the humour may be ironical, or satirical, or sarcastic. Or something else. Look for the humour.

As well, having a sense of humour *around* work can help with the heavy lifting. I once read a puff piece on the TV series *The Handmaid's tale*. The show dealt with unimaginably awful themes – and the actors found themselves laughing and goofing around between takes.

By contrast, I once worked on a TV show with somewhat dark themes where everyone was so SERIOUS. What the work needed was some levity!

Acting Boot Camp II

ROLE-PLAYING

Who we are is not fixed. Around the central axis of our basic personality, we change depending on who we are with. In a very real sense, we are who the people around us think we are. When I head home to my parents, as a grown man with children of my own, it's not just my status that changes. I may also start behaving like a kid again, because that's how my folks treat me. In fact, we play a role *all the time*, depending on who we're with. There's even an equation that quantifies this phenomenon, described by social psychologist Kurt Lewin. This is B = f(P,E) - meaning that behaviour is always a function of who a person is (P), combined with the situation (or environment) they find themselves in (E). As writer Will Storr puts it, we have a self for home and a self for work, a self for Facebook and a self for parties. And, usually, we are unaware how much our human surroundings change our behaviour.[35]

Embracing the idea of role-playing opens up the range of our choices. Our character work should never be reductive, smoothing out any inconsistencies, because in truth we are many people, not just one. In one scene our character may behave as a dutiful son, in the next, a raging patriarch. Our characters can show a whole range of seemingly contradictory behaviours, depending on where they are, making them more watchable – and human.

SUBSTITUTION

Substitution grounds us in the relationship our character finds themselves in. Think about who the other character in the scene is to your character – a best friend, a frenemy, a mother, a mentor, and so on – and for an exploratory run, substitute in a person that you know from your own life, who fits this relationship. Play the scene *as if* to them. This will help you sink into the specific truth of which hat your character is wearing in the scene.

We're not looking for exact substitutions. We're looking for someone specific that gives you the feeling you want. The scene might be your character with her boyfriend. But unless the scripted dynamic and relationship are similar, your actual boyfriend may not fit the bill. Depending on the circumstances of the scene, an ex, or another person altogether, oddly, might work better.

When you come to perform the scene, direct substitution may not be a great idea. Taking someone from the real world and putting them into your imaginary world may potentially kick you out of the moment. It's possible though that your substitution does evoke some useful feelings – it might be

---

[35] For more read his book, *Selfie*.

someone you hate or love – and this is just what the scene demands. If this is the case, as per the method outlined in the *Producing Emotion on Demand* section in the previous chapter, give yourself a half-minute to fill up with that substitution, and the feeling attached to it. Then let your substitution go, focus on your objective, and play the scene.

THE REPEAT GAME

Repetition, or the Repeat game, was originally developed by New York based teacher Sanford Meisner. The exercise trains actors to freely act on their impulses. Trusting our instincts - in acting, writing, directing, in all art - is, in the moment, all we really have.

Meisner came up with the Repeat game to solve the two main problems he'd identified for actors in his classes: that they were self-conscious, and that they didn't listen. The exercise helped actors stop worrying about their nerves and focus instead on their scene partners, because it's hard to truly listen *and* over-think at the same time.

Meisner noticed that when actors put their focus on the other person their self-consciousness left them. They started to not just listen to the words, but notice the *behaviour* of the actor in front of them.

Acting, Meisner surmised, is all about behaviour. Words can lie but behaviour doesn't. We should not just listen to the words, but to the *person*. 'An ounce of behaviour,' he concluded, 'is worth a pound of words.'[36]

The Repeat game isn't about studying to a point where we are acting without a shred of self-awareness or nerves. That's not only impossible, it's not necessary. Rather, the repeat game is a good teacher because it encourages actors to work with and trust more their intuition, all the while without judgement. Doing it, actors experience how it feels to be 'present:' reading the behaviour of their acting partner closely and allowing what their acting partner is doing to affect them. Over time, practising repetition makes us less reverent about the words. Behaviour happens first, and the words follow.

The Repeat Game Exercise

To introduce actors to the repeat game, take them through it in several steps, then finally link it to the text.

Simple repeat

Two actors stand opposite each other. One actor begins by saying the first thing that comes into their head about the other actor. This will be an *objective* observation, such as what the actor is wearing. The other actor then repeats

---

36 From the Meisner Master Class DVD.

the phrase.
It could run something like this:
First actor: 'You're wearing a blue shirt.'
Other actor: 'I'm wearing a blue shirt.'
First actor: 'You're wearing a blue shirt…' and so on.
The two actors keep repeating just this phrase.
Admittedly this is not the most inspiring dialogue, but after a while it stops being about the actual words and becomes about what is happening between the two actors. They are reading behaviour and creating behaviour.

Getting personal
Again standing opposite each other, one actor begins by making a *subjective* observation about the other actor, expressing what they are getting from their partner right now. They can now get personal. Such as…
'You have dark lines under your eyes.'
'I have dark lines under my eyes?'
'You've got dark lines under your eyes.'
But now we can change our observation when one of the actors sees something *new* about the other actor:
'Okay, so I have dark lines under my eyes.'
'You look incredibly serious about that!'
'I look *incredibly* serious?'
'Yes, you look incredibly serious.'
'I look incredibly serious. You look incredibly serious too!'
Don't pause, and don't think about your reaction to the other person. Just state what you are reading. If in doubt, just repeat. Don't get stuck on the meaning of the words; after a few repetitions, their meaning won't matter, they'll be overlaid with whatever you are feeling about the other actor right now. Don't respond to the words, deal with the *behaviour* in front of you – read it, and create it by reacting to it.

Taking it personally
As before, standing opposite one actor starts by saying something about the other actor. That phrase continues to be repeated.
'You look really tired.'
'I look really tired?'
'Yes, you're tired.'
Carry on like this until one of you observes something *new* happening in the other actor; if you do, comment on that:
'You're happy about that!'

'I'm happy about that?'
'Yes, you are totally happy about that.'
'I'm totally happy about that now.'
And so on...
We're still making it personal, only this time we're opening ourselves up to be affected and taking it personally. Obviously, you want to avoid making any personal, hurtful comments. You're offering up on what behaviour you're seeing, and prodding the other actor to get a good reaction from them. You're not making value judgements about the other person.

Repeat with Intention

This is where repetition comes into its own. Close your eyes and zone into your intention for the scene. Open your eyes and, now 'magically' in character, begin repetition. Keep observing your scene partner and commenting on what you see, prodding and pushing them, repeating and reacting fully to what they throw at you. But play your intention hard at them too, whatever it is. This is still the repeat game, so don't use any scripted dialogue. This is a scene improv in character. Now you don't have to worry about getting *too* personal – you're in character, and so are they. You can both let fly. It's an awesome way to explore your character and the scene.

Here are some ideas to guide your use of the repeat game:
- Use statements. Don't ask questions, because if you do, the other actor will have to think of the answer – and we don't want them to think!
- Put your attention fully on the other actor, send your statement, then let their response penetrate your defences. Your response will then create a behaviour that they have to deal with.
- Resist the urge to be interesting. Let go of the obligation to change until you see a change in your partner - then act on that impulse, don't deny it.
- There is no right. There's an adage I describe later in this book: 'always say yes.' If you make a mistake, like fluffing a phrase, you've just given a gift to the other actor, and the game. Keep going.
- If in doubt, repeat. How you feel will be conveyed in how you say the words anyway. If you pause to think of a new response, you're thinking. Forget what your mother told you: don't think before you act, act before you think.

By the way; when I say that I don't want you to think I'm not underestimating your intelligence. Nor am I wanting to somehow dumb you down. Rather, it's an invitation to circumvent just the conscious part of your mental capacity, so you can utilise your full intelligence – brain, body, heart and soul.

Acting Boot Camp II

ACTIVITIES

Another Meisner teaching staple, an activity is anything your character can be credibly occupied with during a scene. It should require a degree of concentration and have importance. If you can find an activity with these qualities it can enhance the playing in important ways. It reflects the simple reality that in our lives we are sometimes sitting around on the couch just chatting, but more often we're busy. A story beat can be revealed when your character finds herself forced to stop or pause her activity by something that is said or done. And *how* you do the activity can also reveal the character's inner feeling. Finally, an activity, just doing something with your hands, grounds the performance.

Think through and rehearse all the physical moves and actions that are written into the scene, such as lighting a cigarette. These moves will be easier to change on set if need be once you have made concrete choices at home. But also think of an activity to offer that your character might credibly be doing, that isn't necessarily written in the script, if your instinct is telling you it may add something to the playing.

In rehearsal or class it can be useful to do a run of a scene with a solo or shared activity to get the focus off the performance and let the words find their natural rhythm. Even if the activity doesn't make it into the final scene, it earths the words, bringing them to life. For example, one actor can be tidying up the space or doing dishes, or both can play noughts and crosses through the scene. Or you can mime an activity that pulls out some aspect of the scene – if they are farmers they could be planting. And so forth.

OUR STORY FUNCTION

Michael Chekhov used to remind his students (the likes of Yul Brunner and Gregory Peck) that all art, acting included, has a *wholeness*; a beginning, a middle and an end. Every play and film and TV series you do, but also every speech you make and every scene you perform, is a little piece of art that tells a story. Even a 30-second television commercial tells a story from the status quo to a change and then a resolution. The audience will always be trying to make sense of any scene they see, searching for the story, which creates this sense of wholeness.[37] Change, the one constant in life, is written into every scene and every story. All stories are parables to the audience about how to

---

[37] Robert McKee, writer of *Story* (the Hollywood bible on screenwriting) maintains that if a story isn't there the audience will make one up in its place - effectively doing the work of the screen writer for them!

understand, cope with, and overcome the challenges presented by change. So, something has to *change* in every scene also, as each scene must progress the overall story in some way. Along with our collaborators, our story function as actors is to ensure the change that the writer intended is clear in our playing.

This change is the *central story event* of the scene. It's what is different or new today. It's the thing that happens, to our or the other character, that is unforeseen and spins the story off in a fresh trajectory. Playing the event alone doesn't highlight it – playing the *change* does. The change is the thing the audience will notice.

So when you prepare, look for the change for your character in every monologue and scene, and also the entire role. As a rule, you want to go into the scene *wanting* something from the other character, and also *expecting* an outcome from the scene. The change point for your character will be when their want collides with the actual outcome, when your character gets or doesn't get what they expected, with all the emotion - elation, disappointment or surprise - that lives in that moment.

Once we have identified an event or change, the way to show that is by playing an *emotional* change for your character. We want to play something emotionally at the beginning that's *different* from the end, and know the moment of change. The shift might be from hope to despair, or love to anguish. It may be a large change or a subtle one. You shouldn't try and play this emotion directly. Map out the emotional travel and then return to intention in the playing. If you've prepared in the right spirit, your understanding of what is required emotionally will give you powerful permission to produce that feeling, without forcing it, on the day.

There are some Improvs for exploring change and travel in the Chapter *Exercises, Games & Group work*.

ACCENTS

Actors will spend thousands of dollars on acting classes and then neglect an area that helps their employability just as much, if not more: expanding their repertoire of accents. No matter where you live, proficiency in a variety of accents will get you more work. But this is particularly true in countries such as New Zealand or Australia. You might be kissing goodbye to 50% of your possible income from overseas shows visiting our neck of the woods if you don't have a passable US and British accent.

Your accent needs to be convincing. If you are shooting a US show in Australasia, certain aspects may not look exactly right to a US audience.

Acting Boot Camp II

In some of the US films I've worked on, Auckland has stood in for Hawaii (*Johnny Kapahala*), Alaska (*30 Days of Night*) or Chicago (*You Wish*). In the case of the TV series *Ash versus Evil Dead* it was Michigan. Because Auckland isn't any of those places, there's a strong emphasis on getting the accent entirely right – more so probably than if the project was being filmed in LA. This can mean having the dialect coach run-up to correct a vowel sound in between takes.

At the time of writing in New Zealand, Amazon Prime's *Lord of the Rings* TV series is casting. They are asking auditioning actors to prepare any Standard English accent: something not too posh and not too regional. There has always been plenty of other work for those actors with a good Standard American accent. Big projects like this have vocal coaches on board who will be crafting accents once actors are hired. However it's still important in an audition to present with a ballpark accent choice you can do consistently and convincingly. You never want to give producers a reason not to cast you.

A good habit to help you learn an accent is to practice a little and often. It's also an advantage to have learning materials that you can listen to and repeat, so you can practice while jogging, walking, or sitting on the bus.

As a general rule, when trying to master an accent, there are three fruitful areas to start with: placement, pronunciation and melody.

It's important early on to place the sound in your mouth accurately. So, for Standard American placement is at the back of the mouth, with big rounded vowels. Kiwi is the middle. Australian is in the jaw.

Another key area to work on is pronunciation – how different vowels and vowel sound combinations are different, accent to accent.

Finally, you need to find the melody – the 'song' - of the accent. This may be different from the pitch of your own accent. For example, Standard American runs 'down down down down' over a sentence, or sometimes 'down down UP down,' particularly if the speaker is asking a question.

For vocal placement, vowel drills and more, for just about any accent, try the App *The Accent Kit*. Choose from the previews the one that is closest to your gender and age that you like and purchase – they cost a few dollars each. *The International Dialects of English Archive* (IDEA) website is always a good (and free) place to visit for examples of any accent in English. For standard American, I've personally found the CD set of *The Corff*'s invaluable. And for Standard English *How to do Standard English Accents* by Edda Sharpe and Jan Haydn Rowles is your go-to bible.

It's sometimes a good idea to model your accent on a real person. Choose an actor of your gender and age who appeals to you, with the accent that you want. Then listen to interviews of them on YouTube. Then you can listen/ repeat/ mimic/ experiment. If that person has read an audiobook you can do the same with that. Listen to them speak a chunk, repeat it, then listen back to both: to them, and your version, comparing and learning from your errors.

If you can find a real person who speaks the accent that's a bonus too. Go and have a beer and converse with them. Ask them to record something for you, or even your lines. When you get proficient enough talk in that accent all the time: make it second nature.

Once you've mastered your chosen standard English accent you can carry on. Sharpe and Rowles' excellent book, *How to do Accents,* has drills for Welsh, Scottish, Irish, and other English Regional accents.

A personal bugbear for me is the lack in New Zealand of the use of our own regional, historical and class accents. If you have a South Auckland, West Auckland, Northland or Southland accent, my advice to you is to learn other accents, but retain your vocal distinctiveness. I cherish those accents when actors present them in my classes. If you are playing a character from a different region, class, or period in New Zealand, make an effort to master that unique accent.

Collectively, the tools of the two Acting Boot Camp chapters give you some great potential tools for script analysis. Using any of these tools will get you better at figuring out what the idea in the writer's head is, and how you can best bring that to life in an entertaining and truthful way.

CHAPTER SIX
CHARACTER – FURTHER EXPLORATIONS

This chapter explores more in-depth character work, including for groups and rehearsals, and ends with insights into playing 'bad' guys, and the power of observation.

The inner life of the imagination, and not the personal and tiny experiential resources of the actor, should be elaborated on the stage and shown to the audience. This life is rich and revealing for the audience as well as for the actor himself.
Michael Chekhov

INTERVIEWING YOUR CHARACTER

If you're working in a group, try being interviewed *in character*. The questions can be general, such as 'what's your favourite band and why?' But they can also be relevant to the play or film. The actor can refuse to answer a question, and can also answer, honestly, 'I don't know.' But you'll be surprised what pops into your head the moment you hear a question: an instinctive truthful response from your character *that you had no idea existed*. Likely it'll differ from the instinctive response you would give. It's reassuring that your character really exists, that he or she is really taking shape.

A variation of this is called 'The Sword of Truth.' In a group or a pair, ask questions of each person, such as: 'what is your greatest insecurity?' 'What makes you feel vulnerable?' 'What are you most afraid of?' Dig deeper by asking 'Why' until you get to the heart of the matter. The actor can answer as themselves or in character (and be under no pressure to answer as themselves) so the exercise serves both to explore character and bond the group.

TALKING THE CHARACTER

Here, in a verbal dump, the actor shares as much as she knows about the character to the rest of the group, talking about them in the third person ('he' or 'she'). To save time you can do this in pairs. You may wish to introduce your character as a friend, and talk about them to the group in that way. Again, you can do this solo – telling it all to an imaginary friend.

Be physical, get up on your feet. Jump from subject to subject and fly off on tangents. The actor can describe the character verbally but also by acting them out – their walk, mannerisms, etc.

TALKING THE CHARACTER'S STORY

A variant of the above is to talk the character's story over the course of the play, episode or film. The actor tells this from the earliest script moment he or she has, right to the end, filling in any gaps (bits in the script where we don't see him or her). This can be in the first ('I') or third ('she' or 'he') person.

INTERROGATING THE CHARACTER

Using the Mark Travis (American film director/ teacher) technique, once you are working with text, the director or teacher can interrogate actors *in character* at the end of a scene, or, during it. Travis uses this technique to get the performance where he wants it to be for the next take.

Always begin by thanking the *actor* for their effort, then switch to interrogating their *character*.

Interrogating the character immediately brings the character to life in the actor's head. It's very useful, if you go through the scene in some detail, for the actor to discover the character's flow of feeling through the scene, making everything specific. You're asking the questions, but the actor is empowered because they realise they know the answers. Child actors particularly love this approach and take to the make-believe aspect of it readily. There's none of the critical element that can creep into direction. It's all a good reminder for the actor of the detail they need to drill down into for their prep; they should know what every allusion, thing or person they mention means to their character.

To do the work of discovering the detail in the scene and character, in a fun way, interrogate yourself solo. With the scene in front of you, record a bunch of questions for your character. Then put the scene away and play the questions back, pausing to answer them in character.

FURTHER IMAGINATIVE EXPLORATIONS

Here are some further imaginative explorations; exercises I've practised at various times as a student, a teacher and an actor. Try them. If they work for you, add them to your toolkit.

Character – Further Explorations

Solo Improvisations

Solo Improvisations (or solo etudes) can be a useful way to spend time 'in character.' Start by putting your character in an everyday situation, at home, alone. It's a normal day; they are just relaxing. They might get themselves a cup of tea or look out the window. We're not after anything dramatic: remove the obligation to be interesting. Sit for 5, 10 or 15 minutes, in character. Get used to just 'being' the character.

The great benefit of solo improvs is that you spend time as the character outside of the compulsion to be watchable, or good. You start to get a sense of how this person feels, who they are - and how they are different from you.

You make important discoveries doing solo improvs as well, which, on the face of it, seems counter-intuitive. We're just sitting there, how can anything *happen?*

Well, because we've done our intellectual work, we're now ready to creatively jam. The undemanding space of the solo improv invites sideways creative connections. Unbidden, our study seems to bubble away in our sub-conscious.

Imaginary Visualisations/ Creating Fake Memories

You can explore your character's back story within a solo improv and create fake character memories. These can come in handy if we want a bit of emotional heft for dramatic scripted moments. Fake memories can give us the necessary lift to support the character's inner life that is written.

Let's say your character is scripted to loathe her Dad and is unforgiving of him, but no specific information is given as to why. You could think of several seminal events in your character's life that have become seared into their memory. After these events, your character will have had layers of socialisation accumulate and obscure what is an essential truth about themselves. But to understand our character we want to peel back these layers.

Start by identifying a necessary or helpful past event to remember in your character's life. Roughly sketch out the rudiments of this 'scene': the where, the time of day, who was there - all the basics of what happened in this emotionally vivid event. Then, start your solo improv and sit in it in character for a while, in the character's present. Then, when you're ready, dredge up the event from your character's past. Treat it like something that you are trying to recall, a dim memory, obscured by time. Flesh out the detail. Use sense memory to create the specifics of that past event. Close your eyes and start adding details from all your senses: that is, remembering/ inventing what you can see, feel, touch, hear and smell; painting the picture of the event in more and more detail in your mind.

As you craft it, the event might look like a still black and white picture in your imagination. Or the created memory might play like a washed-out technicolour film, remorselessly moving to the emotional heart of the event, and then freezing there, allowing you to mine all the sensations, reactions and thoughts that live there for your character.

If this sensory approach to recalling memories sounds familiar, it's because American teacher Lee Strasberg's emotional recall uses a similar method. The difference is that here you are not trying to recall a *personal* memory, but instead invent a *fake* memory for your character.

You can also go in blind, without the previous rough sketch, knowing the important facts about your character. Run a few solo improvs and see what comes up. You may be surprised how readily your imagination starts to fire images and stories at you. These images are often a strange concoction using places and people from your own past and other elements of pure invention.

Once a character memory has been created, you can further refine that memory in more sensory detail in later improvs. When you do this you'll find you can consciously tweak at the memory's emotional heart, turning up or down the emotional 'volume' to suit your needs.

How it may feel is that you are not inventing things about your character, but *remembering* them. There's something particularly satisfying about revelations gleaned in this way. Once you've ascertained the story demands being made on your character, these fake memories can give you the emotional rocket fuel to get where you need to go. The benefit of a 'fake' character memory is that your body really can't differentiate between that and a 'real' memory. Both are remembered through a similar cerebral progression as half-formed ideas bubble up from your subconscious to your consciousness. To an extent you can trick your brain into thinking an imaginary back story is real, at least for the purposes of performance.

Strepsil Man

The Strepsil Man exercise allows actors to experience being 'in character' on a deep level. The name comes from a TVC for Strepsil throat lozenges I did once with director Robert Sarkies, where a see-through lozenge blob transformed into me.

Let's try a similar transformation; from you to your character, and in two steps. Stand up. Imagine, one step ahead of you, an opaque jelly-like substance forming the same shape as your body, but with its back to you. Prepare to take a step, leaving your old body behind, to enter this neutral zone of a body in front of you. Now, take that step. As you do, imagine you're leaving your old body behind you, like an insect shedding its skin.

Character – Further Explorations

When you enter the neutral zone feel all of your tension and worry being left behind. You are relaxed and floppy; ready for the second step. Because now, just one step ahead of you, you can see the writer's creation: your character. They are standing, waiting for you to bring them to life.

Take this physical step into them. Feel yourself wiring into their body as all their nerve endings connect up from your brain to your character's extremities. *You are now in character.* It may feel a little unfamiliar. You're seeing the world through new eyes. Carefully, take this character for a walk. It may feel a little like you are borrowing their body. They are moving, thinking and feeling, and alongside, *inside,* you are observing: how they are different from you, how they feel, how they see and react to things.

When you're ready to come out of character just snap your fingers. This exercise sounds all a little bit spooky, I know! But it can also be an insightful experiencing of your character.

Timeline

The first time I encountered 'Timeline' was with NLP trainer Judith Bedard who was guest-teaching a class of mine in Sydney. Timeline is an exploration of events in our characters back - and forward - story. The exercise is normally done in pairs, though there's no reason why a solo version wouldn't work.

Stand at one end of a biggish room. Set out the bounds of the timeline: in one short step, your character is born. Then, at the end of the room, one step *beyond* the far wall is your character's death. We don't go THERE! But everything in between, each step along that continuum, from birth, till just before death, is your character's timeline. A part of the length of this timeline will be the action of the film, TV series or play, but a good chunk may well be events from before and after that scripted story.

Get into character (use Strepsil Man if it gets you into a deeper character state) and start the journey. If in a pair, one actor steps through the timeline with the other asking questions. The actor who is doing the timeline closes their eyes. With their helper guiding them, they step out on to the timeline and continue with small steps until they hit resistance. Then the actor will find themselves slowing, then stopping; like they've encountered the thick treacle of a specific past character event. The helper gives the actor some time to perceive both WHERE and WHEN they are in this event from their character's journey. The actor can look around and let the detail of place and time become sharper. Once they are settled, the helper asks some questions: 'Where are you? What do you see? What can you hear? How do you feel about what's going on?' Get them to paint the scene in some sensory detail.

When they have done this ask them, 'anything else?' If there's nothing more, help them move on, till they pause again at the next point of resistance. At any time the actor can open their eyes, to 'see' where they are at in the timeline, or if it helps them, walk along (I've seen people happily do this exercise both eyes open or shut).

Timeline gives the actor permission to play with his or her imagination, making memories and back story more real, and discovering events of the character from birth to death, including well outside the timeline of the actual play or film. I think it's preferable to do timeline some way into your character study so the discoveries are better informed. You've already spent time as the character and know their story consciously, both in scripted back story and also their journey through the play or film. Timeline allows you to take ownership of that learning and marry it to some vivid events and memories in your imagination and body.

In English playwright Mark Ravenhill's play *Some Explicit Polaroids*, the character of Nadia is a wounded soul – in several asides she alludes to what must have been an abusive childhood. Although she is light and flippant in her dialogue, her past is betrayed through her present actions, such as sleeping with 'Nick' straight after he hurts her. Timeline could allow the actor playing Nadia to explore her dark past in some detail, which then justifies and underpins her need to spray new-age sunshine all over her present, which is far from sunny.

Sometimes you as an actor may need to spray some sunshine over your character if they have a tough time in their journey over the play or film. Timeline can be helpful in such a case if it gives your character a happy ending *beyond the story as written*. It can be easier to go to the dark places you need to in your work if you know that it all ends well for them.

GOODIES & BADDIES

Often in class, when we're discussing a character, an actor may say something like: 'they are totally sleazy,' or 'she's a *terrible* Mum.' These are understandable value judgements on the character's behaviour. But acting is not a moral art. It's not our job to pass judgement on any character we play. Instead always think of your characters, however loathsome their actions may be, with compassion. Seek to understand their motivations. Fall in love with them, or think of them as your best friend – we tend to forgive our friends a lot. The problem with making a value judgement on your character is that then your compassion is not engaged. You're holding them at moral arm's length.

Character – Further Explorations

Compassion, perhaps the greatest of virtues, comes to us from the Latin 'com' and 'passus,' and means 'to suffer with.' You cannot empathise with your character if you are not right in there alongside them, feeling their trials and tribulations as your own. It's hard to judge a character you have created with genuine empathy. Said English actor Timothy Spall on playing the ghastly Carmody Braque in *The Changeover*: 'You don't play the consequences of their actions, you play what they are doing at that very time… you try and connect your humanity to their humanity.'[38]

French actor Isabelle Huppert in the French film *The Piano Teacher* played a disturbed perfectionist having a sadomasochistic affair with a male student. Her character did the most terrible things, including damaging the fingers of a young pianist who was a rival for her student's affection and making a sexual pass at her mother. But Huppert worked until she adored her character, eventually seeing her story as one of first love unleashing passionate forces. It is an extraordinary performance.

One way to play without judgment these difficult characters – the likes of Shakespeare's Iago or Don John - is by asking yourself their story function. British actor David Suchet will rewrite the script for any role he is playing, as an essay, *with his character taken out*. He can then, by seeing what is missing without the character, figure out how the writer intended that character to affect the story. Rather than asking himself, 'how do I play this character,' he'll ask, 'why was he written?'[39] You can also ask: what made them this way? How far back do I have to go to find the innocent child, and how can I bring that child back into my performance?

Hollywood has long depicted baddies in an odious manner; evil, ugly and mean as well, treating their followers badly. Bad guys like Ralph Fiennes' Voldemort in *Harry Potter*, or Darth Vader in *Star Wars*, are fulfilling an archetypal story function.[40] But villains can also be played with deep empathy, such as Bruno Ganz's Hitler in the 2004 German film *Downfall*. Rather than a stereotype, Ganz started his work with something empathetic, real and tangible; the idea that Hitler was suffering from Parkinson's disease.

'Good guys' can also be approached in a one dimensional manner. Director Stephen Spielberg in *Schindler's List* was unable to resist, at the end of that film, whitewashing his lead character, so demeaning him to the status of

---

38 *Radio NZ National*, 5 October, 2017.
39 'David Suchet - Hercule Poirot, and more,' *Radio NZ National*, 11 November, 2019.
40 As we will discover in the *Telling Tales* chapter these black and white depictions of 'good' and 'bad' characters have hooks sunk deep into our narrative DNA.

a recognisable 'goodie.' Otto Schindler was a real German industrialist who risked his life to save hundreds of Jewish lives. He was also a serial adulterer and a dreadful businessman. In the book upon which the film is based, *Schindler's Ark*, writer Thomas Keneally is content to present these contradictions without attempting to reconcile them. Spielberg, however, redeems Schindler's character in the end, adding in a scene where he tells his wife he is stopping his philandering. In truth, Schindler never stopped cheating on his wife. If he made this promise at all, he broke it. But we are lead to believe that this is a redemptive moment. The film is an extraordinary achievement, but in this moment Spielberg's instincts falter. He assumes that if one *does* good, then one must be shown to be *only* good. Far more refreshing, and artistically useful, is Harold Clurman's take on an actual Saint: 'Joan of Arc should be played as a pain in the ass and how do I know she was a pain in the ass? Because they burn her at the end.'

The idea of evil is a biblical, not scientific, construct. Even biblical evil can be hard to spot. In old Christian art, Satan was always depicted, as Yuval Harari has put it, 'as a gorgeous hunk.'[41] Why else would it be difficult to resist his temptations? Evil can be played with allure as well as empathy. Contemporary TV shows such as *Breaking Bad*, *Ozark* and *Killing Eve* blur the line. We see flawed characters being forced to pick a side.

The depiction of evil is something Albert Speer confronted directly in his 1969 autobiography *Inside the Third Reich*. Speer, Hitler's architect (and later Minister of Armaments) has been described as Hitler's best friend. He felt that the traditional depiction of Hitler as a carpet chewing madman made it impossible for later generations of Germans to understand why Speer himself and so many of his contemporaries revered him - even died for him.

When playing someone like Hitler we must remember that no one ever believes they are the 'bad' guy. Hitler was a charismatic leader whose ideology – Fascism – told Germans they belonged to the most beautiful and important entity in the world: the German nation. He and his followers saw themselves as saviours of the Aryan people. Like all of us, they wished to think well of themselves, even as they did terrible things. If you inflict suffering on others, you are given a choice: either the Fascist story - namely, we are the good guys, this is for the greater good - is true, or, much less palatable, *I must be a villain*. But we'd rather not be villains. We prefer to believe the story. Your character always believes his story and it makes him, however heinous his acts, *a good*

---

41 In his TED talk, *Why fascism is so tempting - and how your data could power it*.

Character – Further Explorations

person in his own eyes. You have to figure out the story your villain lives by and what it gives him. Then you can play him with empathy.

Philippe Sands is a human rights lawyer who has prosecuted numerous war criminals at the International Court of Justice at *The Hague*. What fascinates (and appalls) Sands is how the men he has convicted have committed such deplorable acts as kidnapping women, raping them for weeks on end, and then going home and being loving husbands and fathers. All the while their wives fully know what's going on.

How can we reconcile this? As actors we must recognise that it is deeply human to simultaneously commit evil acts and feel we are doing good. There's an acting adage that says: find the devil in the angel and the angel in the devil. But we can never do this unless we admit to the potential for both evil and good to exist within everyone – including us.

OBSERVING LIFE

I shared a house once with New Zealand painter Mark Braunias. He returned from a fellowship in Prague and I asked him what he did while he was there. 'Mostly,' he said, 'I sat in a café on a street corner and watched the world go by.' At the time I thought this sounded like a colossal waste of time. But now I understand that Mark was collecting raw material for his art, squirrelling away sights, sounds and behaviours that would fertilise his work for years to come.

Many artists work in this way. What they produce is based on their observation of the outside world. This observation is then cast through the lens of their unique view. While still a child, Jane Austen, the British novelist, kept notebooks, jotting down the details of everyday encounters she observed: how a couple squabbled, how a man walked, what the maids said to each other when they thought no one was listening. These were all clues revealing how humans behaved. They became the starting point for the characters in her later novels.

Similarly, in one of his visits to my Auckland studio, Joel Tobeck related how he also used to sit outside his favourite café on Ponsonby road, much like Mark Braunias did, just watching people go by, storing up characters and behaviours. The American actor Bryan Cranston would do the same thing. He'd head for the nearest mall armed with headphones, so people wouldn't think he was listening, and a newspaper, so they wouldn't think he was looking, then get close to the most interesting human behaviour he saw, such as a couple arguing.

How many times have you read an interview where a famous actor bemoans that, because they are so recognisable, they can no longer be a fly on the wall watching their fellow human beings? They have become instead the watched and so been robbed of their raw material: other people. These actors know how powerful it is to work from observation.

Why not make watching a habit? Everyone you meet and everything you have ever seen are all potentially useful for a role you may play in the future. You'll see some extraordinary characters, so 'out there,' in fact, that if you saw them on a stage you'd think they were grossly overacted. But they aren't. They are the eccentric, the mad, the carefree, the scarred and the indelibly sad. Just watching them gives you powerful permission to act *anything*.

As you watch, ask yourself: what kind of lives have these people lived? What has made them look that way? Move in that way? What story does their extraordinary face tell? What are they hiding? What are they hiding from? What's their greatest fear? Just imitating someone's body posture or walk will give you an insight into how they feel. When you adopt their physical characteristics you'll feel emotional changes in yourself, akin to their own inner life.

CHAPTER SEVEN
SCREEN ACTING
Talk quietly, think loudly.
Alan Dale

WORKING WITH THE CAMERA

Acting, says Michael Caine, is a delicate operation: theatre requires a sharp scalpel, but screen demands the precision of a laser.[42]

You'll appreciate this when you watch back your screen work. What many of us do for the camera, particularly when nervous, is too much. We emote. We blink. Without knowing it we smile or are overly expressive. Work to clean up any clutter; pull it back with a simple objective or a clear choice. Clint Eastwood's acting coach used to say, 'don't just do something; stand there!' It takes guts to trust yourself. But once you show them more, you might just be showing them bad acting.

Once you're working, remember that as you go from take to take, scene to scene, it's not always possible to judge with any accuracy how well you're doing. It might feel great, and look average. It might feel average because it was hard work, but look great. Said Sir Ian McKellen to a struggling Hugh Jackman, cast at the last minute to play Wolverine in the first *X-Men* movie, 'Just because it feels uncomfortable doesn't mean it's not good.'[43] Act on your impulses. If the director likes it, great! Move on. If not there's always another take.

Don't be negative about getting direction. Sure, some directors don't overdo praise, but almost all of the time their note to you will come out of what they have just seen you do. In other words, your performance is inspiring *them*. Unless told specifically not to, ADD what they say to what you are doing. Don't junk your whole performance and obediently do *only* what you've just been told. That's not what they want. They don't want a servant. They want a collaborator.

---

42 *Michael Caine Teaches Acting In Film*, (1987) Youtube.
43 Told by Hugh Jackman in *Bafta Guru*: 'It's okay, be nervous.'

SCREEN SPECIFIC TECHNIQUES
What follows are some ideas and tools that are especially useful for the screen.

Reacting
Make the other character the most important person in the scene. Don't act. Listen. And listen with your whole body, the way animals do – as if your life depended on it. Pre-eminently for camera work, acting is REACTING, not acting. Make your performance come out of the other character, in response to what they say and do. You can use key-wording, actions, or the game of arrows, whatever works for you, to figure out what is triggering your response. It's too late to figure out your attitude to what the other character is saying once you're filming – you need to know prior.

Remembering
Remembering is seeing things in our imagination, and the root word of imagination is IMAGE; when we remember things we see them. For every person, past event, memory, thing or place that your character talks about in a scene, if you actually *see* them, then the audience will too. Let people and places you know stand in as substitutions for what is written in the script, with the caution that if this throws you, construct something original or historical.

To illustrate this in a class once I asked an actor to imagine, as she was running a monologue, that she was standing in the front of her house, and to mentally count how many colours she could see. Immediately she was looking at the house, as if a slide of it had been projected onto the wall in front of her. She came to life. These imaginative projections are called different things by different people: 'inner things' by American acting coach Ivana Chubbuck, for example, and 'internal landscape' by our very own Miranda Harcourt.

Vista
Vista is a term I first heard from Miranda. It's one of what she calls the 5 Tools, the others being Connection, Internal Landscape, White Space and Journey. Vista describes referencing in some way the things/ people/ environment that are outside the small frame that the camera – and the audience - are seeing. As with internal landscapes, this technique works for the camera because it mimics how human beings actually behave.

In one of his early film roles, British actor Richard Harris was playing a sailor. In one scene he spat over the side of the boat, then leant over to watch the spit move past on the water. Except… the scene wasn't shot at sea but in a sound studio. With that action Harris created the ocean.

You can make any physical place real when you refer to it with a gesture or a motion of your head: 'up north,' 'down there,' 'Doug's office,' 'your place.' This place then, magically, becomes a fact. If you are referring to a place or person or object outside of the frame, even if it is a hundred miles away, and you have no idea of its precise direction, know where it is in your head and place it with a gesture if you wish.

Equally, and in the spirit of inclusion, Vista can include *whatever is really there, in front of you*. If there is a light on set that is making you squint, then squint. If there's something interesting happening out of the window in the audition room, notice that.

Filming your rehearsals
While we don't want to become too self-aware, if you have a scene coming up that challenges you and you think it may help, then film it ahead of time – even just on your phone. This can be especially useful if you have to play a physical circumstance like an illness or a particular mental condition. For instance, you might have chosen an isolation idea, like difficulty breathing, for a death scene, but want to check if what you are doing plays okay. This is not to nail down 'how' you are going to play it, but about testing an idea to see if it's working.

The Close Up & Awareness of Camera
A close up is the time when the audience feels nearest to our work. With more film and television content being viewed on handheld devices, the close up is being used more often.

Obviously, in a close-up, stillness becomes more important – a small movement will read bigger than it actually is. For close-ups get into the habit of looking at the other actor's eye that is closest to the lens - their camera-side eye. If you look at that eye with your eye that is *furthest* from the camera, your head will naturally turn and we'll see more of you. Don't flick too much from eye to eye, unless you want your character to look shifty. Similarly don't blink too much unless you are playing a low-status character. If the camera has to follow you as you rise out of a chair, be kind to the camera operator and rise more slowly and smoothly than you would in everyday life.

If you want us to see what your character is thinking, make sure the camera can see your eyes. Eye-lids are the shutters to our souls, eyes being the only living part of another human being we ever see. Everything else – the skin, the hair, our nails – is dead. Your eyes let us in. Work to affect the other actor with your eyes and open yourself up to being affected.

Of course it's fine if you wish to deny your eyes to the camera too – that can sometimes be a powerful choice.

For screen, be like a duck – looking placid on the surface but paddling like mad underneath. 'An actor has to burn inside with an outer ease,' said Michael Chekhov. He warned against the advice given to actors to do 'less' for camera. Instead Chekhov would say to do *more* - but veil it. Playing an emotionally repressed butler in *Remains of the Day*, Antony Hopkins made just this choice. He created a huge emotional life for his character, which he then had to push down with strenuous force.

Being in the moment

Being in the moment, or 'present,' is important for live performance, but for the screen, essential. 'Being in the moment' means you're not thinking ahead, nor looking back – you are in the here and now. It looks like you don't know what's going to happen next - because you don't. You are being spontaneous, something that can't be faked.

Sometimes we can be so 'present' during a take that if someone walks behind the camera, or a car misfires in the distance, you may not even notice, such is your engagement. But equally other times you may not be so 'in.' You may hear the studio door creak open, or catch the movement of the camera assist scratching themselves. That's fine too. The bigger mistake is to pretend you haven't noticed these distractions. If you see, hear or feel something, your character must too. In a variation of the emotional inclusion we discussed in Chapter 4, you must include all distractions, accidents – *everything* - in your performance. Great actors know that there is no alternative to this kind of inclusion. We want to be in a state of total belief in what we are doing - but we cannot force it. No matter how 'in' we feel, once we hear 'action,' we must trust that our feelings and reactions and our character's are the same. When we do this we are 'in the moment.'

Letting go and living in the moment can feel pretty dangerous. That's why audiences' love it. 'Danger is about unpredictability and being in the moment;' says British director Nicholas Hytner, 'acknowledging that if you are in the moment the next moment cannot and must not be predictable...' For British voice coach Patsy Rodenburg being 'in the moment' means being switched on, watchful, ready for anything - what she calls being 'in the second circle', having the same alertness you would have in prison, where violence could break out without warning. In Shakespeare's time the sense of danger came from the fact that each actor was not given a copy of the whole script because it took so long to handwrite each one. Rather, each actor got given sheets with their own lines, and just the last THREE words of each of their cue lines. They were 'in the moment' because there was always the danger that if they weren't tuned in and listening they might miss their cue.

So this idea of being dangerous and unpredictable – in the moment – has been sitting in the heart of good acting for some time. To prepare for it, when you're working on a role, stop at any point where you feel you're starting to plan your delivery. You want to discover the 'how' in the playing because you can't be spontaneous if you've already figured out how you're going to play it in advance. For some actors that's what their prep is about, building a secure wall around themselves that protects them from possible surprises. This is a misguided effort. Fear is a given. There's no escaping it. It comes from the unavoidable uncertainty of outcome that is acting, and further - something all good actors know - that the outcome must be uncertain if the acting is to be any good.

As I've said, your prep is about getting you ready to discover something new on your feet. A scene and a role should be discovered in the doing because this is what happens in life, where there are no dress rehearsals. If your prep is about deciding in advance how you will speak, do and feel, it can dishearten you later. As you perform you start second guessing yourself, thinking: 'I did that line better in the car on the way in,' or, 'I reacted on this bit much better yesterday running it with my room-mate.' Half-way through the scene you may stop believing in what you are doing because it hasn't met your expectation. That expectation though is just an idea in your head about what the scene *should* be. It's getting in the way of what it actually *could* be.

Once you're performing, you have no choice but to trust yourself and let them see into your soul: not what you'd like to show them, but what is *really* going on. For this to happen, the higher intellectual brain must hand over control, when 'action' is called, to our inner lizard. Our higher human brain just can't handle the split-second decisions needed. If you run each impulse through some kind of conscious filter of 'would my character do that?' then it's already too late. Intellect is careful. Intuition is immediate. The moment has passed as soon as you stop to think. You've missed out on a spontaneous spark that would have revealed in that moment your version of what it truly means to be human. We must trust our instincts and get on with it. That means acting on our impulses – acting before we can think.

It's risky to fly by the seat of your pants like this. But no actor has yet been shot for screwing up because some impulse didn't work out. There's always the next take or the next night's performance. Consistency is the death of good acting. Once you've done a scene a certain way, why serve up that same version again and again? So long as the continuity matches, it's from three *different* takes that the editor can craft your performance of brilliance. It's harder to do that with three that are essentially the same because you've been straining to perfect one idea. In the trade that's called 'polishing the turd.'

Of course, running on instinct and being in the moment can feel exposing to the actor; somehow rather personal, which is discomforting, because we want to be playing a character. Inclusion, running with all distractions, feelings and impulses in the moment, can feel like *our* feelings, *our* inner world, are on show, not the *character's*. But remember that to the audience your feelings look *exactly* like the characters; blocking something out or pretending to be feeling something you do not looks, to them, like acting. You are always in character. Trust your instincts and jump in. 'Affect the other actor,' counsels British actor and director Mark Rylance, 'release whatever is pent up in you – and change the world.'

TELEVISION COMMERCIALS (TVC'S)

Right now, somewhere, hunched over his desk and scarfing junk food, is an advertising copywriter who thinks he has just written the most brilliant, funny, moving 30 second script anywhere. To bring it to life you just have to crawl inside his head and figure out what he was thinking. You may find when you do that you complete his story – you discover as you search for meaning something the writer hadn't thought of. If you show him that icing on his cake he may well say when he sees your audition tape – 'that's it!' – even if he only just realises it watching your performance. If you can show him you understand his story, perhaps better even than he does, the role may well be yours.

The key to achieving this is to understand that TVC's are short scenes: 15, 30 or 60-second stories. Don't underestimate them. They are storytelling at their most economical, and they can teach you a lot about screen acting. They require a precision in the telling – the ability to discern each beat and moment of action, and particularly to identify the hook, turning point or punchline in the story.

So, what is the story? Identify the beginning (the status quo/ happy days), the middle (the change/ presentation of the problem) and the end (resolution). Find the hook. Identify the beats – these are further points of change. Work out how you can embody the beats and the hook/ change. Whatever choice you make, nail yourself to the mast on it – go there. Better to aim high and miss than leave no impression at all.

TVC's differ from most other screen acting in that, as a genre, they tend to be more upbeat; to be more focussed on the *solution* to the problem than the problem itself. When studying the script for elements such as relationship, substitutions, situations and justifications, look for the positives. If speaking a piece to camera, keep this lightness in mind also. You want to place someone in that camera (the substitution), who you like instinctively and have a warm upbeat relationship with.

While crafting your performance for scripted TVC's is a good idea – it'll give you a modicum of pride in the audition room, for one thing – do remember that the 'look' is a big part of TVC casting. Don't be too discouraged if the role doesn't go your way this time. The casting briefs are usually pretty specific, and they can afford to be picky, as typically the budgets are good and the casting directors can see a lot of actors.

Treat TVC auditions as a useful training ground in audition technique and economical screen acting and you can't lose. If you do get cast, don't drop that part-time job. Invest the money back into classes, professional development, or your next creative project.

CHAPTER EIGHT
THEATRE ACTING

Movies will make you famous; television will make you rich; but theatre will make you good.
Terrence Mann, American actor

THE UPSIDE OF THEATRE

Theatre is less relevant in many people's lives today because of the rise of art forms like TV, film and web-based content, not to mention gaming. But actors should think carefully about turning their back on theatre. It nurtures our abilities in important ways.

Why do so many great screen comedians come from the harsh school of stand-up? Because they have learnt what makes humans laugh – from actual humans. In live performance laughs typically come not on the lines, but on the reactions to them. How are you ever going to learn that, without an audience? In theatre there is always a live audience. The theatre actor is getting direct feedback from people, moment to moment. It's an education in what works in acting. It's no surprise that live studio audiences were introduced into TV situation comedy.

In a play an actor usually has to present changes in their character over time: a day, a month, a year - in some cases longer – over one evening. The theatre actor is *forced* to think of their character's journey over time because they have to pack it all into 90 or so minutes. A screen actor can focus on each scene as discrete entities without learning how to capture the bigger picture in this way.

In theatre, typically, the scenes are longer. Sometimes you're up there the whole time or a whole act. This requires a different kind of concentration from the typical 2 or 3-minute length of a film or TV scene. If you drop the ball on stage you don't get the luxury of another take. You have to pick it up and keep playing. So, you learn *resilience*. You learn to always say *yes*.

On a stage the audience's gaze is not directed via editing as it is for screen.

Theatre Acting

Spectators can shift their attention to anywhere on the stage at any time. This means the actor must be 'on' the whole time. In this way, theatre can develop the acting muscle of *stamina,* in a way screen doesn't.

You also learn respect for writing when you work in the theatre, because the material is usually good. Good writing forces you to work harder. Imagine trying to perform any role in an Anton Chekhov play without understanding what sub-text was – and how to find the humour that lurks beneath the superficially grim dialogue.

It's far more common for a non-theatre trained actor to argue that 'my character wouldn't say this' - and want to change the dialogue to how she would say it. But a theatre actor, with respect for writing bashed into them, may be more likely to figure out what kind of person would say those lines and make them work. Playing many roles has forced them to think in terms of playing characters, not versions of themselves.

For all of these reasons, like salmon swimming home to spawn, many great actors return to the stage regularly. It's a common practice in Australasia, not least because if you want to keep acting you have to do everything, across all media. And if you're working in some low paid theatre co-op, and a high paying screen audition comes along, chances are you'll do a better job of it. Work begets work. Sometimes you need to go to the theatre gym to flex those muscles to get match fit for the bigger screen roles when they come up.

Many of theatre's benefits can indeed be learnt doing fast turnaround multi-camera TV. But that avenue isn't always available as a training ground for every up and coming actor, whereas theatre work of some kind can be found pretty much anywhere. This is perhaps theatre's biggest plus - it gives you a chance to work. In almost any city in the world an actor can usually audition for and get cast in some kind of play. When we know we need to work we can pretty much always find it on a stage. Distinguished Acting coach Larry Moss calls theatre the actors' 'life raft' for this reason.

I don't want to overstate the importance of theatre. I've done any number of badly written theatre shows with unimaginative directors. More and more there is quality writing in TV that will stretch and challenge you. Screen acting will of course also develop technique. And performing in just a few plays, or time in any reputable drama school, gives you much of the learning you need. Stage work has been a portal many great screen actors have passed through because, along with classes, there often is nowhere else to start. But just don't think that time doing theatre won't help your screen acting. It will, because it'll make you a better actor.

THEATRE VS SCREEN ACTING

The most obvious preparation difference between theatre and screen work is that theatre has long rehearsals and TV/ Film has shorter ones - and sometimes, none at all. For screen, the onus is on the actor to do more of their prep on their own. Once you're on set *it's too late:* then directors can generally only tweak, not transform, your contribution. Of course, for theatre you have to do significant preparation on your own as well. And for screen work you should expect rehearsals, meetings and as much collaboration as time and budget allows.

With theatre, in performance, the audience is there in the room with you. It's hard to ignore them, try as we might. In camera acting we can forget the audience is there. But they still are – only there's very many more of them. Subliminally the actor knows this, and it can translate to a discomfort with the camera, and sometimes even a fear of it. The screen actor must develop a relationship with the camera that acknowledges the audience relationship and the nerves it brings (see Chapter 16 *Excitement. Nerves. Doubt. Dread*).

The audience is also closer because the camera often is. So, as a general rule the big gestures or expressions that might go down okay in theatre may not work so well for screen. The camera is less forgiving than someone sitting in row 'H.' It cuts through artifice and sees through lazy tricks. Some of the mannerisms you can employ in theatre acting may not read well in close up.

Having said that, the differences between film and theatre acting styles can be exaggerated. Performance size depends not just on the medium but also what show you're in. Film acting can be BIG: for evidence of that look no further than the work of Swiss actor Christoph Waltz in the film *Inglorious Bastards* – a part which won him an Oscar (at age 56). And theatre acting can be tiny. I saw just the big toe of New Zealand actor Cameron Rhodes bring the house down in a production of *A Midsummer Night's Dream.* And many years ago George Henare (another great New Zealand actor), in an Auckland Theatre Company production of *Wind in the Willows,* gave a most nuanced (and brilliant) performance as Ratty – I can starkly remember his every raised eyebrow and startled blink. Prepping for his mind-blowingly precise work as Olivia in the *Globe Theatre's* production of *Twelfth Night,* Mark Rylance watched the male Kabuki actor Tamasaburo play a female character on stage. The minimalism of that performance informed the extraordinary subtlety he brought to his Olivia.[44] Said Rylance of the role:

---

[44] The production ran first at the *Globe* in London and then on Broadway. This is Shakespeare how it should be performed by, possibly, the greatest living actor of our time.

Theatre Acting

'If you're very still for a long period of time, a little raise of the eyebrow will reach a long way. Because people have projected onto you so many things, that there's a lot of life going on already.'[45]

This kind of restraint can and does translate directly to screen also, where the body can be powerful in the smallest details. You may be doing a film close up, but still need every cell in your body engaged. In theatre and film both, under pressure, you can do too much. Don't overdo it. Remember, you are always enough.

SOME THEATRE TIPS

Theatre is often talked about as the actor's medium. But that's only really that from the opening night when the director traditionally hands over the show to the stage manager and the actors for the run of the show. In rehearsal it's very much the medium of the director - with a lot of collaboration from the actors as well. You'll be doing homework but also embracing the unique collaborative opportunities that exist in theatre, more so than for screen. Get the work up, be gutsy, make discoveries on your feet. Listen to the director and get behind their vision for the show.

Learn your lines *before* rehearsal starts. It's so much more useful to engage with your fellow actors off book. Turning up 'script in hand' to rehearsal is a relic of an earlier age of Rep theatre, where actors would have a new play thrust at them every three weeks. Master any accents and stage skills (dancing, sword fighting) you may need before rehearsals begin. If you haven't done theatre for a while the best investment is to do some one-on-one sessions with a reputable voice coach. Theatre is a whole-body medium, engaging voice, body and spirit. Voice work will release the energy and emotion in the words for you, hugely helping your performance.

Every rehearsal process will be different. Say yes to whatever approaches on offer, even if unfamiliar and frightening. Don't be afraid to own up to your fears and insecurities – these are energy, unless you disguise them behind bravado. Each day perform as if opening night was tomorrow. And then know that performance isn't set: it must change, grow and evolve every day, every performance.

---

[45] 'How Mark Rylance Became Olivia Onstage,' by Ben Brantley, *The New York Times,* August 14, 2016.

CHAPTER NINE
KILLER CONCEPTS

An inspiring idea can be as helpful as blunt knowledge. Here are some ideas to lift your acting up a notch, or ten, in unexpected and surprising ways.

> *The thing about performance, even if it's only an illusion, is that it is a celebration of the fact that we do contain within ourselves infinite possibilities.*
> **Daniel Day Lewis**

MAKE SIMPLE STRONG CHOICES

Some years ago I visited the studio of the jeweller and artist Kobi Bosshard in Otago, New Zealand. His style had not changed substantially since the 1960's – though it had evolved. It was simple and elegant. I admired both his trust in his signature and his courage in not complicating it over time. That struck me as real artistic confidence.

You should aim for simplicity and clarity in your acting too. Your prep will be wide-ranging but the point of it is to come to work with a strong, simple offer on the day. You may not be able, for a while, to see the wood for the trees. So, remember that many great performances have happened when the actor has worked through a maze of conflicting possibilities and arrived at a simple hook – a one sentence or even one word understanding of their character's dilemma in the story. Sometimes this can only be articulated after the event. It can be as simple as playing an objective, alongside a sense of where the character lives in their head.

Here are some examples:

For Natalie Portman in *Black Swan*, her guiding idea was that her character, Nina, needed to stop trying to please others, and please herself.

Closer to home, in *The Lord of the Rings* Trilogy New Zealand actor John Leigh, knowing his character was destined to die in battle, imagined that throughout his character's journey he was being haunted by dreams of his violent death.

Killer Concepts

While filming *Schindler's List*, English actor Ben Kingsley is said to have carried a note in his pocket that described Stern's - his character's - narrative function in the movie. He asked Steven Spielberg what he thought it was. Spielberg said, very simply: 'Witness.' Kingsley's word was 'conscience' (of Otto Schindler).[46]

Doubt is always there, nipping at our emotional heels, and with it comes the temptation to overcomplicate things. That's a given, but at the crucial moment take ownership of the work and back yourself. Work on having versatility role to role. Don't try to pack all your talent into one performance. We work on a scene for hours, then on the day we might shoot it ten or fifteen times in different shot sizes and takes. But the audience sees it just once. For them to comprehend the story, the telling of it can be layered, but it also has to be clear, specific, and uncluttered. Do as little as you need to tell the story - you'll reveal more that way than if you try to show us all your cleverness.

OBSERVE ART

When writing, acting or directing, take your inspiration from source. If you're playing a cop or a prostitute, talk to people who have done those jobs, or go to an appropriate documentary source. If we know something to be factually true it has a tighter hold on our imagination. Equally, go and see great art, in all media. It inspires and stirs our imaginations. Opera teaches that truth and big size can go together, that we can feel our way to a profound emotional experience without understanding a word of the story. Circus dazzles us with its skill and bravura showmanship. Music teaches us the importance of sheer hard graft. Singers lay it ALL on the line. Books are still a fast track to living alternate realities. In my early 20's when I first read Dostoyevsky he utterly blew my mind. If you want to experience being eaten from the inside by guilt read his *Crime and Punishment*. If you ever have to understand what a descent into moral degeneration and hypocrisy feels like, read Wilde's *The Picture of Dorian Gray*.

SAY YES TO YOUR INTUITION

We can never be entirely sure how our acting is coming across. Sometimes it feels dreadful - and it is. Other times it may feel plain wrong, but might just be magic. We just don't know. There's an element of chance in all of this.

---

[46] As described by Paul Scheer and Amy Nicholson in their podcast *Unspooled*.

'Directors supervise accidents,' said Alfred Hitchcock. So, rather than letting a 'mistake' throw you, include it in your performance. Get in the habit of never calling 'cut' on yourself when something goes 'wrong.' You might bail just when something interesting is happening. To us the struggle to get the scene back on track may make no narrative sense – but it may still be hugely watchable. It's not our job to make that call – let the director and the editor be the judge. *Whatever* happens: always say yes. It's a lesson quickly learnt in theatre where you really do have to keep going anyway, no matter what.

There are many examples to be found on the internet of 'A' list actors saying yes to 'mistakes,' incorporating the balls-up and gamely carrying on. Chris Pratt in *Guardians of the Galaxy* literally dropped the ball (actually the all-powerful orb of *universal destruction*) then deftly picked it up and kept acting. Jamie Lee Curtis fell over then got straight up and carried on with her striptease in *True Lies*. The wrenching scream of pain from Viggo Mortensen as he *actually* breaks two toes kicking an Uruk helmet in *The Two Towers* will not be forgotten in a hurry - but only because he stayed in character so the shot could play out. Julia Roberts in *August Osage County* forgot her lines in a scene and so just banged on again and again with the one she could remember: 'eat your fucking fish!' And it was brilliant.

These were ALL takes that ended up being used in the final cut of these films. They are some of their best moments. These missteps are a testament to the commitment of the actors not to call cut and the intuition of the directors watching, who could easily have also called cut when the scene went 'wrong.'

So: once you hear 'roll camera,' get in character and say yes to *whatever* happens until you hear 'cut.'

SAY YES TO DIRECTION

We should also always say yes to direction, even bad direction. This isn't always easy. You may disagree with the director, or take her note as a personal judgement on your choices. You may want to change what you're doing, but find it hard to translate the direction you're getting. But it is an uncollaborative mindset that says there is only one right way to do this scene and only you know it.

When you act you make your offer and then it's the director's turn. Your job then becomes translating their direction into *something you can play*. They have the advantage over you: they can see what you just did. Even if you watch playback, that doesn't even the playing field. We're uniquely disqualified to judge our own work as we do so loaded with expectation. If you thought the take was lousy, then watch it back and it's not half bad, you'll think it's great. If we thought the take was great, and it's only good, you'll feel disappointed.

Film sets and theatre rehearsal rooms are not democracies. As Michael Caine says: 'the director is the guv'nor.' There has to be a final voice. The way forward creatively is to embrace the director's note. The director's offer might feel rubbish, and indeed look like that in execution. That's fine. The director will see that and together you can find a third way. So, that awful take will have been a necessary part of the creative process. Bad choices help us find good choices.

But other times that appalling direction which had seemed so wrong makes sense in the playing. Perhaps the director was inspired. Perhaps it was your sheer craft that made the 'bum' note work. Who cares? It's why Michael Chekhov's advice to his students was always to obey all 'bad' direction. You just never know.

My argument here is not that you should be unfailingly obedient. It's that the best way forward is often to embrace the alternate viewpoint and then assess the result. You're allowed to stand up for your point of view. Creative differences are part of the business. Actors that are reluctant to change with direction, or disagree with directors, or passionately defend their choices, can be good actors. But they can be perceived not as committed artists, but obstructionist temperaments. They sometimes aren't much fun to work with either. So, they end up not being hired as much. Figure out how to contest your corner in a collaborative and professional way.

NAP

In my callow youth I spent time in the New Zealand Army. I did my training then returned for several years doing field exercises as a part-time soldier – a 'Cut lunch Commando' as the Regular's disparagingly dubbed us. In our annual exercises we sometimes played out the plot of Oliver Stone's movie *Platoon*: for days on end we'd march all day, dig a hole to stand and sleep in, get three hours sleep, stand to at 5 am, fill in the hole, and repeat. We'd be shot at (with blanks, I hasten to add), told to run up a hill, or suddenly ordered to build a Bailey Bridge. The only way to survive this kind of madness was to nap. When we were told to halt, most of us would just drop our kit and crash. Those that didn't would get to a point where they'd just fall over. And then you couldn't get them up again.

Film sets may not be quite this rigorous, but the hours are long. If you are in a major role you are on set with make-up sometimes hours before other key crew are called. At the end of the day you have to go home and learn your lines. Or you can be doing theatre, getting home at midnight and be so wired you can't sleep. Then the kids are jumping on your bed at 6 am.

If you want to get by, it can be handy to know how to nap. If you have one of those busy minds that has trouble switching off, learn how to meditate. That will teach you how to calm your mind so you can sleep when needed, anywhere – sitting on a chair or even lying down on the ground.

STEAL

For a recent Shakespeare audition where I was time-crunched, I Youtubed several great actors performing the monologue I was prepping. I wasn't looking to copy their external performance; I wanted to understand the sense of the monologue quickly. It was helpful and reminded me of the successful and long collaboration I had with New Zealand director Robin Walters, where we made many TVC's. At the start of every project an unashamed Robin would sit me down and show me clips from films and ads that had inspired him. He would act out his idea of the character in rehearsal, and so communicate how he wanted the result to be. His style was a little like the French tradition in theatre where in the first rehearsal, instead of a table read, the playwright of any original piece gets the chance to communicate his vision by getting up and performing *the entire play* for the cast, acting out all of the roles.

For our award-winning 2001 Short Film *The Platform* Robin first showed me *Desserts*, the 1998 short film directed by English director Jeff Stark and starring Ewan McGregor, to demonstrate the type of change/ switch/ hook we were gunning for. One morning we drove out to the (single) location with the DOP. Sure enough, Robin acted out the entire film. I copied Robin's performance as best I could and the DOP filmed it. Next Robin made a rough cut on his computer and that evening we watched it. I went into filming knowing exactly what he was after. Robin stole from Jeff Stark, I stole from Robin, brought a few flourishes to the template and voila – something fresh and funny emerged.[47]

The *content* of any effective story must be original – ripped from the entrails of the writer's personal experience. But there is no new story structure under the sun. Novel, film and long-form TV stories can be clustered around six

---

[47] You can find and watch both *Desserts* and *The Platform* on Youtube.

emotional profiles. These are; one, rags to riches – an ongoing emotional rise as seen in films such as *The Shawshank Redemption*; two, riches to rags – an ongoing emotional fall (as in a film like *Psycho*); three, man in a hole – a fall followed by a rise (*The Godfather*); four, Icarus – a rise followed by a fall (for example in *On the Waterfront*); five, Cinderella – a rise followed by a fall followed by a rise (*Babe*); and finally Oedipus, a fall followed by a rise followed by a fall (*All About My Mother*).[48]

It's the same for performances. You're not the first and you won't be the last to play this kind of character in this kind of story. You are standing on the head and shoulders of many actors who have come before you. Each combination of story, genre, writer and director will hint at an acting style and approach that will fit that project. Watch content in that style, either by the show's creators, or shows they reference. Cliché is a near, not a far neighbour, of originality. True innovation comes from something new added to what we know has come before. Cliché results from striving to be original without this knowingness. At best, you run the risk of unconsciously repeating what has come before.

'The best steal,' said Robert DeNiro. 'Steal any trick that looks worthwhile,' said Michael Caine,'because you can be sure that they stole it in the first place.'[49]

DISCOVERIES

Michael Shurtleff, in his book *Audition*, lists 12 guideposts to great acting. Humour is one (see below). The importance of making discoveries is another. Shurtleff encouraged his students to find as many discoveries for their characters to make as they could; to always ask: what's new here? Acting should have the quality of an improv; it should look as if you are hearing the other actor's lines for the first time. Being an active listener means making a series of *discoveries* out of what the other actor is saying and doing.

Let's look at the scene again, *When a man loves a woman*, in Appendix 3. Because the scene is an argument it's hard not to act as if the characters have said all these things a hundred times before. They may well have. But no matter how many times something has happened or been said, the actor's job is to find what is new about it today. In this case the answer is that they break up.

---

48 Incidentally scientists recently found the 'Man in a hole' story arc – a fall followed by a rise – to be most commercially successful – 'Scientists uncover formula for box office movie success,' Mark Brown, *The Guardian*, 24 July 2018.
49 *Michael Caine Teaches Acting In Film, (1987)*, Youtube.

When you read your next script or scene, try finding as many discoveries for your character as you can. Then ask yourself how they *feel* about each discovery; whether it's positive or negative.

ROLE MODELS

Having a *role model*, an actor you aspire to be like, can inspire you, but also help define your contribution in a crowded market of actors. But you can seek out a mentor too. New Zealand actor Kevin J Wilson was of great practical help to me starting out. Or a mentor can find you – this was Sam Neill's experience when British actor James Mason saw him in *My Brilliant Career* and sponsored him for his break-through lead role in *The Final Conflict*.

You can also ask yourself, when in a challenging acting corner: what choice would a great actor make? You may or may not find it helpful to tag that question to a particular hero of yours.

ISOLATION & THE IMAGINATION

One thing I've repeatedly observed in classes is the usefulness of the idea of isolation; of focusing in on one idea, or one part of your body. Isolation seems to excite our imaginations, not narrow them, as you might think. Our imagination is activated by isolation because it loves and responds to specificity and constraints.

Acting isn't brain surgery. No one's going to die if we get it wrong. We actors take it seriously because of the pressure we can feel under. But the fact is what we're doing is dress up. It's not real. The Russians do not say 'to act.' Their verb to describe acting is egrat – 'to play.' They say 'I'm playing' a role. 'Playing,' while undoubtedly fun, has a serious aspect. It involves harnessing the power of our imagination within set constraints. That's what children do. If you think back to your childhood, when play was an earnest business, you'll remember that some days most of the lunch break was spent arguing about the rules of the game - which you then got to enjoy for just the last 10 minutes! But some of that prep is essential because it sets the boundaries of our imagination. Without the constraints you can't then give over to the make-believe of the game.

Then there is specificity. I asked Cicely Berry once how her exercises made such a difference to the scene. She explained that they get the actors to focus on one thing – such as the competition in the relationship, or drawing a picture from memory – and the words are left to do their work for themselves.

Isolation helps our imaginations re-discover that childlike state of play

– of serious fun – by *constraining* our imagination in something *specific*. So, if want to make a given circumstance real, if you need to be hot, or cold, or tired, don't try to be that *all over*. Be specific. Select one idea, or spot, and concentrate on that. For tiredness, try tightness in your shoulders or stiffness in the small of your back. For a cold day, imagine a cold draught on the back of your neck. Rather than trying to play a generalised drug high or illness, research that particular drug or illness and find what the specific outward symptoms or (to use the medical term) *affects*, of the condition are. Then, in the playing, focus in on just one. For instance, if you're schizophrenic, don't play generalised madness. Try *really* hearing a voice talking to you. For a crowded dirty market-place in an earlier century you could perhaps use your nose: imagine the stink of human faeces or a rotting animal. If you're drunk, try that sense of staring at someone as if from the end of a tunnel, while all around you is a kind of blurry whirl. Try… ONE thing; something specific, that you've figured out from your own experience or research.

You can also shape a character around one physical hook. If you're playing multiple characters in a play you can use isolation to switch to each character and help both you and audience differentiate between them. An eight-year-old child can have one child-like mannerism; an eighty-year-old can have a stiff leg or poor eyesight.

Isolation – specific and not generalised choices - works well for audiences as it makes them do some of the work. Instead of showing them *exactly* what is going on they'll see a detail. It will intrigue them because you're not spelling it out. They'll know something is up, something recognisably human, and be made to guess what it is.

Isolation can also help in emotional scenes. If your character is tearfully grieving the loss of a loved one, sometimes thinking of your partner or mother or pet, and imagining they are lost to you, can feel a little too generalised. Try thinking of one particular aspect of that person, something quirky and individual – their unique laugh, a scar, or that remnant of a removed tattoo. The specificity of these images can get the emotion moving in you.

BE AN ARTIST, NOT A CRITIC

The chattering voice that accompanies us everywhere is known in scientific circles as the 'left-brain interpreter.'[50] On bad days this inner voice operates as a personal critic. This inner critic doesn't *really* understand what good

---

50 We discuss this know-it-all bastard child of our pre-frontal cortex more in Chapter 18.

acting is, or where it comes from. But it's very happy to tell you what is wrong with your acting anyway. Our creativity lurks in a primitive part of the brain; an unseen world that knows no limits, is curious, instinctual, and easily distracted. Your higher brain will seek to own, guide, and criticise your artistry. Don't let it.

Your inner negative voice thinks the more you beat yourself up, the better you'll be. While there's nothing wrong with high standards, you can only work from where you're at: right here, right now. You can't build from a place of artistic wizardry that exists only in your head, often as an exalted standard you can never actually attain. Failure is the point, the raison d'etre, of the inner critic. It's comforting to fall short of our expectations because it feeds our vanity – that we are so much better than what we've just served up. It can be discomforting to move to an unfamiliar place of being, if not positive, at least objective, about our work. To say that right now, this is as good as it gets. It's worth working toward making the shift to going easier on yourself.

Self-hate tends to suck the fun and freedom out of the work. I did a memorable exercise with Dean Carey once. We imaginatively constructed my very own inner critic, some middle-aged disillusioned version of myself. We even gave him a name: Godfrey.[51] Now when I assess my work, Godfrey gets flushed down the nearest toilet. So, should your little inner disparager. For most of us our inner critic is overdeveloped and needs no encouragement!

THERE ARE NO SMALL PARTS...

Lead roles require stamina, character and sometimes a little pinch of arrogance to pull off. Smaller roles are easier in some ways – you're not carrying the show on your shoulders. There's also less information to build a character on, and less time on set to get up to speed. Yet these roles can be great opportunities. The great English actor Laurence Olivier maintained that any actor playing a role of any size should imagine it's a lead role. Really good film and TV shows have no average performances in them. *Everyone* is good. If you're in one of these shows you will get noticed and get more work.

What can help you make the most of a supporting role is to look at the bigger picture – the role of your character in the overall story. Read the scripts again and again and get caught up in that story. When you get to your scenes figure out what the story would be if you weren't there. That'll tell you why your character *needs* to be there and why they are important.

---

51 After I'd named my inner critic 'Godfrey,' Dean, with a gleam in his eye, pointed out that his opposite was 'Free God.'

Killer Concepts

CREATIVITY & YOUR INNER ARTIST

James Watson and Francis Crick, the discoverers of the DNA Helix, have spoken of how, in the frenetic pace of today's research, they would have never made their breakthrough. They counted punting on the river or chatting over a pint to be as important as time spent in the lab. Creative problem solving is our business, and it's not always a logical or linear process. It can involve left field explorations to uncharted - indeed, to the most unlikely and tangential - wellsprings. A rich imagination feeds from an eclectic store of experiences. Plain daydreaming and downtime are part of our process too. How often has a great idea come to you on a stroll? Sometimes the answer to our problem is right in front of us, hiding in our over-thinking. We need a break, to recharge, and get inspired. We need to nurture our artistry.

In 2014 I met Fred Van Brandenburg. He was the hugely successful niche architect of luxury New Zealand's getaways such as The *Millbrook Resort* in Queenstown, *Huka Lodge* and *Wharekauhau* in the Wairarapa. But about a decade before we met Fred had started to feel stuck. He'd mislaid his creative zip. He could have bashed on. But in 2005 he travelled to Spain to learn from the example of the late Spanish architect Antoni Gaudi. Gaudi's mantra was that all forms in architecture should be derived from those found in nature. Adopting this principle ignited Fred's professional renaissance. He started to find his mojo again as he began to experiment with new designs. Incredibly, the change in his creative tack would land him in 2007 what is probably New Zealand's greatest-ever architectural commission: the 120,000 metre square, near-complete (at the time of writing) global headquarters of the international fashion giant Marisfrolg, in Shenzhen, China.[52]

Fred hit a wall. He struck out in a fresh direction. He went to Spain and did a hack job on his imaginative world. Julia Cameron, in her book *The Artist's Way*, would say he'd taken his inner artist on a date. She recommends that all creative people do this now and then: think of anything that might benefit our inner artist, then take them out and spoil them silly. It might be as simple as sipping a coffee in a café as you watch the world go by.

Your next artist date could be anything from a ukulele lesson, to a visit to the opera. Watch a rookie's stand up night at your local comedy club, or go to the circus, or an amateur or high school play – the rougher the better! Try learning the tango, or see a documentary film. Visit a town you've never been to.

The idea of an artist's date is somewhat 1990's, but it has power, especially in

---

52 For more on Fred's story see my article, 'Big in China,' *Sunday Star Times*, 16 November 2014.

groups, where the benefits of the experiences can be shared wider. Prominent educationalist Sir Ken Robinson once worked with an architectural firm where every employee, from secretaries to executives, was given money every year to use for their professional development.[53] There were no restrictions on what they could do. Some went to Broadway shows; others on an Arts tour in Rome. The only requirement was that afterwards they had to give an hour's talk to the whole company about the experience. Left field ideas and thinking flowed into the organisation, allowing insights and expertise to migrate across office partitions and departments.

If you're working in a group, sharing your Artist dates extends the personal benefits to everyone, imparting fresh ideas and perspectives. What is shared may have no direct bearing to the work at hand, but may fertilise the imaginations of the listeners in unforeseeable ways.

SELFLESSNESS IS OVERRATED

When I was 12 years old, I was pleased - and a little alarmed - to overhear my Grandmother telling my mother that I'd do really well in my life. 'He's so completely selfish!' she explained, with typical authority. But then, she was a little selfish herself. She had pursued a musical career to the highest level in the early part of the twentieth century, flying in the face of social convention.

I'm not sure that Grandma was entirely right in either of her pronouncements upon me. But I recalled her back handed compliment years later when I watched an interview with much loved British actor Sir John Gielgud. He confessed that he'd lived a very selfish life. I remember being surprised to hear this. Hadn't he given so much of himself to his audiences? By following his passion he had shone bright, not just to the public, but to actors everywhere who, like myself, he had inspired. I was very pleased that he'd been selfish. This made me think: is being a bit selfish such a bad thing?

Oliver Burkeman, until 2020 the psychology writer for the Guardian newspaper, contends that selflessness is overrated. When we're wondering if we should be helping others, he believes it's often a sign that we ought to be directing more energy into what I would call our whims and fancies, and what he calls 'our idiosyncratic ambitions and enthusiasms.' No one is served, says Burkeman, when you suppress your true passions. When you do your own thing, you 'kindle a fire that keeps us all warm.'[54]

---

53 Sir Ken Robinson talking with *Radio NZ National*, 'Creativity in business,' 30 June 2009.
54 'Oliver Burkeman's last column: the eight secrets to a (fairly) fulfilled life,' *The Guardian*, 4 September, 2020.

CHAPTER TEN
TECHNIQUE SUMMARY

This chapter is not a checklist. Rather, use the following as a guide so that when you are preparing for an audition or a role, you don't have to remember how to prep, as well as actually prep. You have the answers; you just need to know what questions to ask.

CHARACTER
The lists
Start with the *character lists*. The lists are how you discover what information the play or film gives you about your character.
After the lists
Fill in the gaps of what the writer has provided with a list of specific questions about your character: the physical facts, social aspects and psychology. Answer the questions verbally if you're time-poor.
Further explorations
- Interrogate your character.
- Observe life – there may be a gift – a walk, a mannerism, or an attitude – out there that you can use.
- Write an emotional diary to chart the course of your character's journey over the film/ play or episode.
- Master any accent/ skills particular to the role.
- Do what your character does: life, job, hobbies. How does doing those things make you feel? What research can you usefully do?
- Spend time in the character's skin with Solo Etudes.
- Ask yourself: what is your character's status? What's the period and how does that affect your character? What are their favourite books/ music? What character traits would an outsider see? What's their body centre/ internal beat? What is the thing they are most ashamed of? What's their big secret?
- How is the character like you? Different from you?
- Find the devil in the angel and the angel in the devil.

SCRIPT ANALYSIS
Lines
Record/ listen, or use active recall to learn your lines. Try the *Script Rehearser App*. Use the *Pomodoro Technique* for time managing masses of dialogue. Move around to get the lines in your body: we need to learn them by *heart*, not by head.

Keywording/ game of arrows
Doing these will make you an *active* listener; meaning that your reactions will best tell the story.

Being an active listener means making a series of *discoveries* from what the other actor is saying and doing.

Actors are *reactors;* everything we say and do is only because the other character has forced us to respond – so everything we say should cost your character something.

Intention/ want/ objective/ need
What does my character want? Why does she want it? What's the importance of getting it? The *Scene Objective* is the change you want to see in the other character's eyes by the end of the scene. Make it something concrete in your imagination; envision what the change will look and feel like. If your character doesn't achieve their objective that will have consequences.

Discover the objective by asking yourself: 'if my character were to rewrite the scene to suit them, what would she make the other character/s say/ do?' Try out a bunch until you hit one that feels right. Never give up on your objective, even if/ when you 'lose' the scene – that is, you don't achieve your objective.

Inner monologue
Also known as subtext or the dark matter: everything your character thinks of saying and chooses not to.

Opposites
This is the thing your character wants *almost* as much as the OBJECTIVE, but is it's opposite, or near opposite. Win or lose the objective, either way, it will cost your character something.

If you're stuck in the scene, play the opposite: do the scene *wrong*. It'll work better.

Obstacles
An opposite is a form of an obstacle; others are any facts or given circumstances that make it harder for you to achieve your objective – a headache, lack of sleep, a noisy bar etc. The other character in the scene is always an obstacle.

Technique Summary

Contradictions
Add layers and nuance by taking the idea of Opposites further and look for more contrasting pushes, pulls, flavours and desires for your character in the scene.

Moment before
Start the scene warmed up by asking yourself, what is your character's 'moment before'? What has just happened? What's on your character's mind? What has just been said? What is your character's need and expectation going into the scene? Where have they just come from? What is their state of being/ emotional mood/ preoccupations/ agenda?

As you prepare, ask yourself: do you enter/ exit at the head/ end of the scene? It's especially important to work this out for auditions.

Relationship and substitutions
We act out different roles (as well as status) with different people: lover, sister, father, a dutiful daughter, a rebel son, a boss, an employee – depending on *who we are with and where we are*. Who is the other character in the scene to your character – a best friend, a colleague, frenemy, a mother, a mentor, a protégé? You'll behave differently with each of these. Do a run substituting a real person that you know from your own life for the character opposite you. How does that shift things?

Make associations and substitutions for every thing and person mentioned in the scene - don't leave acting blanks.

Line & scene actions
What you DO (as opposed to what you SAY) reveals character. Line and scene actions earth the scene because they take the playing out of your head and into your body.

Doing something changes how you feel – the root word of emotion is *motion* after all. And like objectives, opposites and reacting, *doing* can highlight the cost of the scene for your character. Audiences love to see this: no matter how much we try to dodge it, suffering defines our humanity.

Figure out what your character is doing in the scene overall. Are they arguing, or breaking up with a loved one, or making a vow, or being chatted up? Then think about a time you did something similar (personal experience), or when you might want/ need to (imagination). This is your *Scene action*.

If you wish, figure out what your character is doing with every line, every beat and pause and non-verbal action, at a clear non-interpretive level. This is your *Line action*.

Given circumstances
Given circumstances add layers/ depth to our work. What are the FACTS of the play/film - they may not specifically be mentioned in the scene - that affect HOW this scene is played? Where is my character? When are they (time of day/ century/ etc)? Who am I with (status/ relationship)? Given circumstances give layers to your performance.

Humour
Ask: what is the sense of humour my character uses to keep sane and survive?

The world of the play/ film
In a musical you must embody, as part of your character's DNA, the truth that they may burst into song at any moment. If in a comedy farce, you become the sort of person that bounces back from hurt easily. If you'd acted in *The Sixth Sense* you'd need to have explored how living with the dead could warp your mind. And so on, for cop shows, for war films, for period pieces. What is this world, and how must the characters respond to survive in it?

Story
Figure out the reasons for the beats/ shifts/ changes.

What is the *change* in the scene, and your characters emotional change to signify that? Are they thrilled at the end of the scene, or angry? Play something at the start of the scene that is *different* from the ending. Then your character has *travel* through the scene.

This all helps tell the story, as it highlights the event that has been written. But once you know it, forget it all and play the moment.

Doings/ activity
An activity can enhance story beats (when you stop or pause the activity) and reveal the character's inner feeling. Most importantly they can ground a performance. Not to be overdone, but good to have in your arsenal.

Don't prepare the result
Don't rehearse delivery. It's always a work in progress. Because it's a collaboration you don't need to turn up with all the answers, just ideas, and a preparation that has made something real more likely to happen. There is no finished product and no right way to do it. Your instincts are always right.

ON THE DAY

Pull the work back to the basics: Who are you? (character); Who are they? (relationship); What are you fighting for, and what will it cost you to get it (objective/ opposite)? Where are you (GC's)? What's the basic situation (Personalisation)? What are you doing (Scene Action)? What show are you in?

Technique Summary

The details
If auditioning: dress appropriately; men with no make-up, women with little (unless the part clearly demands it). Don't hide behind your hair – let us see your face. This isn't a fancy dress party – they probably don't want to see an SS uniform or a Nun's habit, even if you are testing for a Stormtrooper or a Holy sister. Dress in something that suggests the period/ character for you; it doesn't have to be exact. Be early enough to find a park, fill in the form, visit the bathroom, and not be rushed.

Make the world friendly
Be it a film set, rehearsal or audition room, make it familiar. Touch and handle props and surfaces; make friends with objects and furniture.

Imagine that the camera lens is the *director*: smiling at you, watching and wondering at your performance, revelling in your every subtlety and nuance.

Make the crew (or casting director) your friend – they are your *audience*; they love your acting. For recalls, treat the producer and director, even if just in your mental energy, as people you would love to hang with and get to know.

Place your greatest fan in the room. Someone who LOVES your acting unreservedly: your daughter, best friend, partner. Bathe in their *Approving Gaze*.

Demeanour
Be professional: show the same respect for everyone, high or low. Be generous & humble: let your work speak for you. 'Never be needlessly present or noticeably absent,' said British actor Peter Barkworth.

Just before the scene
Make a connection with the other actor/ reader. Let go and trust you have it, remind yourself of your objective. Step out into the delicious unknown - Go!

Do what people do
Look away, deny us your eyes, stumble on a line. People fail all the time.

Really look, really listen
Let *them* do the work. Don't act. Pay attention. *Really* listen. What part of your body feels this person? Where in your body do they impact you?

Pace
Don't give yourself time to think. If you don't know what you're going to do next, neither do we.

Cicely Berry: 'The audience can hear and think faster than you think they can.'

Keep the wheels turning
Endings are important. Give the editor a cutting point. If you think your character should leave, then leave.

Camera specific techniques
Be aware of the size of the shot. In a wide shot you can be more physically expressive. In a tight close up you can be more still and play the other character's camera eye.

Seeing is remembering: if a person or place is mentioned, or you think of it/ them, then see in your imagination an actual place or thing.

External landscape/ vista: if you think of or refer to an actual place, know where it is outside the frame.

Be in the moment
What is there is there – any windows, barking dogs next door, distractions. If you hear it or see it, so does your character.

THE HEAD GAME
Live, don't act
Living is fun; acting is hard work. The thing that happens by accident is usually more interesting than what you'd planned.

Disobligate
Be yourself. Be eccentric. Obey your fancies. Acknowledge your nerves.
They are energy, and you need it. Say yes to every mistake; never call cut on a scene but commit to it all.

Give yourself permission to fail. Failing is a given; not trying is self-limiting.

'You will only fail to learn,' says American actor and teacher Stella Adler, 'if you do not learn from failing.'

The learning never stops
Aim higher than what your current acting gigs may be delivering to you. Develop a routine of regular classes/ scene work, voice work - and something that helps you inhabit your body with more fluency. Make fitness and accent a daily practice. Take a vow of poverty so you can pay for workshops, travel for work opportunities, spend less time working, and have more time for your craft.

When you get work, that's when the learning *really* starts.

We're not saving lives here
It's dress-up. It's serious, but it's play too.

Personalise this list
Take stuff out, add in your other learnings - anything that helps you. Only you know what works for you.

PART 2
WORK

I think you should take your job seriously, but not yourself.
Dame Judi Dench

CHAPTER ELEVEN
AUDITIONS

Once I made the switch, I was no longer a supplicant. I had power in any room I walked into. Which meant I could relax. I was free. Of course I didn't always get the job, but that wasn't my intent any more. What was important was I always left that room knowing I did everything I could do.
Bryan Cranston

THE STIRRING OPENING BIT...

The audition room is the gateway to the thing we actors all want: employment. Work pays the rent but it also validates us and the investment we have made in our profession. Actors are not alone in having their self-worth linked to work. But no one in any other field undergoes as many job interviews as we do. We will always be rejected more than accepted, and given the stakes, rejection can feel very personal indeed. This is *especially* true if we regard the audition as a failure when we don't get cast.

The focus on employment is understandable. But a healthier view is that we are not just actors, but fully rounded people with a range of interests and passions – who happen to act. If we make auditions *only* about getting the job, we are set up to lose from the get-go. And we'll miss out on the other tangible gains of being in that room – because auditions are much more than just job interviews. Booking the job is only one of many reasons you're in that room.

As well as taking you through every step in the process, from the initial phone call to casting, I aim in this chapter to grow your understanding of the real benefits auditions offer us, give you effective strategies to manage the challenges they present, and develop a winning attitude to them.

THE BENEFITS OF AUDITIONS

An acting career comes down to doing your best in the acting task that happens to be in front of you right now. So, first and foremost an audition represents not only the possibility of *getting* the job but the certainty of actually *doing* it. Think about it. For any role, only you and the other actors who also happen to be auditioning will EVER play that character. For something locally cast there may be only 30 or so of you. So, you're not just presenting your take on the material. You're also going in there to work: to play, to experience, to explore, under conditions of unique stress. When you have an inspired casting director in there it's an acting masterclass.

The great thing too about auditions is that it's just you, the reader, and the casting director in the room. There's no set, no crew, no other distractions. It's an opening night performance for two. It's all about you and your acting. That doesn't happen as much as we'd like. On the job often we're sitting around, waiting, surrounded by people and disruptions that, if we let them, can dilute our concentration. By contrast, auditions have a kind of purity: they really are all about the work.

The other benefits of auditions derive, oddly, from NOT getting cast. First, from the fact it is so arbitrary. You can do an amazing audition and never get close. You're just wrong for the part. Or you're in one of those in-between casting age ranges where, for example, you're too old for the love interest but too young to be the 'Mum'. Or you're right for the role, and it was down to the wire, but then you got passed over for a 'name' actor, or one the director has worked with before. Is that your fault? No. So, the unbridled injustice of auditioning trains you to let go of your illusion of control.

But again, if your 'hit' rate starts to decline, it may be a message to you. Auditions can be your canary in the mine. Maybe your craft is stale and needs a revamp? Maybe your enthusiasm is on the wane? It might be time for a break, a class, or whatever works for you to re-ignite your passion.

The art is in knowing the difference: knowing what is within your control, and what isn't. Sometimes you don't know - and you have to let that go too.

THE WINNING ATTITUDE

We can't make the audition just about getting the job because the chances are you won't. Neediness can lead us into trying to craft the performance we think 'they' want, trying to please the casting director, director, and show producers. This is disempowering, as well as being a misguided effort: often they don't know what they're looking for until they see you do it.

Try and please them and you risk losing sight of what works for you, and thereby what is unique about you. You disallow your artistry, diminish your contribution, and with it your chances of getting work. Over time you risk losing your artistic way.

Rather, your focus from the time you get the audition script should be on doing it *on your terms*. If you bend yourself into unrecognisable shape you may be making the job of the casting people harder. They may get you in because of some quality they saw in an audition for a previous role, only to see that obliterated in your desire to please. Why not play to your strengths and do what you do well? Then the producers and director will become intrigued by you. If you're not quite right for this role, you'll certainly stay in their minds for the next.

Bear in mind that casting directors do fall in love (metaphorically, not actually!) with a good actor. Their buzz is uncovering and nurturing talent, and I've seen them get an actor back, again and again, sometimes for years, to find them a great role. What they love about you is not your brand but your craft and commitment. If you deliver what you think they want you may just end up doing 'yourself' badly. They don't want a second rate you.

Instead, follow your heart and tailor a unique creation. Walk into that room holding in your heart the flame of a combustible idea – that could change the world. Discussing auditions with a group of acting students in 2016, Bryan Cranston likened auditions to handing a gift to a friend that you are pretty sure they will like.[55] That's a warm feeling. You'd be nervous, but you'd be excited also, because you know you're giving something of value: your take, your interpretation of the material. Then they can take it or leave it: your job is done. Australian casting director Dave Newman once asked actor Sam Worthington, in an audition after shooting one take, if he'd like another. Sam thought for a moment and then said something like: 'Nah. Let's leave it at that. If they don't like it... Fuck 'em.'

So rather than an attitude of *getting* something off the casting director (a job), go in to *give* something instead. Value your craft enough to do that.

THE PHONE CALL

The process begins with the offer of an audition by your agent. At this moment remember: no one is holding a gun to your head. You don't have to say yes! If you never audition, you'll never work. But know that you should only be in that room if you want to be. If you can't find a compelling reason to do the audition, you *can* say no.

Do the material and the people involved excite you? Is the script

---

[55] 'Bryan Cranston on Auditons, Acting, Jealousy, and Working in Entertainment,' November 16, 2016 at Point Park University, Youtube.

Auditions

challenging? Is it a great opportunity? Find good reasons to be there. Acting is in your life to serve you. You can't become *just* some cog in the casting machine. Of course you are: you are making up numbers, giving the director a wider choice. But that's why *they* want you there. *You* have to be there for yourself.

Things change. At one time I used to say yes to pretty much any audition. A time came though when auditions started to take a big chunk out of my time, because self-test opportunities were proliferating, and I had two hardworking agents on both sides of the Tasman feeding me opportunities. It began impacting on the other work I loved: writing, developing projects, and teaching. So, I started saying yes only to auditions for roles that excited me. This entailed, in the end, only saying no to a few opportunities. But I was enabled to then bring commitment to whatever I chose. It was empowering. I enjoyed the process so much more, regardless of whether I was cast. And I started finishing personal creative projects, beginning with this book. To do this I had to shed the illusion that I could do everything.

When you're starting you don't know what you're good at and no one knows who you are. You should run with just about every opportunity that comes your way. And you'll want to because there are lots of good reasons to: meeting new casting directors, getting on producers' and directors' radar, earning some money from that TVC to support your self-devised work, and so on. The point is to know that you do have the power to choose. Remember, if you're in that room it's only because you want to be.

PREPARATION

For auditions and screen tests there is often limited information and almost always limited time. The good news is that everyone is in the same boat. In the time available immerse yourself in your audition prep as far as you are able, especially if you are new to the business. This was the tactic favoured by Russell Crowe in his early days and it's as good a way of honing your craft as any – practice married to need motivates. If you prep well you can walk away from the audition knowing you did all you could. If you procrastinate and don't prep as well as you could, the outcome is like a bad relationship break up: harder to let go of if you don't get cast.

Getting the genre right is a big part of your success in audition. There is no point turning up with a comedy performance for a drama. Figure out, as best you can, what show this is and what acting style might be called for. Explore the bios of the creators of the show, watch their work, read the show description – or even better the Story bible, which is made more available these days. This can help you tailor your performance style to suit the show. But just as important in finding the right tone is digging into the writing itself. Trust the words, let them guide your choices. There will be a melody - a rhythm – a weight - to your character's words, that fits that writing better than others.

In a class or other learning situation you can of course look up the trailer to a show, if you haven't seen it. That alone will usually tell you the flavour of that world. I would encourage you to do that, because then you'll learn how to adjust your approach and tone, genre to genre. Equally, if you're auditioning for an existing show, you can watch past episodes. However, you don't get to look at an episode or a trailer if the show is brand new. You must do your research but then take a stab at it. Your guesses will get better with experience, but they'll still be guesses. If you're in the room the casting director can help correct your choice. For self-tapes you just have to club that ball as hard as you can and hope it lands in about the right spot. And of course, even if you 'nail' the tone, there will be some styles of acting you happen to suit better. That's okay: our job is to do our best to serve the material, and where we miss, or fall short, forgive ourselves, and move on.

Read the script as often as you can, if you have it. Adjust your personal 'note' – your energy – to fit that of the character and the scenes, if they differ.

You cannot, as a rule, pick up an accent from scratch in 72 hours, which is the New Zealand Equity agreed minimum notice for any audition. Standard American and its British equivalent are accents called for often and actors should get serious about mastering at least them. For TV and Film competence in the required accent is expected, so accent practice should be part of your daily routine. Holding an accent authentically under pressure, especially one you're shaky on, or if an emotion is called for, is harder than you think. Often our ignorance of the nuances makes us think we have the accent right. Much accent work is drilling and you'll do it on your own.

Learn the lines well, without working out exactly how you will say them. While searching for the words *sometimes* aids spontaneity, nerves will make even well-learned lines harder to recall. So, start on the lines early. It's not always possible at short notice but, if you can, have those lines 'down' at least a few days before the big day. Then you can run the whole scene in your head, over and over, off-book, for a day. But just as important, do let them sink in by leaving them alone for a bit. When you return to them you'll be surprised how well they have cemented in.

Auditions

At some point run the lines with a friend. Just remember that your friend's reading will be much more impressive than your own because they are supremely relaxed. Invite their input too – not a judgement on the quality of the performance, but constructive comments on how it could be different, or better. Good ideas can come from anywhere.

As you prep, look for what lies beneath, so that rather than making the predictable choices everyone else will be doing, you'll discover all the contradictions, opposites and possibilities that exist in the writing. Show them something no one has thought of. Prepare to make an offer that is unique to you that you can make real. It is your unique spin they want, not some unimaginative service to the material.

I got an important early 'break' doing a car commercial. It got me noticed, and lead to dramatic roles. I was cast in that TVC because of an accident. The casting director told me to pick up a soft toy from a huge armchair and exit with it after my piece to camera. I wasn't paying attention – I was too nervous to listen! - so I walked over, picked up the entire armchair, with the toy balanced on top, and staggered out of shot carrying it. The director, Robin Walters, told me later that he'd already been fast-forwarding past my audition but stopped when he saw that. What he had up to that point was thirty actors all doing exactly what the brief had told them. It was brain-numbing. I arrested his attention because I was doing something different.

Some of the best moments in American filmmaker David Lynch's film *Mulholland Drive* come where Naomi Watts' character first reads a scene as she prepares for an audition, then goes in and does it. When she prepares at home she plays the scene two completely different ways - and each is just as interesting. Then in the actual audition she smashes it in another, totally unexpected direction, by using what is in the room (a sleazy, ancient, and already cast male actor). It's a masterclass in how to do an audition. Which version was the 'right' one? None of them of course. There is no 'right' way to play anything, except in our heads.

IN THE ROOM

As you prepare, anticipate as much as you can the environment that awaits you. Who is going to be in the room? It can be quite a shock to wander in and find the director sitting there if you weren't expecting that. Have a mindset that any such challenges or surprises are grist to your mill: embrace the uncomfortable and the unexpected and make them work for you.

Ask yourself what props you can expect or should bring, but don't arrive with a whole lot of complicated mime that you have made essential to your performance. Offer a prop or activity if you wish, but be ready to ditch that choice as the situation demands. Have a haircut, tie back your hair, have a shave or grow stubble and dress in a way that makes you feel right for the role. At the end of the day it is your acting they are looking at. You will not be cast on the extravagance of your make-up or wardrobe choices, and they can distract from your performance. Cover up any tattoos, and do remember that visible tattoos will take time for the make-up department to remove. Think twice about getting these – don't give them a reason not to cast you.

You need 10 minutes to fill out your forms, take your measurements and visit the bathroom, so if you're on time you're late. Get there at least 15 minutes before your call time. Yes, they might be running late, but that's not your business. Once you walk into the waiting room the work has begun: hold the energy of your choices close in your heart.

In the audition room approach the work as a collaborator – someone with a contribution to make – not a supplicant – one who is seeking something. Empathise with the casting director and the reader. You might be a bit stressed, but casting is no picnic either. It's bloody hard work: long hours, tight budgets, actors changing times at the last minute etc. Humanise everyone in the room. Don't put them up on a pedestal. They're just people. They have to pay the rent too.

First up the casting director almost invariably asks you if you want to do a lines run. This is a great opportunity to connect with the reader. They are really important: you are about to perform with *them*. Nervous actors can focus entirely on the casting director and ignore the reader until the camera rolls. Don't! Seek to make a connection with them in the read before the take, and indeed from the moment you walk in the room: be generous, gracious, and available to them. If you start reading their behaviour now you'll react to them more easily once the scene rolls. It will help you feel less self-conscious and nervous. New Zealand actor Tim Carlson has a nice trick to help himself do this – he'll memorise the reader and the casting director's name, and one article of clothing they're wearing. When he gets in his car afterwards he'll check that he remembers this all accurately.

I don't believe in the myth of the 'bad' reader. I think actors that complain about how awful the reader was are more likely to have just had an 'off' audition and be looking for someone to blame. In New Zealand and Australia I have almost always encountered great readers in my auditions. In LA, auditions live in a parallel but different universe. There they want to see as many actors

Auditions

as they can. Consequently you are more likely to get a dry, possibly unhelpful reading from a casting assistant. The interesting stuff tends to happen at the recall. But in Australia and New Zealand you generally get a high level of commitment from the casting director and reader to make your work as good as it can be in the allocated time. In any case, if their reading is a little off, *use that*. Blame them, in the moment, in your acting. Use *whatever* they give you.

In the first take of each scene, do your version. You've prepared thoroughly, so you now have a shot at something real. Fly on your instincts; do it wrong, do it the opposite way if you want. Take a 'big swing,' as director Jordan Windsor put it once in a visit to my Studio. Come in with your choices but work off the reader too. They know what's best for the scene, after all, having just done it with the five previous actors.

You'll almost always get a second or third take, where the casting director gives you direction. You'll be able to run with that because, while your prep allowed you to settle on a strong offer, it also acquainted you with all the other possibilities that exist in the scene. Now you can demonstrate your supreme directability. There should be a sense of excitement around this, of cruising off together to unexplored horizons. You can trust the direction you get from a casting director. They spend more time directing actors quickly for good results than any other industry professional. They have discussed the project with the director, producers, and possibly other members of the creative team. Right now they know this project better than you do. They're on your side because they want you to do a great audition. So, be attentive to what you are told; listening can help you relax too.

Don't be fazed if you get thrown by something unexpected and forget your lines. It's usually a good thing. It probably means you've just done something spontaneous and interesting. And if you can muddle on or – if you have to – ask for a cue and recover, that struggle will be fascinating and revealing. They'll see a team player who can pick up a dropped ball and save on re-takes (and therefore time and money). So, don't call cut on yourself. Never apologise or make excuses. Own the best you can do today.

A lot of the time the casting doesn't go to the greatest performance. Feeling genuinely relaxed – because you are confident in your choices – may be more important than flashes of lightning igniting your performance.[56] Listening, tuning in to the reader, is more likely to bring something alive in you than showing off your Acting (yes, with a capital 'A').

---

56 Katie Wolfe, actor and director, told me that she cast the relaxed actor every time.

ACTING & How To Survive It

SOME GUIDELINES

CHOOSE to do the audition so you can bring your full commitment to it.
PREPARE to make an offer *and* be directable.
RESEARCH the show: don't turn up in the wrong one.
LEARN the lines early.
Have a LEARNING GOAL (see Chapter 17: *Failure & the Mighty 1B4*).
Walk into the waiting room (the audition starts there) with a WORKING ATTITUDE.
Be a COLLABORATOR, not a supplicant in the room.
Be up for something NEW and unexpected.

THE RECALL

It's a day. Or a week. Or even a month - since the audition. You've forgotten all about it and are probably returning to a tranquil and resigned existence. Then you suddenly get the phone call: you have a recall.

The stakes are higher now because you're closer to pay dirt. So, take the pressure off. Remember that actually getting cast will depend on a host of factors, *all* of which are out of your control, except one: the quality of your performance. But a recall is a recognition that there exist 3 or 5 or so actors, including you, that *all* have the requisite competence to do the role. Now it's about a bunch of *other* things: is your hair colouring too similar to another actor, already cast, so the audience may confuse you? Are you taller than the lead? What's your chemistry like with other performers?

Casting decisions can involve producers, writers, a show-runner, a director, clients, network or distributor representatives, all trying to reach a consensus on the casting choice they disagree on least. In the end will the two main producers each have a favourite, one of which is you, but can't agree, so settle on the compromise third candidate? It happens. New Zealand actor and casting director Neill Rea said as much in a visit to the *Actors Lab Studio*: 'I wish in drama school someone had told us that the best actor hardly ever gets the role, and the best audition often doesn't either.' Enough quality auditions will get you work. When you're consistently getting recalls (and 'holds' or 'shortlists') it's only a matter of time.

As well as the casting director and reader, it's likely the director will also be in the room, if only via skype. And there may be a producer – or three or four. Be ready to be outnumbered. More than ever you need to take ownership, to do this on your terms, and see this as another opportunity to collaborate with fellow creatives.

Auditions

Before you walk into the casting office get in touch with how you feel. You might be feeling, superficially, a little nervous. Then when you walk into the room you are suddenly assailed by pure terror. The terror was there all along. You just hadn't acknowledged it. This is why a 15-minute meditation before an audition or a recall can sometimes be helpful – it can help you connect to how you are feeling inside, so you won't be surprised by it later. Or have a sing on the way in to blast out any emotional cobwebs. As Irish Folk singer Damian Dempsey says: 'when we sing we give our soul a cuddle.'

Often what the recall team will want to see first is just what you did at the audition – that's why it's handy to debrief after, so you can remember what it was you actually did (more on that later when we discuss 'The Mighty 1B4'). If they ask, 'do you have any questions?' that doesn't mean they are necessarily dying for a chat. It's usually just another way of saying: 'shall we start?'

After the first take they will hit you with some direction. Embrace it.

If after the work, the director or producer wants to talk, do listen to what they are saying. You give away more about yourself that way than you'd think. Bring the chat to a close before they do – and suddenly you'll see them get down to the nitty-gritty, and the meeting will likely go on longer. Yes, to an extent, *you* are being auditioned as well as the work. But mostly it's the work that they will love about you.

If you signed an NDA (non-disclosure agreement) in the waiting room or when you received your audition material, legally this means you are unable to talk about any aspect of the audition (or test) to anyone until the production is aired. If you do, and this is found out, you may be dropped from the project. Equally, it's standard practice nowadays that any social media comments about a project you have been cast in need to be run past production first.

After your recall you may feel a bit dazed, like the sole survivor of a train wreck. You may feel ecstatic. In either case, if you did your prep you probably acquitted yourself well. But sometimes we prepare well in every sense and then in the room we just *suck*. Something throws us. It can be who we bump into in the waiting room, or some offhand comment we take to heart. I heard a story once from a British ping pong champion. After years of hard prep for the Olympic games, just as he was about to trot in for his critical game, his coach said (well-meaningly I don't doubt): 'Okay, now we'll see if all that training paid off.' And BAM. The pressure piled on, and he walked out to play the worst game of his life.

In the actual moment, acting is more like a sport than science: you can do everything right and still mysteriously screw up on the day. Happily, for the most part, casting directors get this. They know a good actor having a bad day when they see one. They are more forgiving than you might think because they are interested in you over a long career.

Sometimes your best will give you a shot at the role, but the producers just have another idea in their head. It's sobering stuff. But not if you make your profession about the long game. *There will be a next time.*

SURVIVING AUDITIONS

Odds are you'll get no further than the first audition. But that's okay because now that casting director knows you. Early in your career you can go for years getting auditions and not getting cast because casting directors have no idea what you can do; what your abilities and flavour are. New actors on the scene may often only get TVC auditions for a while. But these too are good opportunities. A casting director might have got you in for a TVC but be casting a film next month with a role that's just right for you. If you are not getting repeat invitations from casting directors, that's when you need to start working on your craft (again, one of the few tangible elements in the casting mix you can control). Don't beat yourself up though. Doing bad auditions for a time doesn't mean you are a bad actor. You're just a bad auditioner. But you will get better. It's like figuring out how to pass exams at school. There's an art to it that sits alongside your actual knowledge of the subject.

On the other hand, good auditions do bring a definite benefit in the here and now, which has nothing whatsoever to do with whether you get *this* part. And that's more auditions. Only actors who do good auditions get more. And chances are next time it'll be for a role you are better suited to.

Always remember that every time you are auditioning for a specific role you are also doing a general audition for the casting director and anyone else who happens to see your tape. That includes the producers and the director, who might then keep you in mind for another project, even if you're not the right fit for this one. At a workshop some years ago Dave Newman, an Australian casting director, walked up and shook my hand. It was surreal because we'd never met. But it emerged that over the years he'd viewed a bunch of my self-tests. It was a useful reminder that these missives that we lob off into the dark casting ether do get seen. Remember, casting directors are our natural allies. They want us to be good. It makes their job infinitely easier, for one thing. If they like your work they will go in to bat for you in the casting discussions.

Auditions

So don't forget: every audition is a showcase of you. On display is your craft, which is your ability to understand the writer's intention, and place your performance in the appropriate genre; your talent, which lies in your choices and your interpretation of the material; your flavour, which is the unique energy that you bring to anything you do; and, finally, your commitment - your willingness to take risks, to be directable, to make it about you in the work, not the other way around.

Even if you do great work in there, it may take some time before it leads to actual work. Keep delivering, and the time will come when you and the role get matched up. A student of mine was called back three times for a role in a film. She got close, but no cigar. But she hadn't been forgotten. When the director got his next film greenlit she got a call from her agent. The gist was: 'get on a plane, they want you.'

Good, bad or indifferent, when it's over, walk out of that audition room and *keep on walking*. Do your post-mortem - then forget about it. Until the electronic ink is dry on the Deal Memo, you're getting excited over *nothing*. Don't call your agent to check on things a week later. Don't run off and tell all your friends. The job was the audition and employment from the experience is a bonus. Believe me, if they want you, they will find you.

This is the trickiest part of course: letting go of something you have invested your time and talent in for days - or even weeks, if it's stretched out into the refining torture of multiple recalls, shortlists and holds. Letting go is a Zen art they don't teach at drama school, but I do discuss it in Part Four of this book (The 15% Rule). Magical thinking, or sending out positive vibes, or reading tea-leaves might make you *feel* better, but it won't affect the outcome. Good acting will win out but *over the long run*. If the audition does pop into your head, envision exactly what it would feel like to get that role. Then immediately do the opposite: imagine finding out it's gone. Now, psychologically, you're ready for anything.

'If it be now, 'tis not to come,' Shakespeare, who was an actor himself, has Hamlet say. 'If it be not to come, it will be now. If it be not now, yet it will come — the readiness is all.' English actor Sir Laurence Olivier in his (otherwise rather dreadful) book *On Acting* defined good luck as opportunity plus readiness. In between auditions help yourself by keeping busy. Acting, paid or unpaid, attracts more acting. When you get those audition sides emailed to you, you'll be warmed up, more relaxed - in the zone. You won't have the time to overwork or overthink the scenes.

When I out started out acting my mantra was just to be working creatively, any way I could. I figured the money would follow. I did stand-up comedy, dinner theatre and corporate gigs. I collaborated to produce a series of TV pilots and launched several theatre shows. I acted in some really awful amateur theatre productions. I wrote stories, articles, screenplays and a book. I kept my creative muscle moving. And the professional gigs did follow. The auditions that came along no longer felt like great mountains to scale, but occasional speed bumps along a creative path of my own devising.

When I worked in Australia I'm particularly struck by how confidently pro-active many of the actors there are: developing shows, putting on their own work, writing, testing themselves in all sorts of diverse creative ways. They are very comfortable wearing multiple hats, and dismissive of being categorised or boxed in. The same is true for many young Kiwi actors. I'm in awe of them all frankly. So, my advice will always be to create work, to study, read, watch, experiment, argue, and train - but *never* just sit around waiting for the phone to ring. Get out there and make it happen for yourself. No one else will.

CHAPTER TWELVE
SELF-TESTS – THE PARALLEL UNIVERSE...

The first step to a better audition is to give up character and use yourself.
Michael Shurtleff

THE PEP TALK

These days actors from New Zealand are winning international roles without *ever* having visited LA. If you're working in Australia you can test for something in New Zealand, and vice versa. It's an extraordinary development. Self-tests come with their challenges but - with certain provisos - they dissolve the old tyrannies of distance that used to come with living at the bottom of the world.

In 2017 New Zealand teenage actor Thomasin McKenzie broke into the Hollywood mainstream thanks to a self-test in Wellington for the indie film *Leave no Trace*, which became a Sundance sensation. Frankie Adams was in her early 20's when she was cast in the international Sci-Fi series *The Expanse*, again from a self-test in New Zealand. Matt Whelan told me that for his break out role in *Narcos* Season 2 he shot the self-test from the studio of his Auckland agent, Gail Cowan. Self-tapes have genuinely changed the game, bringing overseas-based roles – and their transformational possibilities for careers - right to our back yard. Sometimes it can even be easier to get an audition for an international project from down under. I've known actors living in LA who couldn't get in the room or even get a self-tape accepted from there, but got in the back door via their New Zealand agent.

As well as one-off tests, now the US pilot season (which generally runs from the end of January to mid-March) can come to you. More and more shows are skipping pilots and going straight to series. Those briefs are making it down our way too. With upwards of 500 actors being seen for some international roles the chances of getting cast statistically are not great. Self-tests are numbers games: you do enough, and do good work, chances are that at some point something will come your way. The auditions are often kept and used by the casting directors as reference material. What have you got to lose?

Self-testing allows the actor to make their offer unadulterated to the director, cutting out the 'middle man.' Some casting directors aren't overly fond of this because it removes the benefit of them affecting the performance in the room. But I think all would accept the principle benefit of self-testing, namely that they stretch small budgets by allowing more people to be seen for any role. It is advantageous to get into the room if you can, especially if you've never met that casting director before, or if you know the producers or the director are going to be present. I certainly wouldn't recommend a sole acting diet of self-testing for an actor. It's hard to grow craft in a vacuum. But if you can't get in the room, a good self-test can pop you into contention. They are becoming more and more common, for local as well as international projects. The global pandemic has embedded them further. Self-tests are here to stay.

Self-tests have other advantages. Doing them will further your relationship with your agent because they will view every test you send and get more invested in your talent. You'll learn a LOT because with self-tests you get to wear your 'producer' hat: you have the luxury of stepping back and reviewing your work. You get to send only the best takes, but you learn a lot from watching the fails. Then if you are cast or recalled you can use the test as a reference to build your performance.[57]

Jonathan Brough, a Kiwi TV director, now Australia based, confesses to preferring self-tapes to regular auditions. 'I can see better what the actor can do,' he told me, 'because they're more relaxed.' How much more relaxed can you be than filming in your own home? Then you can figure out the difference pressure makes and, by trial and error, get on top of it. You can send tapes to colleagues, friends or your coach for feedback. Self-tests can be part of your own self-run drama school. If you don't get a self-test for a few weeks, find a scene and film one. Self-tests are like anything: the more you do the better you get.

Don't fool yourself though that self-tests are enough on their own. Those three breakthrough self-test examples I mentioned earlier - Thomasin McKenzie, Frankie Adams and Matt Whelan – were actors who all had a substantial body of work behind them at the time of their critical castings. If they like what you do the first thing the producers will want to see is your

---

[57] There's nothing to prevent you asking, via your agent, for your audition tapes once you are cast in the more traditional manner, and want to do the same thing.

CV and your show-reel. You want to have something to show them. The more credits you have – never mind if half of it is from drama school or your local theatre – the better the chances of a callback.

THE TECHNICAL CHALLENGE

Before you can embrace the performance and learning aspects of self-taping, you need to get on top of the technical aspects, so you can produce a well-lit take with good sound, an uncluttered background, and with a good reader.

In the main centres of New Zealand and Australia the actors union, Equity offers a self-taping setup, with camera and studio, which you can book for up to an hour. Many agents provide their actors with the same. There are various services in the major cities where you can pay someone to shoot your test or come into your house to do it. And finally, you may have a friend with all the necessary equipment and know-how.

All of these alternatives offer a tempting shortcut to having to organise everything yourself, and that's understandable if you are only getting the odd test. But there are downsides. If you are paying for technical help, and getting a lot of tests, that will soon become unsustainable. If you have to drive across town it does negate the advantages of self-taping at home, where you are supremely relaxed, can take your time, and control the whole event. Also, if you don't have the kit, it means you can never self-tape if you are travelling. Mind you, I've seen excellent quality tests that were filmed on mobile phones (make sure you shoot in Landscape, not Portrait, orientation). You just have to figure out how to make the lighting, background, editing and sound all work.

I've also seen winning self-tests shot outdoors on a shaky handheld phone (while the actor was on holiday) and in a dingy office (the actor was on set at the time). If the producers like the actor they will recall you regardless. That said, always aim to achieve the best technical standard that you can. Why make it harder for them to cast you?

So, if you are getting lots of self-tests, I'd advise you to work out how to do them on your own. Don't wait until you get your next self-test: get on top of the technology, from set up to filming to editing and sending, so you are ready to go when the phone rings. Master how to shoot and edit on your phone, or invest in a digital camera and work out how to edit on your laptop. I use a Canon Eos with an added microphone. It's small, portable, and easy to use. But there are plenty of cheap alternatives out there. Find a lightweight, compact tripod too - something you can travel with.

Frame yourself in mid-shot: from your chest up, with not too much headroom. That way you'll give yourself a range of movement. Check out Australian actor Dacre Montgomery's test on Youtube for Billy in *Stranger Things 2*. Watch for his shot sizes, and strong choices that carry a degree of risk. By this point Dacre was a skilled self-tester. He'd already secured representation in LA and done self-tests off his own bat through his final year at drama school at the Western Australian Academy of Performing Arts (WAAPA). He'd already been cast in the *Power Rangers* movie. Dacre is proof that acting and auditioning are not the same skill set. Talent isn't enough. As with auditions you need to hone your skills through regular self-tape practice.

If possible film your test during the day and use natural light. Set up your camera with the light source behind it. Make sure you squarely face the light so half of your face isn't shaded. When travelling you can keep it simple with just the camera, tripod and laptop, but your set up at home can be as elaborate as you like, so long as it's quick and relatively painless to set up and break down.

A plain background is best with nothing distracting in the frame. A sheet can read fine, so long as it isn't wrinkled. Or you can buy a piece of fabric from Spotlight in the colour of your choice: green is usually best but otherwise blue, cream or charcoal grey is okay. Avoid white. Alternatively, use a blank wall in your house, so long as it is well placed to catch light.

If you don't have easy access at home to a good source of natural light, two small light stands may be your go-to. You can pick up a cheap cell phone holder and stand too, if that is your filming jam.

When it comes to filming your test a good reader can help with useful feedback as well as a great read. Work on getting a pool of friends you can draw on – you can always repay the favour next time. If no one is available, or if you're out of town, use whoever is at hand – your flatmate or partner or a friend, even if they're not an actor. If you are on top of your performance you can hit the beats and moments anyway. The casting team will look past an average reader. The next best alternative is to set up a Skype or Zoom call, placing the screen near the camera. So long as there is not a significant lag/poor wifi, and the sound quality is alright, this can work okay. Or you can do a mobile phone call, with the speaker on. If so, give yourself a photo or reference point to work from.

The worst possible option is to pre-record the dialogue yourself and play it back with gaps – avoid this if you can.

Self-Tests

PREPARATION

Tests inhabit a slightly different performance expectation to auditions, partly because they are even more of a numbers game, with more actors being churned through. At times you can get bombarded with a lot of tests with only a day or two to turn them around. Occasionally, you'll get a lot of pages and scenes to deliver. The first thing you need to lose is your preciousness. Don't over-prepare. In depth character work (as the quote at the start of this chapter contends) may be a luxury you don't have time for. Don't stress if you don't perfectly learn the lines. Certainly for US content and/or short notice that's not a big issue. The producers are looking for an indication of where you may take the role. You can sometimes even get points off for being too polished – they may worry you won't be able to change the performance.

For US tests it's fine to have the scene pages in your hand (held just out of sight) if you are pushed for time. Script in hand you'll just look like a busy professional jobbing actor, so long as an offer is there. For Australian and New Zealand auditions the expectation is generally that you have your lines down, but for self-tests having the script handy, if you need it, is much better than not sending in a test at all. You can get away with the odd sly peek at the lines.

As for auditions, do your research on the producers, directors, and style of the show. In film, directors are king, but in TV, they come and go. Producers, writers and show-runners (often the same thing) tend to run TV land, so don't ignore their vision and style. Look at their previous shows, as well as the directors. It will give you a sense of where to pitch the performance.

LAYING DOWN THE TAPE

If you can, sit down. Keep your physical actions to a minimum. Make sure you can be seen and heard clearly. Check the frame size: loose mid - TICK. Don't zoom in and out during the take. Keep it simple. Have your scene partner as close to the camera as possible for eye-line. If you have a directional microphone place them behind it, or make sure they don't speak too loud if they are close to the microphone. You want them to be audible, but quieter than you. Position yourself a few feet away from the wall behind you to avoid shadows. Unless scripted, don't look directly at the camera at any point in the scene. Set your eyeline: make sure the camera is positioned at eye level or above. Women should wear minimal makeup; men should avoid it altogether. Dress appropriately, and make sure your hair is out of your face.

Once everything's set up, record a test sample. Check it for look and sound. Tweak as needed. Then do some takes of the scene. Don't try and get it 'right.' Treat every take like a rehearsal, a jam, an exploration. Come at the scene in different ways. You can finish with a crazy take, an over-the-top take, or a flat-line 'I'm barely acting' take - if nothing else when you watch them back they'll be helpful for your learning, and it can be useful to have some contrasting takes one way or another (see below).

If you do need to look at your script just glance down, capture the line, look up again and deliver it to your reader. Maximise eye contact by watching them while they are talking. It's your eyes we want to see, not the top of your head as you stare at the pages.

During the take, if you fluff a line just pick it up from the page and carry on. These takes can be the best ones. It's fine to send the odd take with a minor fumble in it so long as you recover. It can be to your advantage: calling 'cut' on yourself on set costs thousands of dollars, so any producer or director watching will love that you bounced back from an unforced error.

Watch out for emotionally charged choices. Except when specifically scripted, it's usually a bad idea. If the test is for a character carrying a show in an American TV series you need to be likeable and show you can save your acting powder as required. The antidote to emoting is to play the objective. Emoting can come across as overacting, and the US standard is naturalism. So, even for a heightened situation, keep it true. Don't be overly seduced by the genre, if it's pulling you toward an outsize performance. Give them a hint, a flavour, but keep it real.

Another trap can be to do a general audition for the character, trying to cram a season's worth of brilliance into one scene, giving them everything you've got. Don't try and show every aspect of your talent; make the test a tease.

Once you have selected your best take of each scene make sure you also have a second contrasting take to keep because, if they like what they see, they might ask for more. Better to then send them a different take on the material than the same, but a second-best one. If I do a bunch of takes I usually end up using the first, which invariably feels the roughest when I do it, but captures that essential acting element - spontaneity.

THE ART OF THE ID

As for an audition you may be asked to shoot an ID (also called a slate) where you give the casting team a feel for who you are, how you look, and to see a full-body shot. For live auditions the ID is usually taken at the start, and it's more important than you might think.

Self-Tests

For a self-test shoot your ID last, once you've got all of your acting out of the way. Unless requested do your ID in two setups. Make the first a mid-shot from the chest up where you state your name and height (in feet and inches if for the US), character name and agent: 'Hi, I'm John Doe, I'm 6 foot 1, I'm represented by Lisa Mann Creative Management and I'm going for the role of Sheriff XY in Fargo Series 9.' Then include a full body shot where you can turn your whole body to do profiles if requested (don't turn just your head for a profile – it's usually unflattering). For tests your ID should be at the end of your submitted tape, but you can have your name, character name and agent flash up as a subtitle at the start of your tape if you wish.

The acting in the test is showing your craft. The ID tells them who you are. Here there is no relationship with another character to play off, so you have to create that connection through the lens. The stance that's easy to slip into is 'I hope you like me and want to work with me.' Invert that. Think about who is in that camera: a bunch of producers and creatives who want you to be the solution to their casting problem. Try thinking of someone you don't know (an actor say) that you would *love* to meet and spend time with. Speak to that person as an equal.

EDITING & SENDING

If you can, master editing and do it yourself. I use *Wondershare* on my laptop and it works for me. But you have to pay for it and there are comparable free editing softwares out there. iPhones come with their own perfectly useable editing software apps. There are some tips on file compression and editing in the Software guide at the end of this chapter.

Regardless of the order you shoot the scenes, always put the best takes first. In LA, most self-tapes are rejected or passed up the chain by an assistant to the assistant of the casting director. Chances are you have to make an impact on some teenage intern in the first 15-20 seconds to get to the next stage. Send one take only per scene – leave them wanting more. You can always hold a take back to send on later once interest is expressed (show-reels can be useful at a later stage too).

Your file shouldn't be too big. 80mb used to be a maximum, but as technology moves some casting agencies are saying bigger sizes are okay. Check this though before you send a 300mb file. Use one of the following formats - MOV, M4V or MP4 - and label the file in such a way that it is easy to identify e.g. Name of Project, Name of Role, Name of Actor. If need be, use a program such as MPEG Streamclip to reduce the file size before sending if needed. The file should be sent (usually to your agent) as a private downloadable link via a platform such as HIGHTAIL (https://www.hightail.com/). You can also sign up for a free Lite account on VIMEO to do this (https://vimeo.com/ - ensure your video is set to private viewing only). You can also send via a private Dropbox link - but ensure it allows for downloading. Do NOT send via a YouTube link - and do not post information regarding the project on social media!

Before you send off your test, check that all scenes are there, the spelling is okay, and that the clip has the ID with the correct information.

THE WAITING GAME

Sometimes you'll have a bad day, or the character just isn't right for you, and the test doesn't work out. If you go back and do it again the next day it'll probably be better. If there's no time to do that let your agent make the call whether to send it on. In any case, be reassured: no one remembers a bad test. As I've said the initial playback is often done by the office junior, and if it's terrible they only look at it for a few seconds, then move on.

Bear in mind though that what you think is your worst effort may be *exactly* what they want… British actor David Harewood was driving a lorry for work and had 50 quid in the bank when he was sent a self-test by his agent. He was so despondent that he dismissed the script (for the series *Homeland*) without even reading it – despite the mounting pressure to support his wife and two daughters. But his manager pressed him and eventually, as he recalls it, 'I propped up my iPhone on the window sill, called my wife down so she could do Carrie's lines, and just pretty much read it. I never even did an American accent.' As luck would have it, his unsmiling sullen intensity was exactly what the casting directors were after. He got the part.[58]

SELF-TAPE SOFTWARE GUIDE

In 'Useful Book and Resources' I've listed some info and links, current at the time of writing, to different programs that you can use for editing and compression of your self-tapes, as well as some explanatory YouTube tutorials about them. See page 286 near the end of this book.

---

58 'David Harewood nearly quit acting before *Homeland*,' *RadioTimes,* Tuesday, 1st March 2016.

CHAPTER THIRTEEN
ON THE JOB

Many of the techniques we've covered so far have focussed on acting tools relating to scenes. This chapter offers additional tools and questions to help you investigate the arc of your character over an entire film, episode, season or play. We also look at the nuts and bolts of what happens on a film or TV set.

Acting is standing up naked and turning around very slowly.
Rosalind Russell

WHAT SHOW ARE YOU IN?
Acting has a long tradition of differing genres of show: tragedy, farce, slapstick, comedy, satire, to name a few. The late Sir John Gielgud said 'style is knowing what show you're in.' Each show, each genre, has 'rules'. For instance, you can't mumble your way through a musical – although that might work okay in a kitchen sink reality-based drama. In a cop show, the mood may be oppressive, tense, and edgy; you might decide that a way into finding the style might be to tell yourself that in every scene the killer is always in the room. In a comedy, you may conclude that your character must have an element of cartoon robustness, to bounce back from all the funny (but also cruel) barbs flying around.

Michael Shurtleff calls 'style' the behaviour chosen by the characters as a way of dealing with the dilemmas of their particular lives. In what ways does the *style* of your show part from actuality? What kind of people talk or behave like this? In what kind of world is it normal to suddenly burst into song and dance (as in a musical), or exist in a constant state of near-panic (as in a farce like Faulty Towers)? What sort of character must you be for this to be 'normal' behaviour? Watch the musical *Chicago* – Catherine Zeta-Jones' and Renee Zellweger's rouseabout numbers pull off the heightened characterisations required, and yet are utterly truthful. In contrast, Richard

Gere's strong and naturalistic performance doesn't quite match the energy of the show when it comes to his singing solo.

As well as genre and style, research the reality of the show. This is especially important if it is a world unfamiliar to you: a period piece, say, or a different culture. What is the reality of living in this kind of world? If your show is set in South Auckland or West Auckland, those are different places. If you haven't been to them, go there. If it's set in the East End of London and you can't go there – watch content from there, preferably documentary, and listen to any relevant podcasts you can find. Documentary has a peculiar power over us, as we prepare and research, because in our heart *we know it is true*. It's the same with observing real human behaviour. We can observe something utterly outrageous, almost clichéd, that we would reject as bad acting if we saw it on a stage – and yet here it is, in front of our eyes. It gives us powerful permission to go there ourselves, broadening the range of what is possible in our acting.

The heightened language that we find, typically, in the plays of William Shakespeare, brings its own challenges. Shakespeare's audience and actors alike had a visceral connection with the spoken word, in a way we don't today. It was a drab world to look at – dyes and paints were expensive – and less than 10% of the population could read. Visually less sophisticated than us, and far less likely to be literate, Elizabethans had a sharper ear. Words, in much contemporary performance, serve mostly to convey information. To the Tudor English, they were a rich auditory feast. Modern English was still in formation. Rich dialects abounded (the rhythm of Shakespeare's own, from Stratford, comes through loud and clear in his writing) with new vocabulary being imported into the language from Ancient Greek and Latin, which was being devoured at the time by Renaissance scholars. If some of his speeches feel a bit long and windy, it might be because Shakespeare really is saying the same thing twice - first, using some classical allusion, then again in a more colloquial idiom. He's speaking to all, high and low: he knew his crowd. In the absence of literal handholds, Shakespeare's audiences got the meaning through the sound of words as much as their sense.

In a Shakespeare play you must find reasons not why the characters are flowery or poetic, but why they yearn to communicate so precisely to every audience member. Said Cicely Berry to Antony Sher: 'Richard (III) is not scared of words in the same way that he is not scared of death, or killing, or anything.'[59] In any Shakespeare play the modern actor might be intimidated

---

[59] From Sher's memoir, *Beside Myself*.

by the language - but the characters must not be.

Shakespeare's characters are also written to live on the edge; more Italian in their passions than we moderns, rather more likely to pull out a dagger and run someone through. Perhaps this was because at the time he wrote his plays everyone was a bit drunk. Londoners in Shakespeare's day drank, on average, 17 pints of ale each week. Many preferred it to water because it was less likely to carry diseases. They drank it with breakfast and every other meal of the day.[60] How would just that one fact affect any characterisation? Or the fact that infant mortality was much higher? Were people more hardened to grief, or more damaged by it? Or both?

Every world created by a writer differs in some way from another. For TV, figure out what is the driving combination of creative forces behind the show as best you can from the muddle of showrunners, producers, writers, and directors. Watch their previous shows to get a sense of how they see and depict the world. For film, watch the director's previous work. Any Baz Luhrmann film, from *Strictly Ballroom* to *Romeo and Juliet*, has an exuberant and flamboyant style. Just as distinctive is a Taika Waititi or Coen Brothers film. We are the children of their vision.

STORY

Read the script, and keep reading it during filming or the run of the play. Each time you read you'll discover something new about the story, your character's function, or why they are there.

CHARACTER DIARY

For any character you play it's probable that their action will not be continuous. There will be gaps of time for your character between scenes. You have to have some idea of what has happened in those blanks. Some of that information will be given in the script. Sometimes you have to make it up with events and scenarios that suit the demands of the story. So, at the beginning of every scene, if there has been a time-lapse, you may wish to make notes about what has happened in the interim that are relevant to the scene you are about to play. Then for any scene in the film or play you'll know where you are in the story.

You can take this further and collect these notes into what you could call a

---

60 *Ye Olde Good Inn Guide*, by James Moore and Paul Nero, The History Press, 2013. Such traditions are not confined to Tutor England. When I visited Hungary in 1992 I found it was relatively common to kick off the day with a shot of strong liquor called 'Palinka.'

Character or Emotional diary. This diary charts the scenes and events relevant to your character, plotting where they are at emotionally throughout the whole story. If you do a diary you'll be able to play an arc for your character over the whole performance, however long it is. Without this construction of your character's journey you risk playing all your scenes with a similar - or random – intensity. So, the character diary helps make sense of a performance, both for you and the audience. Most importantly, it allows you to make sense of your continuity. Some actors write up their character's *real* diary, to help them discover their 'voice,' and how they feel about the events described in the script. Rena Owen did this for her iconic character 'Beth' in *Once Were Warriors*.

Film and TV tend to be filmed not chronologically, but by locations. You might, for example, be playing a cop who interrogates three different suspects in six different interviews over two episodes, but all these scenes are filmed in the same day in one location.[61] The director will call 'cut' on one scene and you'll be reading the next straightaway. You'll have a quick costume change and 20 minutes later you could be filming again. The next scene could well be from a different day in the story, or another episode. You need to be aware of where and when the audience last saw you, as well as what's happened just before your scene starts. When you work in TV in this way, juggling intersecting storylines over a season, the on-set discussion with the director is often around the story, figuring out the nuts and bolts of what your character knows and does not know in any given moment.

An excellent example of how a character diary can work was shown when *Actors Lab Studio* alumni Antonia Robinson visited one of our classes during her filming of the BBC show *Mystic*. Antonia's character was a central one, and her filming was very busy, typically 12 hour days, counting travel, over many months. As well, it was one of her first screen roles and she wanted to be on top of her work. So, to help her keep track over the first four episodes of filming, Antonia, who is an image-based person, wrote up her character's journey over these episodes onto a long paper timeline, recording events and her character's response to them. As I've said, emotion can't necessarily be played directly. But charting out how your character feels scene to scene does help you understand where your character needs to get to. Antonia added in three emotional strands, in purple, red and green, representing happy, sad and jealous (the latter being her character's governing emotion). These

---

61 Typically episodic television is filmed in 'blocks' of two episodes.

On The Job

strands rise and fall through the episodes. You can see Antonia's timeline on page 166.

Some actors like to give each scene a song they can listen to in the lead up that strikes the emotional note they want to hit in the playing. That's a throwback to silent movies, when actors would request a certain song be played while they did a scene to put them in the mood. You can also choose audioscape; for example the sounds of rain, or children playing, to place you where you need to be at the start of the scene. Sometimes sound or song gets you 'in' faster and more deeply than just reading those notes you made earlier.

ON-SET ACTING – THE NUTS AND BOLTS[62]

You may or may not have had a rehearsal process for the TV or film role you are doing. Usually there will be a meeting with the director but if not then do ask for it. Failing that, email her. Don't be afraid to ask the stupid questions. Get an idea of her vision for your character and scenes. Then you'll be able to get on the same page that much quicker.

When you arrive for the days filming you will normally be greeted by a 3rd AD who hands you some 'sides.' These are all the scenes to be filmed that day, printed in an A5 size booklet. Sometimes they are left out for you in the cast bus. Sometimes you get to read the sides in make-up with the other actors.

Then, once you're through make-up and costume you'll be called to set and typically follow these steps:

The Read-Through
This is a 'Line Run' with no actions. Most people have their sides in their hands. But not you (see below).

The 'Block through'
This is where the positions, movements and marks for the scene are figured out. The director usually makes initial offers and 'blocks' the scene (suggests movements) with the actors while the crew watch. This is done a few times with ongoing discussions between the director and the DOP about shots.

The 'Build'
After this there's some time out for a 'build' by the camera crew – laying out tracks or setting up sticks, and lighting the set. This process can take anything from 5 minutes to 2 hours, depending on the budget of the show and the complexity of the setup. You'll figure out the rhythm of the turnaround

---

[62] BIG ups to director Geoffrey Cawthorn – this segment was built on the bones of an excellent handout he gave on a visit to the *Actors Lab Studio*.

pretty quick. Sometimes you'll need to have a costume change or visit make-up. Don't stray too far (here British actor Peter Barkworth's adage is apropos: 'never be needlessly present or noticeably absent...') Sometimes it can be useful for you to stand in near the end of this process for focusses and marks; sometimes stand-ins are used for this, or you do it when you return to set.

On-set runs

Once you're called back there will be one or two runs or rehearsals of the scene, while the camera operator tweaks sizes and focus, and lights are adjusted.

Filming

The standard industry procedure for filming can be a little intimidating initially. Remember that a lot of the calls made in the lead up to filming are there to make it possible for make-up, wardrobe, continuity and sound to do their jobs. You have a job to do too, which is to stay relaxed and focussed while all this is going on around you:

The 1st Assistant Director (AD) calls for FINAL CHECKS: make-up and wardrobe check the actors.

The 1st AD then calls ACTORS to their 1st POSITIONS: Go to your starting mark.

The 1st AD calls STANDBY, then TURNOVER or ROLL RECORD.

The 1st AD may then ask for QUIET for the SLATE. The Camera assistant then MARKS THE SLATE (saying, for example: 'Scene 8, Take 1').

SOUND and CAMERAS Call 'SET.'

The 1st AD calls ACTION.

And you're on.

Remember that call of 'action' is not a starter gun unless a camera move or action is synchronous with it. Begin when you're ready, and keep going until you hear the DIRECTOR call 'Cut.'

Filming usually begins with some kind of wide shot, then the shots devolve to complete 'coverage' – all the mid shots, singles, two shots and close-ups that the Director has devised with the DOP necessary to complete the scene. So, you'll need to repeat your performance multiple times, all the while keeping it 'fresh.'

This is the job you are paid to do: keeping it real, but intriguing, time after time.

CAMERA PERFORMANCE

Your performance must seamlessly include technical demands. You need to be able to hit your mark, have an awareness of where the camera and lighting is, stick to the blocking and continuity, and stay out of the other actors' shot.

You need to be understood, and watch your diction and clarity.

Some actors like to save their full performance for the first 'take.' This is NOT from *their* first take but for the *first* take done of the scene - no matter who the camera is on. If you hold something back till then you'll give your fellow actors a great gift: your performance will only then be revealed to them, and they'll be surprised by it. In subsequent takes they will be able to 'remember' their surprise and play it so it looks spontaneous. That reaction won't have time to get stale. But if you're hitting them with your full performance from the time of the first read on set they may have too much time to get used to it.

As you roll out the takes it will cease to feel *entirely* new. That's okay. There's a great story New Zealand actor/ comedian John Clarke tells about working with Sam Neill in *Death in Brunswick*. Take one of a scene, the crew laughed. Take two, there were a few titters. By take three there was nothing. So Clarke started to mess with it, and take four he got a laugh again. Sam took him aside and told his mate: 'you don't have to change it to keep it funny. It is funny. It's just that they have already seen it.'

Don't look at rushes and be careful about too much monitor gazing of your takes. The director's job is to watch, and buy the take; your job is to present without censorship. The monitor gives a distorted account of the work: you'll only see *your* performance. Art department will only see set dressing; lighting will only see shadows. Only the director and editor can see, and craft, the whole.

ON-SET DIRECTION

Your prep shouldn't scare you to death with a sense of obligation or puff you up with self-importance. You are no more or less vital to the scene than anyone else on that set. Without any one of the crew the whole machine would grind to a halt. The director's outside eye is fundamentally necessary in this mix: their very presence removes the need for us to judge our work.

Listen to the director. If their direction is outcome or result focussed your skill will lie in translating that into something that you can play. But do forget it all just before action and trust that the note you've been given will play. If you're told ten different things remember that you're not expected to bake an acting cake containing all those ingredients precisely. You're better off latching onto the thing that excites or interests you. Treating direction too literally can mean you lose a lot of good stuff the director liked. It's usually not the intention of the director that you throw out every other choice you've made and do *only* what they've just told you. As I've said, their direction is most probably inspired by you. They want you to *add* the note to the mix.

Be unafraid to leap out into an unknown path though, if specifically asked. If you get direction and sometimes the next take is a bit bumpy, don't let it throw you either. The take following will likely be less self-conscious.

If directors ask for more pace they usually mean that we should tighten the pauses between the dialogue – the cues - *not* speak faster.

SOME ON-SET TIPS

- Read the big print once. Then ignore it.[63]
- Keep any business or activity simple – for continuity purposes, shot to shot, it has to be easily repeatable. Settle on any physical actions in the read through then stick to them.
- Be ready for any surprise or change on the day – different actions, locations etc…
- Prepare warm-up lines to say in the run-up to a scene if, as scripted, you are cutting into a scene mid-way.
- Trust how you are feeling – it might be just what the scene needs.
- Stay connected to your feelings. If you feel the stress piling on, do what you do to bring yourself back to calm. Only you know what works for you.
- On set have a rule: don't have sides and don't have a phone. Stay connected to yourself and the job at hand.
- Sometimes the most liberating thing you can admit to yourself is 'I don't know how to act.'
- No one sleeps well the night before the first day of filming.
- No one can tell you how to act.

PROFESSIONALISM

I used to love circuses when I was a boy. One would set up in a park near my house whenever it came to town. I'd visit them out of showtimes and hang out with the circus folk. They seemed exotic creatures, fish that would be out of water in any other kind of home. And in fact a lot of the performers I met really had run away from home to join a place where outsiders found themselves welcome. In the hit musical, *The Greatest Showman*, Hugh Jackman's character, P.T. Barnum, is forging a new kind of show-business, but his deeper intention seems to be to create a family where he and a band of diverse individuals can make their unique contribution, each just as

---

63 Remember, the big print are the stage directions, descriptions of business, and acting tips. Intended to be helpful they can sometimes constrict you in the playing.

important in going to make up the whole.

When I wander on to a film set nowadays it makes me think that film making is the modern-day circus. When the big tent comes down in the circus everyone, from the clowns to the trapeze artist to the impresario, pitch in and help. Likewise, on film sets everyone is doing their bit, big and small, but all equally indispensable. If no one showed up, if there were no lights, no power, no food (or, God forbid, no coffee!) the wheels would come off. The cast and crew feel like my tribe, all of us committed to the single endeavour of telling *this* story. I find myself surrounded by people of all backgrounds and ethnicities and that's also been one of the privileges and unexpected bonuses of the job.

I'm not at all surprised at the variety of personalities in our industry, the richness of the human tapestry of cast and crew. As a teacher, when I ask my actors about themselves, I'll often find out how unconventional their childhoods were, or how they suffer from some behavioural disorder, or how they have been labelled with some kind of mental illness. Such traits, disadvantages in many walks of life, give the creative person their unique perspective and can be positively beneficial – so long as they find the inner mettle to rise above them.

While I relish our rich human tapestry we sometimes also find ourselves working with people we don't connect with, or in a project we're struggling to believe in. Sometimes stress and lack of sleep make us and others less tolerant. Very occasionally we'll witness outrageous behaviour. How to negotiate all this in the theatre, or on a TV or film set? How to be ourselves and do good work, but not impede others' good work? How to enjoy ourselves so that we're genuinely looking forward to going to work the next day? Because at the end of the day, if we're not having fun, what is the point??

The key to a harmonious experience is to understand that you're being paid not just to act, but for everything you do around acting – all the meetings and pre-production calls, the downtime, the time in the make-up chair, even the publicity round. Your paycheck covers all of that. Don't curb your personality outside of work – by all means go home and rant to your flatmate or partner – but at work keep your drama in the work. When you work with international names like James Nesbit, David Wenham or Danny Huston and experience their seamless meld of generosity, friendliness and self-sufficiency, it sets a high example.

When you step onto the set or into the rehearsal room, you're 'on.' Be friendly, approachable and open. You don't have to learn everyone's name and slap every back. But the crew are your first audience, and it's helpful to have a warm relationship with them.

My first ever acting job was in 1994 on Annie Goldson's docu-drama *Seeing Red*. When my final scene wrapped the crew burst into spontaneous applause. I was touched. Teary-eyed and mumbling thanks, I stumbled off the set. On my next acting job another actor got wrapped out ahead of me. The crew burst into applause. I realised this was standard procedure… I've noticed since that if the crew is in a hurry the clap can be pretty perfunctory. It can also be sincere and long. If the crew has taken a collective dislike to the actor, it can be louder and longer! But I still know two things: what a sweet sound applause can be, and how much we cherish the respect of our peers.

ON-SET DEMEANOUR

TV and film sets can be wonderfully social places. It's lovely to catch up with friends, but we are also paid to be ready when called. We want to stay mindful of that little knot of tension in our stomach: it is there to remind us that we have an important job to do. On the occasions you need to be alone go for a stroll. In the cast camper you can read a book or pop headphones on – they serve well as a 'do not disturb' sign.

As a general rule people tend to work again with people they like, or have worked with before. What ends up on the screen is important, but the truth is that most of us are replaceable on the next job if we're a pain in the ass in this one. Casting directors have people on set who talk to them. A judgment will be made, and that casting director may not want to see you again for a while. Producers may note if your 'process' wastes time. Don't second guess everything you do. But that's the way it can roll.

'We're all nervous,' said the late Gordon Jackson, a fine British actor. 'That's where actors' quirks, eccentricities - and demons and bad behaviour comes from – the constant fear.' Acknowledge that under pressure you can be a different person. Be polite even when you'd rather not. Professionalism is one half of the glue that sticks productions of disparate characters together when the natural laws of personality would predict destruction under the stress of temperament and time pressure. The other half of the glue is the feeling that the story we are all pitching in to tell is the more important thing.

The odd day you might be feeling a four out of ten. We must assume on those days a professional persona. But in our acting we want to be raw and real and *not* hide behind a persona. So, if you save up your feelings for the work, you'll not only be great to work with, it'll be a gift to your performance.

AUTHENTICITY

This above all: to thine own self be true,
And it must follow, as the night the day,
Thou canst not then be false to any man.

So finishes Polonius' advice to his son, Laertes, in Shakespeare's *Hamlet*. Pretending to be someone else takes rather a lot of energy. But being true to who you are isn't always easy either, especially if you're still *figuring out* who you are. Be reassured: 'imposter' syndrome stalks us all our lives. We can feel a phoney at being an adult, an actor, a parent. That we may, somehow, at any moment be found out. But 'you' is all you've got. Who you are is why you get the work, and why sometimes you don't. American actor Tim Robbins was once asked if he thought his political activism had damaged his acting career. 'On the contrary,' was his answer. 'People hired me for me, for what I believed in.'

You have to own up to the fact that you'll never create anything, or ever make your way in the world, without crossing someone occasionally. It's inevitable, the way a speedboat leaves a wake. 'If you don't make some enemies in this business then you're doing something wrong,' said Scottish actor Sean Connery. It's important to rub along with the crew. But it's not a popularity contest you have to win. Follow your fancies. Place importance on your values. Speak up on matters you care about.

'Being yourself' means being true to your feelings, no matter if they feel inappropriate, or even a little bit shameful. Said Michael Shurtleff: 'it isn't necessary for you, the actor, to like yourself - self-love isn't easy to come by for most of us - but you must learn to trust who you are. There is no one else like you.' You don't need to act on your feelings every time, but you do need to at least acknowledge them.

I was a barman in theatre bar Kinsela's in Sydney in 1985 and had the privilege of meeting a string of wonderful performers, including the cast of the hit musical *La Cage aux Folles*, international celebrities such as British TV actor James Bolam, and the then stars of Australian TV and film. I learnt that no personality type is a disqualification for acting, and perhaps even more intriguingly, that likeability was no predictor for whether I would enjoy any performer's work. I think authenticity was a better predictor. The more comfortable they were in their emotional skin, be it scarred, spikey or sublime, the more I loved their work.

ACTING & How To Survive It

PARTING TIPS ON PROFESSIONALISM
- Give everything 110%; NOTHING (unless unsafe) is too much trouble.
- In the first few days at a new job keep a low profile and have your social antennae out, as there is a different vibe on every set or show: find your way in.
- We love to gossip. Take everything you hear with a grain of salt. Don't have a pre-judgement about anyone you haven't yet worked with.
- Be generous to other actors, for instance on their close ups: you get back what you give out. The best way to be interesting in your work is to be interested in the other person. If other performances are better, yours will be too.
- If someone is rude or unprofessional, stand up to them.
- Don't interfere in another actor's performance, ask them to change it to suit you, or offer advice (unless solicited and then, cautiously). The other actor's choices are the director's business, not yours. Focus on what you are doing and what the director is telling you. If the other actor isn't giving you what you think you need then use what they are giving you anyway and hit the beats and moments you identified in your prep.
- Be ready for accidents, surprises and screw-ups. They are part of the process. Try and anticipate what might go wrong and work out how you can help. When shit happens, be part of the solution. Be a team player.
- Don't be that person who fights everyone else's battles.
- Be that actor who saves the production money, rather than costs it. Don't, without good cause, consume the production's most precious commodity: time.
- Be prepared. There is no excuse for not knowing your lines, or your accent being out. The crew arrive ready to shoot and you need to be ready to act. Nine-tenths of the battle is preparation. Then you can relax and enjoy the day.
- Learn from your mistakes *without* ruminating on them. Do your best, debrief as needed, forgive yourself - and move on.

A Post-script: Resolving conflict in the workplace

On set, when conflict arises, a stiff upper lip is sometimes required. As British wartime Prime Minister Winston Churchill said: 'a problem ignored is a problem solved'. That's true for most acting jobs because most don't last long. We can endure most types of professional horror if we know it's only for a limited time. We have to put up with things sometimes. Rehearsal rooms and film sets are not democracies. A hierarchy is at play. You must know your place. As an actor, it's not your responsibility to fix a colleague's bad behaviour. That's the director's business. You are an equal with all the cast. Your job is to find a way to work through everything and everyone that's thrown at you.

On The Job

Turning the other cheek won't work though if, despite your best efforts, a conflict actively interferes with your work. Sometimes, there is a serious, inappropriate behaviour at play which needs addressing.

In the first instance you may decide to discuss the matter with the relevant colleague directly. If so, don't over-rehearse the conversation. Bring it up in a matter of fact, calm voice, beginning with a positive comment. Then they are less likely to get their back up.

On the other hand confrontation, for many reasons, can be difficult. If the person concerned is older than you, or holds a more senior position, you also stand to lose reputation or jeopardise your future employment.

So what are your options? First, you can take the matter, in confidence, to the Director, Producer or Production Manager (or Stage Manager in the theatre) and ask for their help. If you have a genuinely serious workplace issue in progress and the production is unable or unwilling to assist, your next port of call is your agent and Actors union. They will be able to advise you based on similar situations they have faced before. In this #MeToo era you'll find a more informed and pro-active response than in times past. And of course, if a law is actually being broken, you have legal recourse.

Taking on bad behaviour is not easy if it means standing up to those in authority. If you do call out a bad egg, fewer people will ever suffer from that individual, and that person too gets a chance for reflection and redemption. Thankfully, improper conduct remains very much the exception rather than the rule, at least in Australasia.

The consequences of speaking truth to power may not be as grave as you fear, and you'll certainly earn the respect of your peers. In 2016 during our filming of the TV series *Dirty Laundry* I chatted to Jennifer Ward-Lealand about her leadership of New Zealand Equity during the bruising *Hobbit* labour dispute some years before. John Barnett, then head of heavyweight TV Production house South Pacific Pictures (SPP), had declared that she and fellow union member actor Robyn Malcolm were 'damaged goods' and could struggle to find work.[64] And here she was, playing the lead in a TV show! The likes of Jennifer, Robyn, and Penny Ashton have shown leadership on tough issues. Their careers remain robust.[65]

---

64 'TV producer: Unions fed frontwomen to mob,' *NZ Herald*, 25 October, 2010. By Derek Cheng.
65 Penny Ashton called out Auckland's *Pop Up Globe* on the overall gender bias in their casting.

CHAPTER FOURTEEN
PREPARING FOR A ROLE - ACTORS SPEAK

For this chapter I asked seven actors to discuss how they prepared for important roles in their career. I've also provided some examples from my CV. I hope one take out for you at least will be that there is no 'right' way to prepare, just as there is no 'right' way to act.

This is the true joy in life, the being used for a purpose recognised by yourself as a mighty one; the being a force of nature instead of a feverish, selfish little clod of ailments and grievances complaining that the world will not devote itself to making you happy.
George Bernard Shaw

LISA CHAPPELL
Lisa is perhaps best known for her iconic Logie winning role as Claire McLeod on the Australian TV series, 'McLeod's Daughters.' But she has had an extraordinary career spanning many decades, and has been proving herself to be a talent as a writer as well. Lisa is a much-loved occasional teacher at my own school, the Actors Lab Studio.

My preparation for McLeod's Daughters
Creating Claire McLeod from the Australian TV show *McLeod's Daughters* was an interesting process as seemingly we had nothing in common other than both being women.

She was a true blue Ocker and I was a Kiwi girl. She was born, raised and lived on the land. I was born, raised and lived in the city. She grew up surrounded by men, I grew up surrounded by women. She could muster, dock, drench, shear and ride and I couldn't do any of the above. But the more I worked on the scripts the more I realised what we did have in common were our values. We were both hard-working and loyal and tried to do the right thing by people. So that was a start. We had a similar moral code.

My instinct told me to role model men, not women, for her, so I used a lot of my Dad who was hardworking, passionate, a loner and emotionally shut down when I was growing up (now he's an open book!) I also soaked up as much as I could of our head animal wrangler Bill, who, like Claire, had spent his whole life on the land and working with animals. He was a character. Sandpaper hands, sandpaper communication and sandpaper wit. He walked like he was still astride a horse, picking for a fight while heading up hill through a gale-force wind. I became Bill's shadow, a bit of a stalker really, in lighting setups I'd hang with him and pick his brains about anything farmy; crutching, flyblow, how to use a whip, and if I had a scene off I'd track him down and offer to do some menial task just to clock up some more time with him.

We had such a short prep time for this show, and as I was starting from scratch with the riding and all the farming skills, I chose to live out where we were filming and spend all my weekends at one of the wrangler's properties soaking up the atmosphere in this alien world as they drank beer from 10 am watching cowboys break in horses and rope steers and inevitably break a bone or two which appeared to be part in parcel for their world. Boy, these guys were tough. I saw Bill's bone sticking out of his thigh after being tossed off his horse and crushed against a wall by a raging bull and he didn't utter a sound.

My first director, Don Crombie, helped with a great piece of advice for me which was, 'She doesn't smile. When she does it's rare and special like a rainbow.' That was tricky for me. I had no idea I smiled so much! So that was a good awareness and a specific physical discipline to take into each scene which also helped me find her.

So: Bill, Dad, no smiling, substitution work for our life passions, empathy for her emotional history, allowing my humour to infuse into her and a shared desire for love – these all helped create my beloved Claire. May she rest in peace.

TAMMY DAVIS

Tammy Davis (Ngāti Rangi, Atihaunui a Paparangi) grew up in Raetihi, and studied acting at Northland Polytechnic before landing his first major role (alongside fellow graduate Clint Eruera) as Mookie in the feature film 'What Becomes of the Broken Hearted?' Following supporting roles in 'Whale Rider", and TV dramas 'Jacksons Wharf', 'The Market' and 'Mataku,' Tammy starred in feature film 'Black Sheep,' and Taika Waititi's short film 'Tama Tū,' before securing the role of Munter in long-running TV series 'Outrageous Fortune.' He won Best Performance by a Supporting Actor at the 2008 Qantas Film and Television Awards for this role. Tammy made his feature film direction debut on the 2015 film, 'Born to Dance,' released in 2015.

He currently co-hosts the breakfast show on George FM and is, of course, still active as an actor.

Munter and me

When I first auditioned for *Outrageous Fortune* I was told that the character was originally written as Pakeha but that my audition was the best lol. I don't think that's true. I think a decision had probably been made somewhere to brown it up a bit.

Anyway, I was cast as Munter, the dim-witted friend of Van West, twin of Jethro West. From the first time I met Ant Starr I knew that we would work well together. We met on the set in a scene and he asked if he could kick me in the head. I replied yes that's ok, and after the third kick I picked him up off the bed and threw him to the ground. We were good from then on.

In pre-production it was hard trying to communicate who Munter was to the crew. The ideas were very cliché when it came to his make-up and costume. Here he was, about 21, and the tattoos that adorned his skin were ones that mates of mine had done ten years ago. I decided to outsource and then come back with ideas and this paid off: the tattoos that I ended up wearing for 6 seasons - 109 episodes - were ones that I had gone and had designed by friends.

I was very lucky in the first season to be kind of left alone to develop the character on my own. The production team knew that if they got the family dynamic right that they were onto a winner. The character was written as a dope-smoking hopeless crim but I decided to grow Munter myself and take him in a different direction. I made him loyal, loveable, interesting, courageous, smart and cheeky.

On set, I continued to take direction and grow as an actor. With no one to guide me I wanted the character to be memorable. I decided that he could make mistakes but that he would always grow from them and never make them again. I didn't want him to be just an idiot that would at some point be discarded. All this paid off and the role got bigger and bigger from there on in.

Preparing For A Role

I followed my training and saw an opening to self-develop the character and I did. Don't be afraid to make the character your own and don't be afraid to see parts of yourself in the character. If it works trust the process and go there. Be patient and trust your instincts. You might end up finding a character that we can all identify with.

NEIL MELVILLE
I met Neil working on the Australian TV series 'Playing for Keeps' in 2019. He has many television, film and theatre credits in a career spanning over four decades. Says Neil: 'I have always loved finding characters and creating 'real reactions to imaginary stimuli' - as Hayes Gordon described the art of acting. Because auditions are such a big part of our working lives I asked Neil to discuss one. The role he auditioned for was for a male character who was also homosexual, and a female impersonator/ drag queen.

The *Torch Song Trilogy* Audition
I was asked to audition for the play *Torch Song Trilogy* many years ago. It is the story of a drag queen wanting to adopt a child with his gay partner. Such a subject was outrageously controversial at the time and the play was written with fierce humour and a deep underlying anger. I approached the scene given to me by wanting to understand the life of a drag queen. The scene was set in the dressing room of a theatre as the artist removes his makeup to reveal the person behind the mask. The dialogue, peppered with sarcastic wit, reveals the weight of oppression facing this man embarking on a taboo want: to adopt a child as a gay couple.

To prepare, I arranged to spend an afternoon with a drag queen. Terry was unsure whether to accommodate my request but I managed to find a conduit via a professional choreographer who arranged for me to meet Terry's boyfriend, a very straight looking film industry executive, Paul, who invited me to one of Terry's 'Revues'. From there, Terry would be able to observe me from a distance before deciding whether to commit.

The first I knew of her acceptance was when a stunningly beautiful blonde sidled up to me, slid her arm through mine and said seductively: '*So, you want to learn to be a drag queen do you darling?*'

We arranged to meet at her flat in St Kilda that Sunday. My girlfriend at the time sat outside with Paul while Terry and I sat alone in the living room for hours discussing the world of cross-gender.

Terry explained that she was in the process of a full sexual transition. She had to complete a psychiatric assessment programme and was on a course of hormone treatment before undergoing surgery to complete total gender transition. Her commitment was inspirational and the challenges daunting. Beyond the social, physical and emotional challenges was her concern to maintain her feminine beauty.

Terry thumbed through a book of photographs of famous Hollywood stars explaining the tricks they used to enhance and highlight their natural features. Her knowledge and appreciation for these details was profound. I realised in Terry a quality that I had not applied to my understanding of the text before I met her. Gender was of less consequence than the fact that my character was confronted by the reality of ageing. He was revealing his face in a mirror. The underlying fear provided the crack in the humour that opened the door to a vulnerable human being.

I felt liberated by what Terry had taught me. Ironically, Terry's final words were even more enlightening: *'You won't get the role Neil. I know you will do a great audition because you care. But you won't get it.' 'I won't?' 'Darling, there is no way that you are ever going to hide that chin. But I know you'll be good.'*

Terry was right. I didn't get the job. But I did relish the preparation and what it taught me. My audition felt powerful. I was very engaged, I loved performing it and the American director was very kind and complimentary. He stood up, walked to the front of the auditorium and praised my 'sensibility.' He then said candidly, and inoffensively: 'I thought you did an outstanding audition. But unfortunately I can't offer you the role.' 'Probably my chin,' I replied.

He just smiled and I left richer for the whole experience. Tony Sheldon went on to perform the role brilliantly. But preparation brings its own rewards. I highly recommend it.

EMMETT SKILTON

Emmett is a New Zealand born actor, director and screenwriter and has worked in over 40 productions in film, TV and stage. Most Kiwi's would recognise him as the young God-in-the-making, Axl, from TV3's 'The Almighty Johnsons.' Emmett is also an occasional teacher at the Actors Lab Studio.

General approach

I read a lot. I find ideas sink in deeply when I read, which is why I have strongly paired reading with the rest of my preparation for a character.

My goal is always to find specific biographical life events about the person

I'm playing. If a book about them exists, or of someone in a similar era/occupation/experience to them, I'll read it. I'm looking to use the material as touchstones to build my version of the character, so I can justify every word my character speaks, and every step they take.

My preparation for Sam Giancana, *The Making of the Mob: Chicago*

It's easy to look at a role and say, 'Okay, they're THIS kind of person.' This can especially be the case when playing someone 'bad'. We take their outward actions for face value, then make stereotypical choices toward making them all bad. But of course, no one is ever ALL bad, and there must be a reason behind their behaviour. Plus, the character is already written to *do* bad things, it doesn't mean he should *be* bad while he does them.

So I go into the history of the character. What's come before? What has shaped them to want what they want, to do what they do, in the way that they do it? Outward actions have an inner reason, and without the why, you just have a whole bunch of ideas.

For the role of Sam (Salvatore) Giancana, his biography, '*Rise and Fall of a Chicago Mobster*, was my key to finding those 'inner reasons'. After just a few pages the complexity of Sam Giancana was so apparent, leading me to discover so many pivotal touchstones.

Among many, an example of a touchstone I found is when Sam told his young daughters he was away at college while he was in fact serving time in a corrections facility in Indiana. This information can be taken two ways: he is deceptive, sure. But it also tells me he is protective and cares for his family. This to me is a very honourable trait and one which I found I could use to build a 3-dimensional version of Sam Giancana.

Detective. Derek Mois, *Murder is Forever*

Another character I had the honour of playing was Derek Mois. A true-life detective with the Omaha Police Department, he was famous for cracking a case that saw twin double murders committed 5 years apart. The information was clear in the story: what he was experiencing at each crime scene, how his hope built only to be frustratingly knocked down. But what was *not* clear to me was: what happens in the scenes, in the *years*, we don't see on screen?

As there was no book on this Detective, I sought content from a person in a similar walk of life.

The book was about an IT expert from San Diego who pursued his lifelong dream of becoming an FBI agent in his early 30s. From hopeful to miserable,

I saw this individual's expectation versus his reality as the weight of his career took a toll on him, most apparently his guilt, as crimes went unsolved.

This information became an important touchstone in building my version of Detective Mois. Knowing he had two connected murders years apart, with family members waiting with bated breath for any information, would have brought Mois deep guilt. This could then not only stem from the victim's family but from his own love for his family, his wife, his parents - who are all unsafe with a murderer on the loose. All playable aspects, and all very present at different times throughout the episode.

Another pivotal discovery in this book was this FBI agent's moment of deep frustration and fury in finding no answers to a particular crime. We are so often exposed to quick crime-solving thanks to Hollywood portrayals, but this is actually less than 1% of the cases. So for Detective Mois, an experience like this was again a valuable touchstone for me to use.

An important aspect is how I embody these touchstones. It depends on the event or memory. I may explore through meditation while walking the story step by step in my imagination. Others I say out loud with large and clarified actions, physically speaking the experience into my body. Other times a softer approach works, just sitting in the feeling of experience.

JOEL TOBECK

Joel is an award-winning actor and is rarely out of work – a major achievement for any actor anywhere in the world. He was born into a theatrical family and has played lead roles in the American television hit 'Sons of Anarchy' and the Australian series 'The Doctor Blake Mysteries.' In 'Little Fish' he played against Cate Blanchett, was Geena Davis's husband in 'Accidents Happen,' and has worked with Ben Mendelsohn in 'Tangle.' Joel is also a teacher at the Actors Lab Studio. When I asked Joel to talk about preparing for a particular role he decided to talk about his process for ALL roles. So, here it is: Joel's technique – or more accurately his cure for your technique.

How Joel prepares for any role

To me, this is like asking 'How do I read a book?' Instinct is a huge part of my process. We've all read books. We all have an imagination. We all trust these imaginations while we are reading. We visualise what the writer is describing. We create our own journey of the story. So, to me, that is the important ingredient to preparation. Trusting our own interpretations and responses to what we are preparing for.

Preparing For A Role

Unfortunately, I've found that a lot of actors don't trust this natural response and spend too much time picking at minute details of the story or character, and ultimately end up sucking all the fun out of what they are doing, leaving no room for imaginative preparation, play and (most importantly) spontaneity. That's fine. But man: how exhausting. It's supposed to be fun!

Tell the story

If study and analysing is your thing, all power and respect to you. Just don't forget about the organic, innate and fun parts of yourself; the parts we used as children to unapologetically express our ideas. Don't let these get left behind. Embrace the story. I was working with a young actor recently who was giving a not very interesting performance because he was worrying too much about saying the script 'the right way'. I pulled him aside and said. 'Don't say the words, say the feeling'. He instantly became an actor feeling something, and the words just flowed.

Remember. It's not about the performance, it's about the story. Tell the story.

Be in the moment

Personally, I LOVE walking on to a set or into a rehearsal room not knowing what I'm going to do. I thrive on the danger. But, it took me a long time to trust that side of my process. It takes practice and patience. You have to be ok with falling down with your pants down around your ankles in front of everybody. I've fallen many times. It's embarrassing. Get over it.

I love to be directed. I love an acting challenge, and being thrown a curveball by a director or even another actor is like gold to me. One famous actor asked me to 'ramp things up a bit' in a scene we were doing once... That's like being given the keys to the kingdom... 'I'll show you Mr A-lister!'

I've also had directors shoot my ideas down in front of everyone... It hurts. So what?

Observe people

I've spent hours and hours sitting in cafes or airports watching people go about their business. Not taking notes or consciously trying to capture a particular aspect of what they are doing, but just watching. It all gets stored in your creative-vault to be called on later... Or not.

For many of my roles I have found there are parts of the character that remind me of things I may have observed years ago. It's awesome fun.

Be open

Keith Richards from the Rolling Stones has always said that he is a conduit, where the riffs and musical ideas come *through* him rather than *to* him. I believe we actors are the same. Leave yourself open to 'The Acting Gods' or the 'Universe' or whatever you want to call it... Be open, be ready. This is how I like to work. When I have my doubts about my ability - especially when taking on a new project - I remind myself that I will be ok... Just let it come in.

A very famous drummer when asked what makes a great band said: 'The band doesn't play the music, the music plays the band.' Beautiful.

Interesting is interesting

We all want to be good and have people like our work. But, don't tie yourself up in knots trying to please anybody. Your ideas and offers are yours. You have a right to have them. Trust them! If the director has another perspective on things then, if you have to, work it out. There is usually a middle ground, and very rarely will you get told in no uncertain terms that you are wrong. Remember you may bring something into the room that no-one was expecting... That's gold!

Look at all the actors, artists, writers and musicians you admire. You love them because? They are them!

Again what works for some won't work for others, and that's cool too. Use whatever resonates for you to help find the result: it might be a passage or a quote from an actor's biography, some life experience, a particular moment from a voice or scene study class, or even one particular teacher who has a way in their teaching that just makes you 'get it'. You can take bits from here and take bits from there, and sprinkle a bit of this on that and make your own dish. It's like traditional Indian cooking. One village's recipe for Kadai Chicken may differ from another's. It's still Kadai Chicken. As long as it tastes good it's working.

I've worked with a lot of actors, some famous and others not so famous, who will break everything down and know the character inside and out and constantly ask questions about why why why? – and others who just wait until we get onset and the only work they've done is learn the lines. And some who just want to get to the bar before it closes. We are all unique. We are all valuable. As a well-known actor said to me once when our plane hit some bad turbulence sending me to white-knuckle hell, (holding up a glass of wine) 'Just go with it man!'

BRONWYN TUREI

Bronwyn Turei is a graduate of Unitec's Performing and Screen Arts in Auckland (2005). Her screen credits include four seasons as a core cast member on the hit

Preparing For A Role

NZ show 'Go Girls,' Holly Collins in Season 2 of 'Brokenwood Mysteries,' Aroha in 'Dirty Laundry' and Arataki in the web series 'Awkward Love.' Bronwyn has an extensive theatre resume, performing with theatre companies all over New Zealand. She is also a recorded singer/songwriter.

Natalya and Me

In 2017 I was offered a role at Circa theatre in *Three Days in the Country* by Patrick Marber (adapted from *A Month in the Country*): Natalya Petrovna, the fiery, formidable, intelligent, isolated and extremely passionate wife of a wealthy estate owner, stuck in a gilded-cage-life and a loveless marriage, torn between the adoration of her husbands' best friend and the lust for her son's idealistic tutor.

Our experienced and fearless Director Susan Wilson shaped every subtle power play and character interaction. The cast was phenomenal, I was floored by the talent I had the honour of going on this journey with. Gavin Rutherford, Peter Hambleton, Harriet Prebble, Carmel McGlone, Irene Wood, Ken Blackburn, Jason Whyte, Simon Leary, Andrew Paterson, Maia, Alex and Shaun (three students on placement) and two high energy boys sharing the role of my son. I was suitably terrified, this being my first lead role on stage in years. Up until that point I had been happily plugging away at supporting roles, multiple character pieces and singing my alto heart out in Musical Theatre ensemble.

I was living out of my suitcase staying in Lower Hutt with Alix Bushnell, (one of my endlessly generous best friends) so every morning I would leave early and sit in traffic for an hour doing vocal warmups, articulation exercises, singing at the top of my lungs to The Rock FM and run lines I'd stayed up learning the night before. As I am chronically early to everything I would spend the extra hour and a half before rehearsal pouring over the many notes from the days before, work on the lines for the upcoming scenes, and find my way into Natalya's headspace. Ken and Jason would arrive early too most days. I have such fond memories of mornings spent chatting about life over a hot cuppa in the green room upstairs with those two kind and fascinating men.

My biggest challenge was grounding myself. I tend to rush, to not trust that I am capable of holding a moment. And I move. A lot. It's like I have too much nervous energy sometimes and it usually comes out through my fidgety feet or flailing limbs. Sue's direction was all about finding my centre and planting me there. I learned so much about how to tap into my power as a woman and as an actress.

Another element which I always find invaluable to my process (especially if it's a period piece) is getting my hot little hands on stand-in costume items ASAP. In this case it was heeled boots and a gigantic heavy full length multiple layered skirt. I couldn't sit down without a straight back and had difficulty breathing. Who needs to breathe, right? It had its own sassy way it swished when I moved angrily across the stage, it was coy and girlish when I twisted my hips, and when I needed the quiet strength of stillness it kept me rooted to the spot.

Overall, I felt as though for the first time, with the luxury of such a complicated character and the time to explore it, I had tapped into a more mature level of understanding my own performance potential.

You'd think that would be enough, right? If only I were that smart.

Just for kicks I also said yes to doing a piece called PSA in the Wellington Comedy Festival - which we had around 4 rehearsals to throw together. We performed it to sold-out houses for 5 nights while I was in the thick of *Three Days in the Country*.

Parodying New Zealand politicians couldn't have been more different. I would finish an intense emotional Natalya rehearsal for the day, find a spare piece of floor in an empty dressing room, power nap for 20 mins, wake up, wash my face, put my show makeup on, gather my wigs and run down to BATS to make people laugh. Then I'd drive back home to the Hutt, shower, learn my lines for the next day and pass out curled up with my script.

I learned so much about my craft, my capacity to push myself and how much you can truly achieve in a day. Natalya was a pivotal role in my continuing education and an important verse in my ongoing love song to Wellington and it's beautiful arts industry.

Long may we dance.

JENNIFER WARD-LEALAND
2020 New Zealander Of The Year, Jennifer Ward-Lealand (CNZM) is a New Zealand screen and theatre actor whose many screen credits include the 1993 movie 'Desperate Remedies' as well as appearances in 'The Footstep Man,' 'Shortland Street' and Australian comedy series 'Full Frontal.' She's an experienced theatre director also and has won many awards and accolades. She is fluent in Te Reo Maori, is President of NZ Equity, and mother of two children.
Marlene Dietrich
When I look back at the roles I've played, two, in particular, stand out for the different approaches I've taken to prepare. In 2003 I was engaged to play the

role of the stage and screen icon, Marlene Dietrich, in the play *Marlene*. I was reluctant to take on the role at first because I knew it would be a big job, primarily because she was not a fictional character and examples of her work were very much in the public domain. I figured I had to play her very well or not at all! Thus began what would be nearly six months of prep.

Reading is a crucial part in any actor's development, and not just the quick fixes from Wikipedia but the boots n' all biographies and reference books. I amassed a huge pile of these, exploring everything from Marlene's wartime work to her wardrobe. This was all a huge help in providing me with context as I was learning the script. I watched every film she made, recording snippets of her voice to learn her particular vocal patterns; and of course her music recordings were the soundtrack to my life for that period. I needed to learn the 'song' of her speech as well as the actual songs. By this I mean observing and articulating the intonation, locating where in the lyric she might swoop, and the different vocal qualities she employed. Having a musical background was definitely a plus.

If this all sounds inordinately technical, it was - it was plain hard work. But it's important to state here that my job was not to mimic her but to *act* her. Yes, creating an iconic image and feel was crucial, but it needed to be a complex performance; I needed to bring craft to the role - where I took a breath, where my focus was, what I visualised and how I engaged with the audience. I knew I needed a kind of fearless openness that would demand the audience's attention. This is what I focussed on in rehearsals.

As I write this, it is nearly seventeen years since I played Marlene Dietrich for the first time - and I've continued to play her at arts festivals and venues throughout Aotearoa and Australia. I'm delighted that the work I did right at the beginning has meant that there has been a continual demand for the show. And of course, as I've improved as an actor, so the show has grown and deepened.

Darcy in *Vermilion*

In 2017 I was fortunate to be cast as Darcy in the feature film *Vermilion*, written and directed by Dorthe Scheffman. Here was a beautifully complex role to get my teeth into - a composer/performer deeply committed to her musical life but who has been perhaps less successful as a mother, and now finds herself unwell and potentially unable to continue her creative practice.

I knew that there would be pressure on me during filming. It was a low-budget production which meant few of the usual comforts one can expect on a film set and I was in practically every scene. I needed to be able to find an efficient path to expressing Darcy's emotional complexities - a process that would allow me to go deep, fast. For this, I engaged the very fine acting coach, Brita McVeigh. In our sessions we explored Darcy's primary inner conflicts: how to be creative musically *and* to be a good mother. This is a dynamic I intrinsically understood as an actor and a parent. By imagining situations where these incompatibilities were at play, and focussing on how this actually *felt* in my body, I created a physical and mental point of reference to draw on. This was such a useful tool for me during the shoot. Even when time was short all I needed to do was to hook into that feeling and then depending on what the scene required I'd be able to expand or contract that sensation.

As an actor, I'm always looking for the biggest challenge in the piece I'm working on. Where there is something that I don't yet know or understand, something that I need to integrate into my performance, then I need to do that work before I step in front of the camera or on the rehearsal room floor.

PETER FEENEY
My preparation for four roles

These roles embraced a range of challenges: directing and acting at the same time, hands-on research, and telling true-life stories. They demonstrate that there is no 'one size fits all' method to unpacking a role, at least not for me. My endgame is to create the preconditions where something real has a chance of happening. I don't have any single reliable way in. I don't believe in rituals. I let the material speak to me and guide my approach. It's the advice actor Kevin J Wilson gave me early on, and it's stayed with me ever since.

Milo in *Milo's Wake* – Theatre - 2005

I directed this production, a play written by the Australian writers' Mike and Margery Ford, and also played the title character because, honestly, I couldn't find an actor to play it.[66] It was a lot of firsts for me: directing, playing a big lead role, and singing (about 17 songs altogether). I had a lot to prove and, potentially, a lot to lose. There's nothing like a good risk to focus you!

I wanted the rehearsal to have all the elements each actor needed to do great work, but which I'd not to that date always found in the professional productions I'd done. I was interested in what I'd heard about the *Globe*

---

66 Three actors, for different reasons - Stuart Devenie, John Callan and Kevin J Wilson - all turned it down. They may have said they couldn't sing, I can't remember. I can't sing either of course, but I didn't let that hold me back!

Preparing For A Role

Theatre in London and wanted to find a play where the audience had a reason to be there and had a role to play. I was also quite keen on the idea of bringing theatre to the people where they gathered, using a non-traditional venue.

Most of all I wanted to find a play I adored and understood and, if possible, one that could play in a New Zealand setting. It took me over a year of steady reading, but I found *Milo's Wake* in 2001 while I was working at the Queensland Theatre Company. I burst into tears on the second to last page and immediately understood that was the challenge – to get the audience to that point every night too.

As I was directing as well as acting I felt I had to be totally on top of my acting game before rehearsals started, so I could be there for the other actors. In a workshop with Australian director and teacher Rob Marchand I evolved the character - particularly exploring the aspects of grief and guilt, important for the Irish Catholic Milo who felt responsible for the recent death of his son. I got Conor McSwiney, the Irish owner of our chosen venue for the play (*The Dogs Bollix*) to record all of Milo's lines and then hammered in the dialogue, at the same time learning the accent, listening to the recording over and over while I built a new deck for my parents.

Some months ahead of official rehearsal the cast and I began identifying the various themes and ideas around the play: the fact that Milo and his family, the O'Conors, were migrants, and what that kind of upheaval must have meant; their Irish heritage and what that implied; and how the death of their son Aidan the year before had affected them.

We then divided these aspects up as individual research projects. Each cast member (and I ended up with a wonderful cast: Susan Brady, Hannah Marshall, Ashley Hawkes - and in 2006, the late Peta Rutter) went off to look at the history of Ireland, or migration, the nature of grief - and so on.

We drove around as a cast till we found the first-ever house the family lived in – a humble brick and tile in Avondale. Then we found their current house: a grand Mt Albert bungalow. It looked like the proud home of a successful self-made businessman. As we hung around the front gate the owner came out and invited us in. This was an unexpected bonus: I was able to see the room where mine and Aidan's epic confrontation, a pivotal part of the play, took place. Every night I saw that room as Milo described his death.

Conor McSwiney helped us find an Irish migrant family to visit as a cast, where we stayed for an evening, chatting and singing songs. We discovered Clare Connelly, who ran the Irish dancers in Auckland, and Susan Brady (playing Milo's wife Maura) and I learnt how to waltz to an Irish tune. We became immersed generally in the Irish community in Auckland and started to unconsciously copy and assimilate ways, tics and aspects that suited us.

We discovered a lot more: like how all the cheerful sounding jigs we were singing were themed around terrific loss and grief. How emigration out of Ireland tended until fairly recently to be a one-way trip, which is why wakes were held for those emigrating. For those remaining it was like a death; they would never see these people again.

By now our rehearsals were underway. We explored the text via physical, vocal and imaginative exercises. We passed each other's monologues around, sharing them all, taking a line in turn, becoming collectively committed to the storytelling of the whole play. We worked in the performance space as much as we could, and it started to feel like home.

A week before opening I was out with our publicist Sally Woodfield on a promotional trip, handing out flyers to Comedy Festival punters. Sally decided it would be a great idea if I went in character. I wandered into a theatre foyer and for the first time, Milo got a trot outside of our narrow rehearsal circle. It was revelatory. People responded to the character (a bit of a hell-raiser) with *unreserved* delight. This was immensely reassuring, giving me confidence that with the character of Milo I had created something real.

It's always an unknown, our actorly explorations, in what will actually be of use, what from our investigations will stick. But as a minimum, investigations, adventures and rehearsals are shared experiences, bonding actors together. It's as much by working together in a focussed way, as well as what works, that the result arrives. The night we opened I was able to look to any actor on stage and find home. We had become a true ensemble. The play was well received with full houses and ripping reviews.[67] We DID get the audience to tears every night, largely by honouring the play as written: in the first act they got to sing, tap their feet, and laugh – which opened them up in Act two to go anywhere emotionally.

I should add that the whole enterprise was bloody hard work and any remuneration was ridiculously out of proportion to the hours sunk in. That's theatre for you. But it was worth it.

Angus in *Black Sheep* – Feature Film - 2008

The main element of prep that went into creating the role of Angus, in director Jonathan King's iconic Sheep zombie movie, was research. Jonathan and I agreed I should spend some time on a high country sheep farm: Craigmore

---

[67] Admittedly the house capacity was only 120 for our Auckland seasons, but give me a small house packed to the gunnels over a cavernous venue populated with the same number of punters every time.

sheep station in South Canterbury. It was a visit to this same station that had inspired Jonathan to make the film in the first place.[68] Forbes Elworthy was the incumbent there; he'd recently decamped from London, where he'd been working as a banker, to run the family business. His father had been head of Federated Farmers back in 1983 when I had studied at Lincoln College, so I was somewhat in awe of the family even before I arrived.

It was eye-opening getting the feel of a big sheep run. Forbes himself was the real deal: tall, handsome, ruggedly elegant, an Oxford graduate - descended from gentry who had been granted this turf in the nineteenth century. We spent several nights at the shearer's quarters at the top of the farm, sitting around a burning briar, sinking Pinot Noir while Forbes communed with London on his Blackberry, buying and selling stocks. Far below sparkled the faraway lights of the town of Timaru, which Forbes declaimed should be dynamited. This was somewhat disconcerting, considering that my ancestors had slaved their drunken Catholic guts out building the place.

Forbes was everything my character wanted to be. My character, Angus, was anxious to prove himself, to be more than he was. I could imagine Angus attending some Farmer Expo, running into Forbes, sucking up to him, putting his foot in it somehow - and then running home to buy the same *Rodd & Gunn* shirt he'd seen him wearing.

Jonathan and I wanted to chart the unravelling of my character from country squire into raving monster (literally, by the end of the film). For that to work, I decided that the monster was always in him, and he knew it. Everything he did was about trying to keep it in check: top button done up under his tie, not a hair out of place, and so on. His obsessive tidiness became a symptom of his controlling behaviour, which also explained his scientific attempts to control and tame nature. This was all an instinctive response to the chaos of his inner self, brought on by the early death of his father. As his grand plans unravelled Angus became more fractured as his controlling tendencies collided with his increasingly disastrous reality. In the delicious confrontation with his brother in their father's study, finally, he gives in. He's relaxed, happy and himself for the first time. He is the monster.

A tale of 2 Tele-movies: *Abandoned* – 2015 VS *Siege* 2012

Here I'd like to briefly discuss two roles I performed based on real-life characters.

For *Siege*, I got to hang out with my actual character, Armed Offenders Squad

---

68 Forbes was in fact Jonathan's step-cousin: his step-father's nephew.

(AOS) Sergeant Paul Symonds, who trained us in AOS techniques. Paul was opposed to the film initially. He objected to operational inaccuracies, and felt it was too soon to be making it, just three years after the actual events. He'd been a friend of Senior Constable Len Snee, whose death began the 50-hour siege of the film's title.

This was my first time dealing with the collision of fact and drama. Some discrepancies made it harder for me to engage and commit to the story I was telling. It was a challenging shoot for me, although the final result was well-received.

Still, there was a useful take out. A few years later I accepted the role of John Glennie, the real-life skipper in the telemovie *Abandoned*. Now I understood that my role was to portray the *character* of Glennie as written, which I did with as much skill and faithfulness to the man as I could. The story, the historical veracity of the script, was not my responsibility. I made a call early on not to discuss the script at all with Glennie during our several chats. Once I'd made this decision, I was able to get on and do my job. Filming off the picturesque Tutukaka coast, on the water every day, working with an incredible cast and crew, was a pleasure.

Preparing For A Role

Above: Lisa Chappell as Claire McLeod in *McLeod's Daughters*.
Below left: Neil Melville as Barry Edwards in *Killing Time*.

Right: Tammy Davis as Munter in *Outrageous Fortune*.

Right: Emmett Skilton, fresh out of drama school, swinging a sword as Axl in *The Almighty Johnsons*.
Below: Joel Tobeck as police chief Stephen Tremaine in *One Lane Bridge*.

Below: Bronwyn Turei as Natalya Petrovna in *Three Days in the Country*.

Preparing For A Role

Above: Jennifer Ward-Lealand as Marlene Dietrich in *Marlene*.
Below: Peter Feeney in his all-time favourite role: Milo in *Milo's Wake*.

Above: What is Angus about to do with that sheep?! Peter Feeney in Jonathan King's *Black Sheep*. *Right:* Antonia Robinson showing an ALS class her Character Timeline for Natasha in the TV series *Mystic*.

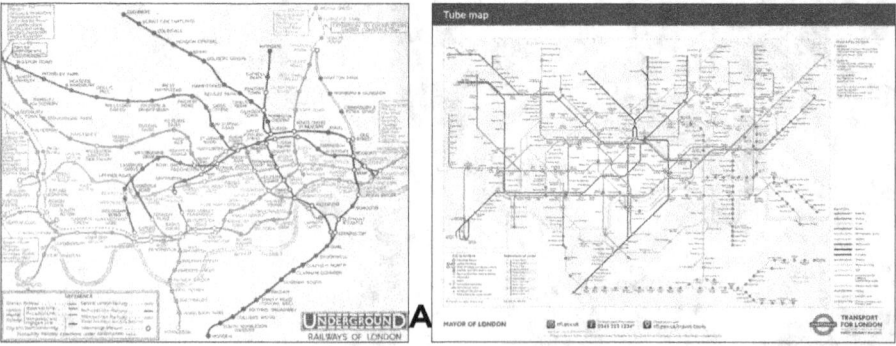

Above left: The London Underground map, 1932. *Above right:* Henry Beck's 1933 map - illogical, intuitive, and the model for Underground maps ever since.

PART 3

THE HEAD GAME

Once and for all you must stop worrying about success or failure. Your business is to work step by step, from day to day, steadily, and to be prepared for the inevitable mistakes and failures, in a word, to follow your own path and leave competition to others.
Anton Chekhov, playwright, to Olga Knipper, actress, 1899

CHAPTER FIFTEEN
LEARNING AND THE LONG GAME

There really has to be a feeling of wanting to learn that's more important than wanting to succeed.
John Cassavantes, US Indie Film director

ADVANTAGES OF OWNING A CONSCIOUS TECHNIQUE
Every scene, every character, every job, every audition, every role - will challenge you in new ways. If you've got an instinct for how to play a scene or a role, listen to that. As Meisner said, technique is just for when you need it. When Britain ruled the waves it could start or end a war just by sending a gun-boat up a river because behind that, everyone knew, sat the might of the Home Fleet. Owning a wide-ranging acting technique gives you that kind of clout, creatively. It doesn't mean you have to bring all of your understanding to shoot every role completely out of the water. It means you know you have many guns to bear *if* they are needed.

Your personal technique is the trust in your own intuition that the sum of your learning and experience gifts you. Even the choice to NOT have a conscious technique is a creative choice – an attempt to connect back to original impulses. But without craft of any kind the danger is that your focus will go on to all the wrong things: how you look, how you feel, and worrying if your the work is any good. Technique gives you a creative funnel for your neurotic energy. For the most part, without a technique of *some* kind, you'll enjoy accidental and occasional acting successes, without ever knowing why something worked or not.

Louis Malle, the French Film director, loved the moments his actors couldn't explain. We all know that slightly dazed, train wreck feeling after a take, that Malle relished: that moment when his actors relinquished control. It's when something rather magical happened and we have no idea how. But a working life of such blinkeredness? That might drive you crazy.

Child actors don't have a conscious technique. They soak up ideas like human blotting papers. Learning by osmosis from a young age is how we were built to learn – look at how toddlers can pick up two or more languages before they even begin school if they are spoken at home. And this was, before the advent of drama schools, how everyone learnt: by being a member, willingly or not, of a theatrical family. In later life though this lack of understanding - of *how* what they do is any good - can make some ex-child actors feel undeserving of their success. The same can be true of naturally great actors, those who rely purely on their gut; on internal forces beyond their understanding. Because results come easily for them they can undervalue their achievement. This may be why Marlon Brando ate himself to an early grave, daring us to revere him no matter how fat he became. Richard Burton did the same thing, but with vodka. Obviously these are individuals grappling with outsize personal demons. But the point is still valid I think.

Actors without a technique can also be unable to communicate craft as they don't have an understanding of how it works in them. By contrast, a hard-won conscious technique, one that you comprehend, gives you a common language to use with directors, your fellow actors, and other collaborators. You'll be able to understand what's good in your own and other performances, and you'll be able to communicate this. That conscious understanding is at the heart of meaningful collaboration, setting up actors for much more than a career in acting but creative contributions of all kinds – editing, directing, teaching, writing, producing, and more.

LEARNING & YOUR ACTING
Your technique is not like a school trophy you can win, plonk on your shelf and forget about forever. It's not fixed. It's a flow, a journey, with no destination. So long as you keep evolving as a human being, your approach to acting will mutate too. And the exciting truth about learning is that our brains love it. Studies have shown that the brains of adults learning new things become awash with hormones to an extent only comparable to our peak learning state as toddlers.

There's learning that can only be found on the job: the day after day zombie-like tiredness, freezing exteriors wearing hardly anything, that nagging hamstring injury, having the other actor rushed to a costume change leaving you emoting in your close up to a lighting stand.

And yet, while work is undoubtedly a great teacher, on its own it's not enough to sustain you. All actors - great ones included – have found themselves, when their craft starts to ossify, returning to a learning environment.[69] When you're working you can slide into bad habits. Because there are professional consequences to failure you can stop taking risks in your work and so stop growing your abilities. Learning situations are the antidote to actors becoming too outcome focussed – a natural response to the unrelenting professional pressure to be good.

Different people comprehend and utilise teaching in different ways. Delay can be the way we learn. When I attend a workshop or masterclass I'm often painfully slow on the uptake - but then later, on set or in an audition room, I'll try something new and fly. Once a lesson sticks though, it's there for life. You may forget it, but you'll remember it when you have to. My therapist passed away some years ago. He had been a great help to me at one time of my life. When he died I was completely unprepared for how distraught I was. Then, some time later, in a time of challenge, one of his wonderful sayings came back to me. I realised that although he was gone, his teachings would always be with me.

SPECIALISATION VS RANGE

When a person comes to study acting they are sometimes learning two things: how to act *and* how to learn. But if they have already achieved proficiency in at least one other performance arena – such as competitive sport, music or dance – they bring singular advantages to their acting apprenticeship. They've had experience in handling pressure; in how to have 'grace under fire,' as Earnest Hemmingway defined courage. And they understand that an audience is out there – and even, that they are the point of it all.

I've had students from other performance backgrounds, such as circus or musical theatre, and when I plonk them in front of a camera for the first time, they totally get what's required. They are open and share everything with that lens. Intuitively they know there is an audience at the other end of it. They already know that performance is not a private thing.

Also, these students have already, in another performance arena, learnt how to master a difficult thing. This achievement, be it in sport or performing arts, gives them an understanding that mastery takes time and effort, and

---

[69] If you get a chance watch the *Working Shakespeare* series where the likes of Helen Hunt, Robert Sean Leonard, Emily Watson, Samuel L Jackson and Claire Danes act – some of them, frankly, pretty averagely - in a Cicely Berry masterclass. It's a lot of fun watching Cicely verbally flogging Samuel L; she's one of the few teachers in the world I imagine with the mana to be able to do that. There are snippets of this on *YouTube* too.

that setbacks are mandatory.

Yet sometimes those alighting at acting from these backgrounds feel like failures: the gymnast who because of injury cannot continue, or the musician who can't bear to play the violin anymore. It turns out that a great many actors come to acting fresh from a string of failed endeavours. Like distinguished British actor Zoe Wanamaker, who tried and failed at everything except acting, before she settled on it, they couldn't 'stick' at anything else. Sampling can look and feel a lot like failure. But once Wanamaker found acting, grit came easily to her. She went on to have a great career (appearing most recently in *Killing Eve* Season 3). Grit – the ability to persevere in any given task in the face of adversity - *isn't* necessarily an inherent character trait. Perseverance is much easier if you are doing what you were born to do.

In 1993 Anders Ericsson published the results of a study of a group of violin students in a music academy in Berlin. His key finding was that the most accomplished students in their late 20's, the ones that had left the academy and gone on to have professional success, had put in an average of *ten thousand hours* of practice by the time they were twenty years old. In his 2008 book *Outliers,* Canadian writer Malcolm Gladwell seized on the findings, concluding that: 'ten thousand hours is the magic number of greatness.'

Gladwell's conclusions however oversimplified the original findings by seemingly arguing that almost anyone could become an expert in a given field *just* by putting in enough time. In fact, the meaningful insight from the 1993 study was somewhat more nuanced: becoming accomplished in any field, in which there is a lot of competition, requires a lot of work. 'People have a tremendous capacity to improve their performance,' said Ericsson, 'as long as they train in the right way...'[70]

Since the initial study, further research has shown that it takes about ten years of study to become a chess grandmaster. Authors and poets have usually been writing for more than a decade before they produce their best work. And it takes on average about a decade of hard slog and research between a scientist's first publication and her most important publication. Stretching our scope to include acting, Ken Rea worked out that for actors starting in their late teens, working through drama school or classes, then into work, mixed with unemployment, it typically might take a journey of 20 years to

---

[70] *Peak: Secrets from the New Science of Expertise,* by Anders Ericsson and Robert Pool. Published by Houghton Mifflin Harcourt. Copyright © 2016

reach a level of real mastery in their work - just when, he observed ruefully, many of them are about ready to give up.[71]

Of course, if we are going to devote ourselves to one endeavour single-mindedly for so long, *how* we practice is important. If we don't find a way to make it fun then at some point we are going to have to stop.

Practice is important, but so too is range, argues American writer David Epstein.[72] His work, based on extensive study and research, has found that in most arenas, particularly unpredictable and intricate ones like acting, sampling widely *first* - gaining a breadth of experiences, taking detours, experimenting relentlessly, and juggling interests - is more important to final success than early specialisation. 'It's never too late to be what you might have been,' asserted Mary Ann Evans (aka George Eliot). And it turns out she was right. Across many fields and professions not specialists but *generalists* are more likely to achieve eventual success.

So we find that almost all Nobel prize winners have diverse interests, alongside their winning field of study. Their hobbies are everything from amateur theatricals to playing a musical instrument. Most successful athletes have typically gone through a sampling period where they try different sports before settling on their final choice - usually somewhat later than the norm.

It's true that a few activities, like golf or chess, can reward early specialisation. This is because they don't have too many variables – such as an opponent whose moves are unpredictable and simultaneous to yours. But, conversely, acting is a collaborative and complex multi-headed beast. It's a profession where a broad life experience bestows a way of seeing the world that gives an advantage. A background in competitive sport, music or dance is enormously helpful once people turn to acting. But so too is an upbringing that's a bit out of the box. This can be anything from being raised in a cult, as River and Joaquin Phoenix were, or just being highly itinerant like Joseph and Ralph Fiennes' family who moved around England constantly. Tom Cruise was also an itinerant - an 'Army brat'. Anna Pacquin was born in Canada but moved to New Zealand when she was young, winning an Oscar for the Jane Campion film *The Piano* when she was nine.

Says Julianne Moore, who changed schools a lot growing up: 'when you move around a lot, you learn that behaviour is mutable. I would change, depending on where I was. I would go to one school and everyone would

---

[71] In his book, *The Outstanding Actor*.
[72] *Range: How generalists triumph in a Specialized World*, Macmillan, 2019

dance one way and, then, at a new school, you'd notice that no one picked up their feet when they danced. You're like, OK, I'll shuffle my feet like them. You learn that there's no one way to dance or be. For some reason, a lot of actors come from these peripatetic backgrounds – army kids, missionary kids, kids of salesmen. It teaches you to watch, to reinvent, that character can change.'

So what's going on here? Well, it turns out that acting environments are (to use David Epstein's description) by definition wicked, not kind, working situations. There are multiple variables and many moving parts. No role, working situation or set of collaborators is ever the same. Directors and producers attempt to corral all this uncertainty and reduce risk by returning to familiar faces in new projects. But some degree of variability is creatively helpful. A 2005 study of Broadway hit musicals by Brian Uzzi and Jarrett Spiro showed that it is a combination of team cohesion and tension, a mix of the old and the new, which produced at least the best *box office* results.[73]

What is useful, as well as the depth that comes from doing the miles with acting, is a broad range of experience. That breadth makes us better creative problem solvers – and creative problem solving is the name of our game. Range makes us more likely to stop and figure out what opportunities and challenges any particular script or role holds for us, rather than just jumping in and ritualistically applying a set formula.

Here's an example of how range, the outsider's perspective, helps with figuring out thorny problems. In the early 1930s Henry Charles Beck devised a plan of the London Tube. Rather than focussing on accurate distance and geography, like the existing, complex maps, Beck pared the sprawling Tube network down to a tidy drawing of coloured, crisscrossing lines, thereby producing the most familiar map on the planet (you can see it on page 166).

But Beck wasn't a designer. He was an electrical draughtsman. His direct inspiration was the electrical circuit diagrams he was used to working on, which simply showed connections without scale. Beck's design went on to become the template for every Underground Railway in the world. His was the outsider's view: a whole new way of looking at map making.

Acting for you might be a life-long career or just a phase in your personal and professional development. At the start, you've no way of knowing. All you can do is take the leap and commit. It's only through action that you can

---

[73] 'Collaboration and Creativity: The Small World Problem,' *AJS* Vol. 111, Number 2, September 2005

figure out if something is for you. Acting may not be. But committing will ensure you'll get the most out of your time in it. Acting will add breadth, insight, and skill to whichever occupation you finally settle on.

Having a varied life experience brings direct benefits to your acting as well. In my case I did a string of different jobs when I left school – everything from a stint in the army, to working on farms and ski fields. I studied Science, then Arts, which lead to politics and finally to postgraduate study in Russia. When I settled on acting, one of my early jobs was playing a Russian speaking operator in a Telecom ad. I eked out the money and it kept me in the acting game for six months. I never would have got that ad if I hadn't studied Russian language and lived there for a time. Craig Hall, who has had an enviable Trans-Tasman career, loves motorbikes: he rode them in the New Zealand feature *Savage Honeymoon* and again in *The World's Fastest Indian*. His Scottish parentage came in handy in 2007 when he was cast with that accent in the big-budget movie *Waterhorse*, and later for *Razor*, the 1920s version of popular Australian series *Underbelly*. No life experience, even a negative one, is wasted in acting.

Perhaps that phenomenon, of some individuals collecting early an artistically useful range of emotional and practical experiences, may explain how occasionally a rookie actor will turn up in class possessing a seeming innate ability to pick up a script and just make sense of it. From what I can tell from a conversation with his agent, this is what happened with Kiwi actor K J Apa, whose break came in *Riverdale*. Says British actor Peter Barkworth: 'some actors are born great… and once they become good, God has done the rest for them.' It may take a while for those that count – casting folk, producers and directors – to find them. But they've got what it takes, seemingly buried somewhere in their DNA.

Yet talent isn't measurable, and early on it isn't always obvious. You can always get better – and that's true for everyone. The trick is to be patient and stay in a learning mindset, weathering occasional career squalls, staying on course, and keeping curious.

FLEXIBLE VS FIXED MINDSET

Actor Peter Barkworth describes the end of a great stage performance with another great British actor Antony Quayle. Barkworth turned to him. 'I enjoyed it tonight,' he said. 'We were acting really carelessly.' Replied Quayle sagely: 'it's a lifetime's work, learning to be careless…'[74]

---

74 Peter Barkworth, *About Acting*.

Learning And The Long Game

Watching someone play the violin we can tell that it was difficult to learn. We can see the sweat, the hours practicing, the sheer graft it's taken. If we see a concert pianist perform, or study the detail in a great painter's canvas, the technique is obvious. By contrast *anyone*, with no training at all, can stand up and act. Compounding the illusion of ease is that great acting looks effortless. We might say, after seeing an extraordinary performance, 'wow, they're so talented.' That's probably true, but it's not the full truth either. No one has thought up a system for measuring talent, except in the results. There's work buried in that performance, only so deep you can't see it.

If you believe in the idea of talent then you'll also believe that if you're talented you shouldn't ever fail and you shouldn't have to work too hard. If so, after your initial happy run, you will then find that it *is* hard. This may lead you to conclude that acting is not for you; you're not a 'natural,' or you're not 'talented' enough. That would be a shame because the failure would be not in your talent, but only in your attitude to learning.

Larry Moss says that being positive is a big risk. You might declare, when you hit a wall, or fail horribly at a role; 'I'm just no good at this!' You think that being tough on yourself in this way is virtuous. But it just gives you an out. Staying in the game takes stamina; that is, the ability to experience a setback, stay positive and learn.

This ability to grow from failure, rather than be demolished by it, is greatly helped by having a *flexible* learning mindset. Such a mindset says that we mustn't expect to be amazing straight away, and our current limits do not define us. When failure hits this mindset tells us the fail is not the end of the story: it's not 'never,' but, 'not yet,' says psychologist Carol Dweck.[75]

Examples of this flexible learning mindset abound in sport. Said New Zealand Silver Ferns captain Katrina Rore: 'I've never been the most naturally talented athlete. But I make up for that with hard work.'[76]

A rather less helpful belief is that of a *fixed* learning mindset. This thinking says that you are either talented or you are not. End of. Such a mindset interprets failure as evidence that 'I shouldn't be doing this because I'm no good at it.' That's not fun or fulfilling. It's an attitude that won't help you stay the course.

I know all this from direct experience. All through my 20's I'd dreamed about acting but kept putting it off, trying other things instead. It was as if I

---

75 See her Ted Talk: *The Power of believing that you can improve*.
76 'Netball: Former Silver Ferns captain Katrina Rore opens up on shock omission,' *NZ Herald*, 16 December, 2018.

had to eliminate all other avenues first. This was not necessarily a bad thing. I was doing what David Epstein might have called 'sampling' – committing to different endeavours, then moving off them, as I circled closer and closer to my actual calling.

However at the time I just felt like I was moving from one failure to the next. Acting was my light at the end of the tunnel. So long as I never committed and risked failure, just the idea of doing it one day gave me a strange kind of sustenance.

I did finally start acting at age 27. I was single-minded, made the necessary sacrifices easily, and then, six years in, I was cast as a lead in Sydney based Mini-TV series, *A Difficult Woman*. All my dreams had come true - but rather than loving the whole experience I found it rather stressful and nerve-wracking. It turned out doing acting wasn't the magic bullet I'd hoped for. I was still me. I faced a choice. Either to stay in the game – and learn a new way of living, where I no longer regarded failure as an ending, but instead as information - or to leave the profession, and forever be the victim of my restlessness. I decided to stay and find my rightful place in the profession.

So it should come as no surprise that I personally believe that acting – or anything at all that you are hotly passionate about - can be a recipe for self-improvement. Neurotics and artists have a lot in common, but the essential difference is that an artist creates something out of their anxiety. In my case a more flexible mindset has allowed me to add writing and teaching to my job description, and to get better at experiencing setbacks as bumps in the road, not end games. I've learnt that happiness doesn't come directly from any single result, but that a creative life can be fulfilling and meaningful. I'm pretty sure I would have learnt none of these things if I'd not stayed in the game and faced my demons.

THE FOUR STAGES OF LEARNING

Actors can get put off learning a practical technique. It takes time, and they can feel it gets them 'stuck in their heads.' It's important to know that applying technique gets easier and over time becomes second nature. But while new tricks and tools are being bedded in, the learning can feel cumbersome. These stages pass, and at the other end of the journey are new artistic possibilities.

The 'Four states of competence' model (originating in the 1970s) describes the journey involved in the transformation from incompetence to mastery.

Stage one is *unconscious incompetence*. The actor is just starting out; there is much they don't know. They are aware of this but have to rely on what they *do* know, which forces them to trust their intuition. This gives them a powerful permission, namely, permission to fail. Beginner's luck comes from having nothing to lose and everything to learn.

Actors can dislike moving out of this first stage of happy ignorance. Because with stage two, *conscious incompetence,* comes the realisation of everything we *don't* know. But there's a powerful lesson from stage one to keep: that there is no way to be intuitive without risking failure.

Stage two, *conscious incompetence,* can be tough. Self-consciousness can come into play. With more experience we now start monitoring ourselves and second-guessing our choices, presenting what we think is expected of us, rather than our own truth. We 'get in our head' because after some success we now have something to lose. We also start to recognise our limitations. This is mortifying, but the acceptance of our limits allows for their potential expansion, impelling us to move and train. Practice, determination and patience will see confidence in our intuition restored. Hard learning tends to stick better than quick mastery anyway; if you're making mistakes now, you'll be making better mistakes later. Just because you're not having fun all the time doesn't mean you're not making progress.

How you train is important. Benjamin Franklin said: 'tell me and I forget, teach me and I may remember, involve me and I learn.' You don't want a teacher who tells you what to do. I had this experience with an old school director, Elric Hooper, at Christchurch's Court Theatre. Every actor's move, every turn, and every inflection existed fully formed in Elric's head on the first day of rehearsal. We actors had a month to catch up. We existed to perform his will. It's an external directing style exemplified in Mike Leigh's film *Topsy Turvy,* where we are given insights into how Gilbert and Sullivan might have directed their Victorian-era Operettas.[77]

My real learning under Elric started after opening night when his dead hand of command was removed. When taking your first steps you don't want someone like Elric. You want someone who asks you the hard questions but forces you to make the connections yourself. It sounds counter-intuitive, but slow learning, multiple failures and creative obstacles, makes for learning that sticks. This is why the ancient Greek philosopher Socrates would never give his students answers: just more questions.

Some teachers though can't resist sprinkling helpful hints along your path.

---

[77] See the video within the article 'Pleasure in the Process: A Rehearsal Scene in Topsy-Turvy,' by Ari Aster, 30 July, 2019, *The Criterion Collection* - www.criterion.com.

After all, you're a paying customer. They want you to make progress. But fast learning fades fast. I've talked to actors who have trained in the best drama schools across the world. Years later the teachers they spoke most fondly of were the ones whose approach still mystified, even perplexed them. Often they were movement or voice teachers, working at a deeply intuitive level.

Stage three is *Conscious competence*: 'I grow and know and it starts to show'. Here we continue practising and experimenting, failing and learning, slowly expanding the repertoire of tools that work for us. Gradually, without even perceiving it, we shift in fits and starts to stage four: *Unconscious competence*. More and more we are sufficiently confident that we can trust and follow our impulses and let our quick, rough and ready intuition fly. We've attained that freedom of beginner's luck, but with much greater awareness. We've learnt how to prepare in such a way that we can let go in performance. We've learnt a technique - and now we can forget it.

The last two learning stages can happen quickly once we get moving into the habit of regular practice. Like a toddler learning to walk, the first steps are always the hardest.

Now awaits the ups and downs of learning over a lifetime. It's a grand adventure with many rewards, not the least of which is getting to know yourself better. There's no end game because we can always improve. But once you've mastered the basics of your chosen craft you'll have a sensible respect for everyone else's competencies – directors, writers, cinematographers, musicians, scientists, doctors etc. You know now what it takes to get good at anything.

CHAPTER SIXTEEN
EXCITEMENT. NERVES. DOUBT. DREAD.

I don't know that I ever find working pleasurable. It's always an exquisite agony – you're always eternally dissatisfied with what you've done. That's why you keep wanting to work, otherwise why would you do it?
Australian actor Cate Blanchett (of performing *Hedda Gabler* in 2013)

LITERAL VS IMAGINATIVE CHOICES

Some years ago I spent four lonely days in a Melbourne hotel room, toiling away on an important role. The feeling grew in me that the work wasn't coming together. Instead of excitement rising in me, there was dread. My response was to work harder, trusting blindly to a process that had worked in the past. Yet, as I've said, acting is a wicked game. Each role we find ourselves in brings the unexpected, the unpredictable, the perverse. We can learn to relish this wicked game, and the challenges each role brings. Or we can seek refuge in ritual, literalism, and playing it safe.

As already discussed, actors are expected to turn up with an offer and prepare in such a way that they can change that offer after direction. The director does a parallel investigation before she meets you. She has wracked her brains about how this story speaks to her and why it must be told. She's related that back to her own life, her fears and beliefs, and thought about how each character feeds into the overall story. You too must make these demands of yourself, preparing imaginatively so that once you've sifted through the artistic possibilities you've found your 'in': something that excites you - and scares you a bit too maybe - an offer you should hold close to your heart, like a precious flame that must be nurtured.

Making literal, unimaginative choices in your prep means playing that is aligned only with what the words say, not what your imagination can add to them. It's playing the scene like everyone else and not making the scene your own. It's working from a place of fear and the familiar. Literalism inhibits your individuality, and hence restricts your full creative expression.

Once you've prepared imaginatively, the challenge is to honour your choices in performance. Trying to 'get it right' stifles your acting. Instead you must trust your instincts all over again. Your choices will live if you embrace the idea of 'inclusion,' meaning acting on your impulses and feelings no matter what. That way you'll bring your full personality to the work. In the end, terrifying as it is, it's your humanity people want to see.

If you prepare an offer imaginatively but then take no risks in the playing, staying in your comfort zone and denying your impulses, your work will be reliably predictable - and uninteresting. If you don't prepare but only rely on your instincts in 'the moment' you can be inspired, of course, but your offers may not be true to the scene as written.

Why do we sometimes second guess ourselves or play it safe? Because with the playing comes what Olivier called 'you bastards!' and Stanislavski (of the auditorium) 'the black hole.' This is the audience and with them our old enemy; fear. Fear of not being good enough, or of being good, and above all, fear of failure. Too much fear will lead you to censor your choices, not follow them. Fear and nerves can be exhilarating, but can also seize you up, and your offer won't make it through to shine.

PERFORMANCE PRESSURE

We can all act brilliantly in our lounge or bedroom, or in the park running lines with a friend. We all have some happy place where great acting comes easily to us. It may be a scene group or even a class. Once you've done good work there, you know you can do it – which is important. But when we come to perform it is in a more unfamiliar environment with that pressure of an audience added. Even in an audition an audience exists – the casting director on the day, but later the director and producers who will view the tape.

There's no getting away from the audience. They complete the work. [The origin of the word audience is from the Latin *audiēns*, which means to hear or listen.] We can't be storytellers if we only have a story. That's only half the job. We need someone to *hear* that story. 'Most people live in almost total darkness,' said American novelist James Baldwin. 'People, millions of people whom you will never see, who don't know you, never will know you, people who may try to kill you in the morning, live in a darkness which — if you have that funny terrible thing which every artist can recognise and no artist can define — you are responsible to those people to lighten.'[78]

---

[78] From Baldwin's 1962 talk at New York City's Community Church, *The Artist's Struggle for Integrity*.

Excitement. Nerves. Doubt. Dread.

Under performance pressure we can find ourselves in our heads, self-consciousness cauterizing the good preparation we've done. It's tempting to blame our process. But our technique is fine. Our prep is fine. It's our head game that has failed. We have not prepared for what happens to the work when the pressure of performance is added.

That pressure can do strange things. The late Richard Harris was prone to getting sick while working, as American actor Charlton Heston complained about in his published diaries.[79] Interviewed while filming *The Elephant Man* Anthony Hopkins was surrounded by medicines and potions to keep a flu at bay he'd had for the entire shoot. Actors dread getting sick because it's almost impossible to get well under conditions of stress.

It's no secret also that many fine actors get nervous at times to the point of actually vomiting: Ben Kingsley, Helen Mirren and Joaquin Phoenix, to name just a few. Stage fright in 1995 led to a 17-year absence of British actor Stephen Fry from the stage. Barbra Streisand had a 27-year break from live performance when she dried up mid-song in front of 135,000 people in 1967. For two decades after 1974, Ian Holm didn't get back on stage: 'The very thought of acting made me dizzy,' he said. Bill Nighy once described a stint in theatre as 'like agreeing to be ill for a couple of months.'[80]

'Remember that you're supposed to be scared,' says Nighy. 'That's the normal, healthy reaction to have.' Fear is our constant companion. No actor is entirely free from it, and actors adopt a myriad of coping strategies. Dustin Hoffman was known for running endless awful sexual puns between takes to defuse the tension. Oliver Reed drank himself to an early grave (and a posthumous Oscar for *The Gladiator*). Samuel L Jackson was a crack and cocaine addict until just a few weeks before his astounding break out screen performance in Spike Lee's *Jungle Fever*. It's even possible that if the use of performance-enhancing drugs disqualified you from an Oscar, as is the case in sport, quite a few of them would have to be handed back.

Acting, also like sport, is about the ability to perform to the best of your ability *on demand*. By contrast, a visual artist has deadlines but they can always hold back a painting from an exhibition if it's not quite right. An actor, like a pilot landing a jumbo jet, is on NOW and must deliver no matter how they are feeling, at 8pm on opening night, or 6.30 am when that magic

---

79 Although it's possible he was just hung-over on those days... See *Charlton Heston: The Actor's Life: Journals, 1956-1976* – an engrossing read, more so than his later autobiography.
80 The examples in this paragraph from 'Stephen Fry, stage fright and how to avoid it,' *The Guardian*, by Matt Trueman, 21 Sep 2012

word is spoken: 'action.' One medical study found that the stress an actor experiences during performance can equal that of a car accident.

Fear and nerves are an entirely logical human response to the combination of being watched in an artificial environment, with inflexible deadlines and uncertainty of result.

Nerves are just excitement compacted under enough pressure. Once we start things usually go fine and we wonder why we put ourselves through it. But sometimes things don't go fine. In the end, acting becomes all about the head game: the spirit you bring to the work. Our job is to produce beauty under pressure, elevating ourselves above our nerves to make it about, as Russian actor Stanislavski said, 'the art in you; not yourself in the art.'

This chapter is about that: how in performance to be confident, back your abilities, and give yourself permission to present the fullest expression of yourself.

LEARNING TO LIVE WITH NERVES & DOUBT

Our original desire to be actors is often conceived alongside doubt, which can be fed by the precariousness of the profession; the stretches of unemployment, rejection in auditions, and so on. But doubt is also embedded in the creative process.

When we start work on a scene or a script it's just chaos. We only have questions. We work until we've found a way in but don't ever end up with any absolute certainty of outcome. That discovery can only be made in the heat of the moment. Great actors know how bad their acting can be. This drives them into serious investigation, but again and again they are surprised if they are any good. Then it starts all over again with the next role. The reason he keeps acting, Joaquin Phoenix has said, 'is I hate the last thing I did. I'm trying to rectify my wrongs.' In a similar way but in a different field Giametti, the Italian sculptor, said that for him all creativity begins in doubt because 'my work consists in moving from one failure to the next...'

No wonder this job we've chosen is so nerve-wracking! Some degree of fear, nerves or doubt is understandable, unavoidable, and even necessary to the work. Acting is not therapy. It's actually a challenging and exacting vocation that may demand you do therapy - or yoga, meditation, or surfing – to cope with the pressures. But while calm and confidence helps it is impossible to hope that we can feel perfectly relaxed every time we act. On the day we have to perform on-demand, no matter how we happen to be feeling. We can do as many downward dogs as we like and still feel jaded, sick, or frightened.

Excitement. Nerves. Doubt. Dread.

There is no 100% reliable way to entirely exorcise our negative feelings *every* time. I believe (quite strongly) that acting systems that demand this of actors are setting them up for failure.

What *is* 100% reliable though is putting our difficult feelings to good use. I once saw Irish Folk legend Damien Dempsey perform. He walked on stage, a bag of nervous energy, placed his hands in the praying position and whispered to himself for a long 20 seconds. Then he let fly with all that energy in his body, supporting him through a 90 minute set of pure magic. By owning his nerves he was able to channel them. (I'd love to know what it was he whispered to himself). It may be that your baggage this day may well be *exactly* the right emotional state you need for the work. David Mamet contends that how we are feeling is *always* right for the scene. Our sub-conscious is, he argues, like a little micro-computer. It's working away, unseen by us, to produce an emotional state that however uncomfortable it feels is precisely the feeling we need to play the scene - if only we would trust it.

Get in the habit of exploring the feelings in your gut as you head into a take or are waiting, quaking, in the wings. Is there not a power here that you can harness? Is your body not trying to tell you something like; 'hey, let me out!' Whatever things happen to be going on in your life, however you're feeling right now, think about how you can *use* that. You can transform something truly bad into acting gold. We are one of the few professions in the world where every life experience we've ever had – good, bad and ugly – is potentially useful. Everything is usable raw material - forever.

Some days when you're acting you're going to feel close to zero. Other days your confidence will be pushing ten. But you still have to work both days. Technique is the thing that will get you through the 'zero' day. The chances are *it won't look any worse than the 'ten' day*. The scene where the actor is struggling to hold it together can strangely be more interesting for the audience to watch. As Bill Nighy says, 'you have to operate whilst your head is attacking you.' A technique is much more than an insurance policy, but some days that's exactly what you need it to be.

But it's also a mistake to try and *pretend* you're not terrified. If we own up to our fear and still bash on even though we are scared, audiences will see not *you* - but *your character* struggling against difficult feelings. If we deny our feelings and don't find some way, even subtly, to include them in the work, they'll see the actor immediately.

This means you need to be okay about just 'being' you, and unafraid to bring that to the work, even if how you are feeling feels wrong or inappropriate. When you do that your full personality and all of your feelings become available for the work. When you present your work without judging how you happen to feel you will give a truly authentic performance.

This, I believe, is the key to the excellence of Mark Rylance's acting; he has found a way to include everything that is going on within him and the other actors around him without any hint of censorship or shame. He welcomes expression of his inner life through his acting. That's obvious when he talks about his work. For example, his Olivia in 12th Night was more grief-stricken when he himself was mourning the loss of a step-child and then, one night he found he was able to shrug that heavy feeling off, changing the performance radically. Interpreted either way, his playing was equally interesting, because it was so entirely authentic.

If you are nervous, let's see it. If you're excited, don't hide it. If you are scared, admit it. We become an artist when we can hold in our performance the complexity of all our feelings. Then we can live them for the benefit of the audience, authentically experiencing something real.

Working against our ability to acknowledge our negative feelings is the modern-day preoccupation with 'positive thinking.' This can lead to rituals, such as positive affirmations, that bolster our sense of confidence. But boosting our self-esteem in this way may not translate into better results. All our energy can go into getting us into a mental state where we are *ready* to work, when ultimately it's the *actual* work that makes us feel better.[81] Positive thinking can become an end to itself. But to *be* good we don't always have to *feel* good. In our acting we need *all* our feelings in the work, including the nasty and difficult ones. How do we know which ones to choose, and which to chase away?

It's normal to feel stressed or anxious ahead of a performance. But know that these jagged feelings are not a predictor of outcome. They are an ancient evolutionary adaptation at work; your body's way of telling you that something scary is about to appear around the next corner. You don't have to do anything. You don't have to make yourself feel better. It can be unwise to wish your feelings away, because that churning may be exactly what's needed. Your body might be doing just what it needs to, and you shouldn't second guess it's chemical and hormonal processes.

It can be a bigger worry if you are not nervous at all. Are you scared when

---

[81] For more on this idea read Oliver Burkeman, *The Antidote: Happiness for People who can't stand positive thinking.*

Excitement. Nerves. Doubt. Dread.

you go out on a date with someone you don't like very much? Of course not! But if you go out for a drink with someone you're smitten with the chances are you'll be a gibbering wreck. Nerves show you care enough to have something to lose. I did a workshop once where the teacher asked who in the group was nervous, and who wasn't. When he split the group up along those lines the nervous actors performed with greater focus and precision. He might as well have asked: 'who here is 'ready?' If the work is too anodyne, if you're utterly calm, it's simply not as satisfying, and not nearly as rewarding. Who knows, you may be in the acting game *because* of the excitement and fear it brings, not despite it.

PERFORMANCE: THE ULTIMATE ACT OF COLLABORATION

Australian actor Barry Otto once told me how his daughter Miranda grew up as a theatre brat. She and her buddies – the children of other Sydney theatre luminaires – would think nothing of putting on a Christmas show at the *Belvoir Street Theatre*. The late Sophia Hawthorne blew everyone away with her extraordinary debut as Juliet in *Romeo and Juliet* for the *Auckland Theatre Company*. Her father Raymond explained to me that she knew that world from growing up in it. It was almost in her DNA. Likewise, Joel Tobeck's second home was the *Mercury Theatre* in Auckland, where his mother was an actor.

With their numerous crew, lighting rigs, trucks and bustle, film sets can be alien and unfriendly environments. A theatre can feel on first encounter like a large cavernous maw, sucking up all your acting energy. The trick in your professional work is to feel as relaxed and familiar in these strange environments as you would be in your own home – much as these children of entertainment families were able to do. In the same way when filming a self-test at home you will be supremely relaxed. You won't stress about the bad takes because you know no one will ever see them.

So how do you make the audition room or set or theatre a place you feel at home? A start is to understand that when we perform we are in a social milieu. We prep alone. We worry alone. But most of us are extroverts, and even if we're not, acting is still a collaborative medium. We must embrace this. If you have a technique then on the day you can be confident you have a robust offer to make. However, what you bring to set is not just your homework, but yourself.

You can only truly be in the moment if you feel safe. And the way to make yourself feel safe is to engage with the people right in front of you: the other actors and crew. We need time on our own, but don't forever be disappearing into yourself, running off in your breaks to read your script notes. It's too late. That was then, but now you're in the arena. Now you want to work in a warm and friendly atmosphere. The only reliable way to do that is to create it yourself.

When I work with actors I admire I'll see them joke about and have a laugh with the gaffer or costume stand-by, then switch into great work on action. Roger Lanser, DOP of the film *Much Ado about Nothing*, told me Emma Thompson did precisely that. I'm not surprised. All these great actors are not pissing about – they know when focus is needed. But they are a wonderful energy to be around. How do they distract themselves like that and then still do great work a moment later? They goof around because it *helps* the work. It relaxes them and everyone around them.

There is the odd actor who seems to have to create a different atmosphere: a chaotic, destructive or negative energy. They may do great work. But no one is going to want to work with them again unless they have to. Don't be that actor.

Acting is not a popularity contest either. You needn't slap everyone on the back and crack jokes endlessly. But remember: the work is done. Let the play begin. Have fun! Sure, you're nervous. But that's just your body telling you a difficult task awaits – not that it's necessarily going to go badly. Not only do you have a right to enjoy this; your work will be better if you do.

MICHAEL CHEKHOV'S ADVICE TO ACTORS

Conviviality is one approach to help you relax in the high-pressure environment of a film or TV set. Actor Michael Chekhov advocated a variation of this. His advice to actors was to make the entire milieu feel hospitable by making friends with the camera, the crew and the set.[82] He was a theatre trained actor, so the core of his idea was that the actor needs to find, on set, a substitution for the missing relationship with the live audience.

The Camera

The camera is not your enemy. Michael Caine says, 'ignore the camera – she'll love you all your life if you do.' So you could pay that camera no mind, but send him or her friendly vibes. Or imagine that the camera lens is actually the *director*: smiling at you, watching and wondering at your performance, revelling in your every nuance.

---

82 Michael Chekhov began acting in Russia in the early 20th Century when film was an irrelevance. He ended his career in Hollywood, where he learnt how to adapt his ease in theatre to a film set. He won an Oscar soon after his arrival, and top actors flocked to his classes.

Excitement. Nerves. Doubt. Dread.

The Crew

Scratch even the most seasoned crew member and you'll find someone who delights in a well-acted scene – otherwise why would they even be here? Develop a relationship with the crew if you can that parallels that of your ideal audience: one that is warm and welcoming. Make friends with them and have an inner sense of goodwill to them (or the casting director, if in audition). If it helps you can imagine them to be an enthusiastic audience, loving everything you are doing.

The Set

As actors we're expected to pretend people we barely know are our loved ones and handle that prop as deftly as if we'd used it all our working lives. We must look comfortable and cosy in a bed surrounded by strangers dangling light meters or microphones with a camera two feet from your head. Do yourself a favour and make yourself as familiar as possible with your surroundings in advance. At home, imagine the upcoming environment. Test your props and activities. When you get to work visit the set and get acquainted with any props, the furniture and layout. Imagine the set as a welcoming and familiar place. Feel fabrics, lie on the bed, sit on the sofa: make yourself at home. Take in sounds, atmosphere, textures. Give objects a back story, if it helps you, or sneak onto set a few character objects of your own.[83]

THE APPROVING GAZE

Let's circle back now to the story that began this chapter. After those four lonely days of toiling away in that Melbourne hotel room, I rocked up for my first day of filming on *Hunters*, the US Sci-Fi show. The show-runner Gale-Ann Hurd came on set to watch my work. Another actor may have been delighted. However I was already anxious, and when she showed, I felt that she was willing me to fail. Of course that's *highly* unlikely. She had cast me, after all, in a significant role (incidentally off a self-tape). Nevertheless, that day I felt like I'd been singled out.

In high pressure situations such as this, it's possible to feel a very real sense of being judged. But it's also often true that the person doing most of the judging is you. Under the stress of knowing great things are expected, the fear of being found wanting can arise. This is, in fact, an ancient feeling. If you didn't bask in unreserved approval in your childhood you may be driven

---

[83] In the film *Black Sheep* the smoking cabinet atop the filing unit in Angus' study is my Dad's. It helped give me a sense of tradition, continuity, of the father handing on the legacy of the farm to the favoured son.

to seek that affirmation in acting. But alongside your childlike desire for approval can simultaneously exist a sense that somehow it isn't for you.

At times like this the actor has to dig deep and find within them the sense that they do belong and that great results can belong to them. Remember, you are not that child anymore. You are a great big ugly adult. A mind game that can help here is to imagine that over in video village (where the key crew, director, producers - and maybe the show-runner! - gather) is your number one fan, someone who LOVES your acting unreservedly. You could make this your daughter, your partner, or that stranger that's been stalking you since they saw you in that television commercial last year. Imagine them in the room, giving you a thumbs up. Bathe in their *Approving Gaze*. Then do the take and make them proud.

NERVOUS HABITS

Actors starting out can have a particular mannerism or nervous tic they need to overcome. This may be something they only do in their acting or something they do in their day to day life also – but it doesn't play so great on camera. Nervous mannerisms might include excessive blinking, eyes darting off randomly, blushing, foot-tapping, over the top facial expressions, repetitive hand gestures, or fidgeting of some kind.

Such tics or habits are not at all uncommon. Many years ago, watching my tapes from *Shortland Street*, I noticed that I was looking repeatedly off camera. I was looking away to read the lines in my head. I changed how I learnt lines. In recent years I had to work on a tendency I have to smile when I'm nervous. I'm a middle-class male, and it's typical of my tribe to smile when nervous - to be polite, or to overcome a sense of awkwardness and make myself and others feel at ease. The antidote to this nervous habit reminding myself to smile only when my character found something funny.

As a teacher, when I point out a recurring nervous habit in an actor it may initially surprise them to hear they are doing anything unusual. But it's also almost enough just to have the conversation. Awareness is nine-tenths of the fight. Underlying the mannerism is always a misdirected nervous energy. As technique grows the nervous energy will diminish. The actor figures out a way to directly deal with the issue. For example, if their eyes are darting around, they'll practice looking people squarely in their camera eye.

Because of such adaptations, actors may inherit a quirk (say, intensity of gaze for our recovered eye darter). But that's not necessarily a bad thing. The late Alan Rickman was loved for his distinctive, somewhat languid voice. He

Excitement. Nerves. Doubt. Dread.

consciously developed this voice to overcome a speech impediment caused by restricted movement in his jaw - a condition with which he was born.[84]

BEYOND NERVES: DREAD

So nerves are mandatory, even needed. Nerves are energy, and they tell us that we are focussed on the difficult task ahead. More often than not your nerves will go once you start acting because you have something to DO. Reliable confidence comes from not just doing the work but having a quiet pride in it. Pride *and* work neutralise nerves and doubt. But even so, as we approach a challenging acting task, our trepidation can get tipped into dread.

Dread is when we are so frightened that we can't function properly. Our prep is nullified because our excessive fear is blocking it from getting through. As we know, story moves through us, from the writer to the audience. We're just the middle men. Too much fear can obstruct this flow.

Exercises for Nerves

Here are some exercises and activities that will help if your nerves are tripping into dread more than you'd like.

1. *Feeling of ease*

Michael Chekhov noted that monumental works of art, such as Gothic architecture or the marble sculptures of Michelangelo, managed to achieve an ease and *lightness*. This fills the observer and makes her also feel lighter. From this Chekhov deduced that an actor needed this ability to express herself in a light and easy way; even when performing heaviness and depression, there needed to be this sense of art in play. As English art critic John Ruskin wrote: 'grace is ease in force.' A sense of lightness is easy to watch, it draws us in. Chekhov came up with two practical applications of this idea.

The first was a simple command to actors if they were tense or nervous, NOT to 'relax,' which only reminds us we are tense, but to stand and walk with a feeling of ease. Working from the outside in, the physical lightness alters our inner, heavy mood.

The second was a more involved exercise to develop a sense of ease in the actor. Here the actor remembers moments in their life when they felt heavy and gloomy, or light and happy. Comparing them, the actor realises that heaviness or lightness lived in their muscles as well as their heads at those times. Using lightness as their guide, the actor makes movements through space with a feeling of lightness and ease – much as you might with the

---

84 As revealed in an interview with *NPR* (National Public Radio), www.npr.org, December 20, 2007.

similar *Laban* effort.

2. Give yourself permission

Before you work anchor yourself by standing strongly, feet apart. Push your energy down into the floor, as if you were planted in there. Tell yourself: 'here I am. I am enough. If that means I'm messy, or gauche, or loud, that's fine. I give myself permission to be seen, to be heard, to take up space, to get it wrong, to make mistakes.'

Look for the flaws, the ugliness, in your character. Go for the dark side – there's a lot of power there. Take a risk. If something doesn't go to plan, this too can be a great gift. 'The pessimist sees difficulty in every opportunity; the optimist sees opportunity in every difficulty,' said Winston Churchill.

3. Externalise your attention

One of Russian theatre actor Stanislavki's early discoveries was that if an actor is given something to 'do' – a simple action – they relax. He found this out when he suggested to a nervous actor that he count the planks on the stage floor while performing. Techniques we've covered, like the Repeat Game, are about putting our attention off ourselves and onto observing the behaviour of the other actor. You can also put your mind onto something else that isn't you and your nerves: try *listening* to what people are saying in the waiting room or off set.

4. Personalise your nerves

If nerves and doubt are a recurring part of your performance, why not incorporate them in your preparation? If it suits the given circumstances of the story, personalise these feelings for your character and make them an emotional obstacle in the scene. Come up with reasons, such as character traits or back story, which make sense of why your character might be wrestling with doubts and fears. This way, you use these feelings to make the scene better (high obstacles make you work harder to attain your scene objective) rather than pretending they're not there. The audience will sense the inner conflict and see a heroic play against.

5. Inventory – Own your nerves

Then again, feelings will arise in performance sometimes that we haven't anticipated. Before a performance do a quick diagnostic; a check-up to explore how you are feeling. Better to discover it now than be ambushed by it later. Get in touch with how you feel and ask yourself where are the feelings in your body? What colour, shape, texture are they? Go into them, feel their radiation, own them. USE the feelings that are there, including fear, as a way to get into the scene. These emotions may not be as far from what's required

Excitement. Nerves. Doubt. Dread.

as you think.

6. Meditation

Meditating can give your brain a rest by diminishing the intensity of that chattering voice that accompanies us everywhere – what is known as the 'left-brain interpreter' (more on that in the *Living* section). The big contribution of Transcendental Meditation (TM) was to suggest to busy Westerners that just 20 minutes twice a day is beneficial. Vipassana is meant to be one hour twice a day but you can do one or two sessions of that practice in the smaller time frame of TM.

As a long time meditator, I can sit on a busy set, and relax to the point where I can nod off – which can be very restorative if you've had to get up at some ungodly hour to get to your makeup call. Meditation can also come in handy the night before your first filming day. As you wrestle with your 2 am anxiety attack, it can help you fall asleep again.

7. Stretch and yawn

Stretching releases tension, and yawning opens up the back of the mouth and releases tension in the mouth. Returning to the lines after yawning you'll find your voice richer - and possibly an octave lower.

8. Breathe!

If you're feeling nervous, take some long deep breaths, in with the nose, out with the mouth, with long exhalations. Hum quietly up and down your range. Breathe in for the count of 4 and hold the breath for the count of 4 then let out the breath for the count of 8. Repeat 3 or 4 times.

9. Ragdoll

Bend forward slowly vertebra by vertebra. You can go up and down several times. Then shake it out.

10. Bluehead/ Redhead

Mossad, Israel's secret service, is purported to use this concept when training its agents, and it was adopted as a strategy by New Zealand's *All Blacks*. The idea is that during a game the players can have either redheads or blue heads.[85] Redheads are all about anxiety and stress, where the focus is not on task, but the outcome. Blueheads are calm and task focussed, locked into the process: living in the moment.

Here's a useful exercise around this idea, based on one I observed Lisa Chappell do in one of her visits to the *Actors Lab Studio*. Close your eyes. Think about how you're feeling right now, and one word to describe it.

---

85 Paul, 'Rugby: How the All Blacks stopped being chokers.' *NZ Herald*, 1 Jul, 2017.

If there's some acting coming up, it might be something like 'excited' or 'stressed.' Let's say that right now it's 'nervous.' If in a group, open your eyes and gaze your feelings across the circle.

It's important to find your actual emotional state before you begin flipping and changing it. You can only work from where you're at, no matter how uncomfortable that is.

Now close your eyes again. This time think about something that makes you feel calm. It could be the person you love. Open your eyes with that feeling, and give it a one-word name – it might be 'chilled' or 'calm' or 'ice cream' – anything. Again, gaze it across the circle – and see if the person watching can guess the word in your head.

If you like you can also give this word a posture – it might be hands-on hips, or arms around yourself – whatever feels right.

The original feeling you had (nervous) you could look at as your 'red' head: outcome focussed and anxious. The feeling you found when you thought of your beloved is your 'blue' head: calm, clear and in the moment .

Once you have a posture figured out for each word, you can play with moving physically from one feeling to the other – from a posture that says 'I'm nervous' to a posture that says 'I'm nervous - but I'm also calm and clear.' You now are working toward a quick physical shorthand for moving from red to blue head as needed.

POSTSCRIPT

That day on the set of *Hunters* I squared off against the formidable New Zealand actor Sarah Peirse – and delivered my best. When we cut on the scene I walked up to Gale-Ann, the show-runner, and asked her what she thought. She pronounced herself satisfied. But I knew better. A week later, I was quietly dropped from future episodes. The entire experience - the prep and the performance - felt like a colossal fail. Failure, or the threat of it, along with our other constant acting companion, rejection, stalks every actor's career, no matter how successful. Understanding and living with failure is part of our job description, and it's the subject of the next chapter.

CHAPTER SEVENTEEN
FAILURE AND THE MIGHTY 1B4

If you never stink you never know what it smells like to have a rose in front of you.
Kevin Spacey[86]

RETHINKING FAILURE

Acting is getting out of your own way so you can listen to your instincts and let them play. I've believed that ever since, aged 17, I saw a Hypnotist perform at the Theatre Royale in Christchurch, New Zealand. The show itself was somewhat cheesy. The hypnotist machine-gunned us all night with dreadful puns. But man, did he know his business. He pared down about 20 audience volunteers to a handful he found to be the most suggestive. One of these was a slight, bespectacled hairdresser. Painfully shy, when introduced he was nervous to the point of paralysis. But once hypnotized he became transformed, slipping between characters, showing an incredible range of accents and emotion. He was the undisputed star of the evening.

This was a guy who went through his regular day hiding under a gigantic bushel of inhibition. But this night for us he *was* John Wayne, whipping his horse along, firing his six-shooter, and babbling authentic dialogue. He *was* James Bond, captivating every woman in the audience. He was hilarious but utterly convincing.

If you're interested in being as uninhibited, relaxed, and confident in performance as this young man was under hypnosis, you must take account of what failure means to you. Our fear of failure cannot be entirely overcome, but it can be confronted and understood.

For most of us failure is the thing we'd do anything to avoid. But great acting is far more likely if you can sincerely give yourself *permission to fail* in your work. This is because intuition and permission to fail are linked: 'there

---

86 In his (now unavailable) online Masterclass.

is no creativity, no originality, no success and no progress without risk,' Judith Weston tells us.[87] Fear of failure can suck the fun, learning – and finally, success - out of your career.

IMAGINING FAILURE
Experience is simply the name we give to our mistakes.
Oscar Wilde

One day, and not so soon after my searing experience on *Hunters,* I found myself chaperoning my son on the film set of the docu-drama *Chasing Great,* about All Black great Richie McCaw. Arlo was playing the young Richie in a series of dramatic recreations. Over lunch I chatted to one of the directors, Justin Pemberton.[88] He told me the film was in large part about how the All Blacks, and Richie in particular, had come back from failure.

Until 2011, Pemberton told me, in the history of Rugby World Cups (starting in 1987) the All Blacks had to that point only ever won the first. That 1987 win had actually inspired the young Richie to become an All Black. But they failed to win in 1991, 1995, 1999 and 2003. Then, in 2007, now as Captain, Richie led the team to the shock quarter-final loss against France - which again knocked them out of the cup.

Widely acknowledged as the best team in the world, there was clearly a problem here for the All Blacks - and it wasn't to do with skill or fitness. The problem was with their head game. Now, for the first time, psychology was put front and centre as the team tried to figure out why they were folding under extreme pressure. Mental skills coach Gilbert Enoka's brief was to find ways to stop the descent into chaos in the heat of critical matches. He sampled and hit upon various approaches, finding one of them with psychiatrist Ceri Evans. One of Evans' key messages for the team was that positive thinking could get them only so far. The players also had to think of everything that could go wrong in their game and have strategies in place to deal with that.

This isn't so different from what many actors intuitively do. Early on in her career, Jennifer Ward-Lealand was cast in the hit Australian TV sketch comedy series, *Full Frontal.* At the time it was a great 'break' for her. Although she'd performed in a lot of comedies in the theatre, TV sketch comedy was a new arena for her. So, on the tram heading to her first day of

---
87 Weston, Judith. *The Film Director's Intuition: Script Analysis and Rehearsal Techniques,* Michael Wiese Productions. Kindle Edition.
88 He co-directed with Michelle Walshe.

rehearsal, as she told me, 'I made the decision that, even if I was out of my comfort zone on this show, I was going to have a great relationship with the director - and that everything would go well.' At the time Jennifer could not have put a name to what she was doing. It was not a bland positivity. It was a brave assessment of her abilities heading into what she knew would be a challenging situation.

Judith Weston calls this counter-intuitive brand of thinking *imagining failure*. It's the idea that in advance of any challenging event we honestly consider our doubts, concerns and fears. We face each and every failure that might ensue. So, forewarned, we can then develop a strategy to deal with them.

Positivity is that ability to deceive oneself a little about reality so as to carry on marching. It has its place. Study after study has shown that optimistic people not only achieve better life outcomes but live longer as well. But positivity is not a creative cure-all.

We may think it's courageous to exorcise all doubt about upcoming creative events and be relentlessly positive about outcomes. But, says Weston, that's just bravado: brashness born of ignorance. Bravado is when you do something without thinking. It's a form of denial; pretending you're not petrified when really you are. You fail because you don't see the dangers coming, and after failing a few times, you start to 'play it safe' - which is sure death for your artistry.

By contrast, *real* courage is when you know something is frightening - but you do it anyway. When you imagine failure in this way you're not only dealing effectively with *anticipated* problems but adopting a problem-solving mindset so you're able to more successfully deal with *unanticipated* problems as well. It's highly empowering to look failure squarely in the eye. Then on a film set, or in rehearsal, or live performance, you're part of the solution, not the problem.

I was surprised to read recently that our chances of surviving an emergency are far higher if we have a plan in place before the emergency hits. Not just A plan: pretty much ANY plan will do. Why would this be? Why would it help to have a *terrible* plan to escape a burning plane? It's because you would then be in a state of mental readiness. The plan can be adapted, but the mindset is harder to change at the moment the shit is actually hitting the fan. It turns out that in any hairy situation the key is to anticipate as many negative contingencies as you can. In a performance situation this allows you to get on and enjoy the rush. Then if things do go to custard you know you're ready.

Imagine you haven't done theatre for a while, and you're cast in a main bill role. Rather than trusting solely to your talent, you could do an amateur show quietly somewhere to get your skills up. Of course, going into an acting job you can never have all the answers. It's a wicked environment: there are too many unpredictable variables. But it helps to be ready for anything.

THE MIGHTY 1B4 & YOUR ONGOING LEARNING

When I worked with him [Stanislavski] in Paris, he said, 'I cannot see you in the morning. I've got to work on my lisp for two hours.' This was a man in his seventies, the head of the Moscow Art Theatre, two years before he died. He knew he had this problem, and he worked on it.
Stella Adler

If you watch the documentary film *Chasing Great* you'll learn that, since the age of about 12, All Black Richie McCaw has trailed a 1B4 exercise book around all his life, writing advice to himself about his game, examining where he's gone wrong, how he could get better. Buy yourself an exercise book. Scripts will come and go - but the Mighty 1B4 is forever.[89]

Before any important acting event, such as an audition or first day on a job, you can use your 1B4 to do a *pre-mortem*. Here you write down what you'd like to achieve, what you are *ready for*. These are the personal challenges you're setting yourself for this particular acting engagement. For example, for an audition, your ready for's might be anything from: 'I'm going to engage with the reader from the moment I walk into the room,' to 'I'm ready for using my nerves *in* the work,' or 'I'm going to *really* give myself permission to screw up.' These are little acting goals personalised to you and tailored to this single-acting event.

After the event you can also use the book to do a quick debrief. Always start this *post-mortem* with something positive: write down the three *best things* from that event.[90] *Then* write down what you might have done better. When the next acting event comes around you'll open up your 1B4 and find these suggestions, and they will, in turn, influence your pre-mortem for that next event.

Your failure imagining is an important part of your process too. However

---

89 It doesn't have to be an actual 1B4 of course! Any notebook will do.
90 This simple but useful terminology was drummed into me in three masterclasses taught by Dean Carey and Brett Woods in Auckland over several years. The phrasing is also applicable to scene work (see Appendix 2). I believe a similar technique is still taught at Dean's own drama school.

Failure And The Mighty 1B4

I don't recommend that you actually *write down* your worst acting fears in the 1B4. Reading all that negativity may risk it becoming reinforced or ingrained. Rather, the imagining of failure should happen in your head. And you don't want to do it 5 minutes before the acting event! Run through the potential catastrophes a few hours prior, then forget all about it. The mental work is done: now you're ready for anything.

Get in the habit of doing this – the pre and post mortems, the failure imagining - for all your acting events. You don't have to write a novelette; just jot down a few lines. You're wanting a snapshot of a creative moment in time. And soon all of your creative activities will start to feel like the *same* experience: a learning opportunity. In our acting we're all on different places on a learning escalator. So long as we're moving that's the important thing. If we're progressing, we're open, we're curious, we're growing. There's no top of the escalator, just stops along the way. The stops are the acting events: the first day on set, the audition, the opening night. But now they're less of a big deal. They're just one in a string of performance events. With the 1B4 our artistic life is defined not by any single incident that makes or breaks us, but by the flourishing of our understanding of our craft, and how it bears up under pressure.

There will be times when your acting is a bit stuck, when you are using your 1B4 a lot as you search for answers. But it's a mistake just to use the book when things are going badly. It's important to acknowledge your acting strengths, be grateful for them, and understand how and why it is that you do good work. Making those ongoing head game notes in the 1B4 allows you to keep a sea eye on your personal psychology.

Your 1B4 notes are also helpful once you get cast. The original audition might have happened a month before your first filming day; you can go back to your notes from the audition and touch base with what you were going for on the day.

Once I had a recall as MC of a panel show. It was an environment utterly unfamiliar to me. I'd be juggling live comedians, a mock audience, cue cards, a teleprompter, ad-libbing, and references to a video screen - all at once. There was plenty to be nervous about, and yet I wasn't. I sat in the parking lot trying to figure out why I wasn't even just a tiny bit nervous. It worried me because I thought it was likely I'd be ambushed by nerves in the studio. I couldn't figure it out, so I came up with some ready for's, imagined everything that might go wrong and how I might respond - and charged in. The recall went well and those nerves never turned up. It was only doing my post-mortem that I figured out why I'd been so relaxed. I didn't have any lines to remember.

Would I have figured that out without my mighty 1B4? Quite possibly. But the 1B4 made it more likely because it makes curiosity compulsory to the process. In this case it made me examine a positive event in a way I may not have. And that discovery – that nerves were mostly about lines – set me on a path of trying to figure out how to give my scripted work the same sense of ease and freedom as an improv. That investigation ended up with me discovering 'active recall' for myself and my students (see Chapter 3, 'Learning the Lines'). For me there's a delicious feeling in this. I'm able, in my 50's, to still learn new things.

The idea of continuous learning isn't a new one. Mike Alfreds talks about 'permanent training.' This is the same thing, it just sounds like less fun. Alan Dale is a Dunedin born Kiwi actor with a busy LA based TV career. 'No matter what age you are,' says Dale, 'get a good teacher and don't think you know everything because you don't. There's always another lesson.'[91]

And yet, while a ballet dancer or an opera singer can have the same teacher or mentor their whole lives, for actors, teachers and directors tend to come and go. We must take responsibility for our own learning. The Mighty 1B4 means that learning is no longer scatter-gun: it's laser tailored just to you.

That's why of all the advice in this book, my plea for you to use a 1B4 may be the most important. This little exercise book has the potential to give you ownership and control over your evolving results. Having a long term vision for your acting is fine, but in your craft the best improvements happen in increments. For that to happen you need to know where you are on your learning journey. You can only do that by regularly checking in on yourself. Then you'll be able to intuit where the next step, the next change, the next class or career move, where the next risk needs to be. Embrace the 1B4, or some version of it that suits you, and you'll enjoy continuous learning all your life.

Without being in tune with your head game, giant leaps, taken on a whim, can lead to disappointment. Consider a jumbo jet flying from Sydney to Hong Kong. The plane is hardly ever pointing directly at its destination. It's usually off course. But it's by knowing where the plane is exactly in space that allows the auto-pilot to make the necessary corrections to bring the plane on course. Without the 1B4 you're likely to discover the hard way that you are way off track - and have to make a sudden course correction. Your 1B4 is your true north, connecting you to your acting head and heart so you can

---

91 'Alan Dale: Kiwi star on the rise,' *NZ Herald*, 3 May 2015

make the necessary incremental corrections along the way.

The alternative to this engaged curiosity is a kind of wishful thinking that says 'she'll be right.' Actors that don't work in increments of improvement tend to make global statements about their acting like: 'when my acting doesn't go well I clam up, stop responding and get resentful.' Such statements tend to give voice to the inner critic and can easily become self-fulfilling prophecies. Much more useful is a statement like: 'that last class I felt I let myself down, I wasn't happy with what I did. In the next class I'm going to be less judgmental and stay open.' Now you've got something practical to work on and that in itself will be progress – you're not stuck anymore.

For your entire career, your acting will remain a slippery fish. Certainty will escape your grip. Disappointment will be a regular companion. But acting is also endlessly fascinating and will obsess you for a lifetime because the learning never stops. Don't wish for the best. Take control.

FAILURE IN YOUR LIFE
Failures are finger posts on the road to achievement.
C. S. Lewis

In 2007-08 I wrote, performed and toured New Zealand with my one-man show, *A Night with Beau Tyler*, a satire of the self-help movement. My character was someone who had peddled positivity and success all his life, but hit a wall and decided to peddle failure instead. As I wrote and researched I found that success and failure were not discreet entities. Anyone who had known success, it turned out, was no stranger to failure either. Numerous quotes, which I used in the show, testify to their counter-intuitive symbiosis. So, Walter Reuther, the American Labour leader, said: 'If you are not big enough to lose, you are not big enough to win.' Opinioned that most quotable of British politicians, Winston Churchill: 'Success consists of going from failure to failure without loss of enthusiasm.'

That failure might have an intrinsic value was initially surprising. So was the revelation that relentless positivity wasn't only not enough for the All Blacks, it was actually the thing that got them into trouble. For sheer skill they were the best sports team in the world – but one that choked when things started to go wrong. Once they sorted out their head game their undisputed skill did the rest. But there's a caution there. The head game can never become an end in itself. The skill and prep must be there. Performance psychology is not a substitute for hard work. It's the bit you do at the end to make sure all your good work will not be wasted.

Acting is not a perfect science. It's fraught with missteps, mistakes, and bad acting days – or months. It's a long game, and the path to success is bedecked with fiascos and fuck-ups. Career disasters don't always make it into the flattering celebrity stories that adorn the front pages of glossy magazines. But failure is sometimes necessary for progress. Some lessons can only be learnt the hard way. To learn a new language, you must commit to speaking it badly for at least two years. A toddler must fall over about one hundred times a day to learn how to walk. Risk, accident, failure: you don't get anywhere without these elements. Success is the sum of countless failures.

As a five-year-old taking instruction on riding a bike, after falling over and scraping my knee for the tenth time, I bellowed at my mother: 'I CAN'T know!' But I learnt to ride the bike. Contrary to what we might assume, short term achievement doesn't always translate into long term learning. If you're struggling and failing now that's not necessarily a bad thing. Anyone who has ever achieved anything will tell you that it was at some cost to themselves. And once you start to look at failure more curiously it opens creative doors. You may realise also that your characters are also failing all the time – this is why they are forced to try different things to get what they want.

Bad experiences aren't much fun at the time. But they often bring positive legacies. As an example, learning can be difficult for dyslexic people. So, from an early age, they find creative ways to solve problems and understand things. Creatives are then more than twice as likely to be dyslexic than the general population: Tom Cruise, Whoopi Goldberg, Kiera Knightley, Anthony Hopkins, Steven Spielberg, Harry Belafonte, Steve McQueen, Jim Carrey – and many more – are dyslexic. We actors are always looking for that counterintuitive choice. These actors have the advantage that they already see the world differently.

At the same time, as Cicely Berry has ruefully observed, dyslexics are also over-represented in our prison population. Great challenges can grow our resilience - or crush us. Those in the US prison population are two to three times more likely to have lost a mother or father. But for others the loss of a parent can make greatness more likely: 67 per cent of British prime ministers from the start of the 19th century until World War II lost a parent before the age of 16. A third of American Presidents lost their fathers when young. The stats run similarly high for eminent persons across all professions.[92]

---

[92] 'Successful Children Who Lost A Parent — Why Are There So Many Of Them?' October 16, 2013, Robert Krulwich, *NPR* (National Public Radio), www.npr.org.

Failure And The Mighty 1B4

A successful lawyer I know puts his success down to being remorselessly bullied at school. Because life wasn't easy he learnt to handle adversity from an early age. Some learn the hard way how to survive in the face of adversity. When the adversity is removed, they can become sprinters in life, and thrive.

There are graduations of failure. At one end is a career stalling, a big opportunity squandered, or a relationship break up. At the time they feel immortally wounding. But the unexpected boon from a big failure or setback can be that it gives you clarity. It strips away the unnecessary and brings our lives into stark relief.

The great celebrity example of this is *Harry Potter* author J K Rowling. When she was a solo mum on the benefit she stopped pretending, in her own words, 'that I was anything other than what I was, and began to direct all my energy into finishing the only work that mattered to me… I was set free, because my greatest fear had been realised, and I was still alive, and I still had a daughter whom I adored, and I had an old typewriter and a big idea. And so rock bottom became the solid foundation on which I rebuilt my life.'[93]

One day I came home from High school upset because I disliked my teacher. 'Even bad teachers have something they can teach you,' my Dad told me. 'Look for the gift.' Failure can hide unexpected treasures. Mourn and grieve. Feel sorry for yourself. Then look for the gift.

We shouldn't, however, try to construct meaning out of *every* failure we encounter. Sometimes shit just happens and there isn't a redemptive or inspirational narrative to find. Rather than a rush to meaning sometimes the victory can be being able to honestly stare an almighty balls-up in the eye, shrug and realise you need to walk away.

Only you can make these calls. The point of this chapter is to awaken you to the idea that a *solely* negative view of failure will not serve you. Don't despair if you're working on something and fail follows fail, because that's the way the creative process often works. Talent isn't enough. Visionary Technologist Kevin Ashton believes dedication is just as important. His proofs range from Mozart, who toiled over his compositions, to James Dyson, who built 5,126 prototypes over five years before creating a cyclone-based vacuum cleaner that worked – the reason, perhaps, why the things are so incredibly expensive![94]

---

93 From J K Rowling's 2008 Harvard Commencement address, republished as *Very Good Lives*.
94 Ashton is the author of the book *How To Fly A Horse: The Secret History of Creation, Invention, and Discovery*.

BRINGING FAILURE INTO THE HEART OF YOUR WORK

You have to step into the void, I reckon. I always felt that I didn't quite know where the front foot would land...
Sam Neill (quoted in *The Power of Us*)

Humans aren't built from scratch. Evolution renovates and adds to what is already in place. Some of our neurological plumbing isn't that different from what you might find in a lizard. And studies are showing that while we may think that our more modern higher brain, our conscious thought, is running things, ancient unconscious motors drive much of our behaviour.

For example, if we find ourselves in a threatening situation, we're likely to respond with a panic or startle reflex. The startle reflex reaches our autonomic nervous system, or ANS, via our ear, about five milliseconds after a stimulus like a loud noise (more on the ANS in the next chapter). The panic reflex kicks in seven milliseconds later, generated by a primitive emotional processing core at the base of our brain, the amygdala. We have no conscious control over such reactions - it takes a whole *half second* for sensory information from the outside world to be incorporated into our conscious experience.

So we find that the *unconscious* processing abilities of the human brain are extremely fast: about 11 million pieces of information per second. The estimate for *conscious* processing is much slower, something like 40 pieces per second.[95] That's why when we're hitting a fast-moving ball with a bat there's no time to figure it all out consciously. The only hope we have of hitting that ball is if we don't think. When we're acting our unconscious reactions will also always be faster. But letting go and taking a big swing in our acting can feel scary. We can easily try and corral our impulses and instincts. We want to pull them back because we don't consciously control them: we haven't made a story up about them yet (more on that in the next chapter).

That's because our conscious, higher brain is a bit of a know-it-all. It thinks it knows best. It likes to think it's in charge. So, arriving that half second behind them, it will try to censor, tame, interpret, and adjust our instincts. But in the moment of performance good acting comes from ignoring the good sense of the higher brain and trusting your first impulses. It's a dare to yourself that you can step off the cliff and somehow be alright. Without that courage - to take that step out into the unknown - you remain ruled by fear.

The type of acting that will not get you cast is 'good' acting, if that means

---

95 David DiSalvo in Forbes Magazine, Jun 22, 2013, *Your Brain Sees Even When You Don't.*

playing it safe – acting fully in control. But if you fail, you surprise yourself, and go straight to where your instincts live, into interesting acting: acting out of control. Many of the working actors who have visited my Studio have spoken of a career-changing moment of revelation when they were faced with a stark choice. This was whether to stay safe or step out into that void. For Joel Tobeck it was an early role in the US syndicated TV series *Hercules*. For Dominic Purcell, it was the callback for his breakthrough role in *John Doe*. For Colin Moy it was filming the climactic scene for the movie *In my Father's Den*. All of them in a moment of fear and challenge felt everything drop away as they realised they just had to step out of the box.

The acting gem sits alongside the steaming turd of a failed impulse. You can't have one without the other. You have no way in the heat of performance of knowing if some instinct is going to work, or tank. Over time your judgement will get better as your instincts are honed. But you can't second guess; you can't genuinely surprise yourself and the audience without *really* acting on your impulses. If you do you'll still be scared on occasion, but less ruled by that fear. Ironically, if you're trying to do good work all the time, it's much harder to find out what works for you.

For me, the real fail is preparing too literally, in a way that protects you, not exposes your deepest beliefs, and arriving with a predictable performance. You fail too by not understanding your character and the guts of the scene and the script, because you set up your instincts for failure. Your impulses may then not be grounded in the truth of the writing.

I can't tell you how interesting it is in class to watch an actor struggling, dropping the ball, picking it up, drowning in fear. Then suddenly they take your breath away with an impulse that just flies. We can applaud this - and then talk about the screw-ups. And so the learning begins.

In a recent scene class at my Studio, two actors performed a scene from *First Reformed*, the recent Paul Schrader film. In the scene the priest, Toller, is visited by a parishioner, Mary, who confesses that her husband wants to kill her. In one take the actor playing Toller, after hearing this news, placed a hand on Mary's knee. It looked 'wrong:' all of us watching immediately jumped out of the scene. Later we all agreed that this was not an appropriate gesture for a priest to make to a parishioner.

The actor did this because he hadn't immersed himself sufficiently in understanding the relationship between Toller and Mary. If he had thought a bit more about the pastoral nature of the relationship, he'd not have made that gesture. In time, as he acquires technique, he'll get that right. But equally, there is no denying that the *impulse* underlying the gesture, *to comfort Mary*, was spot on. That instinct can play very powerfully on camera, even if the given circumstances dictate that the actor must resist the urge to touch her.

It's the same with emotion. You'll be acting, and suddenly feel teary, or get an urge to laugh. The impulse is a true one and must be trusted. But how to play it? Here your *judgement* comes in to play. Judgement comes from experience, which is simply the sum of our mistakes. You'll get better at making an instantaneous call whether that emotional expression is appropriate for the scene and the character, or whether it needs to be pushed down. But regardless, the impulse itself is wonderful. An emotion suppressed is even more interesting to watch.

In the 1981 film *The French Lieutenant's Woman* there is a steamy love scene between Jeremy Irons and Meryl Streep. Such scenes are always difficult to film, and on take three Jeremy accidentally plonked poor Meryl onto the floor a bit hard and she banged her head. She then – completely inappropriately – giggled BUT kept playing, going straight back into serious passion. It was authentic human behaviour *because* it was so unexpected. And sure enough, that's the take the director chose.

You can't plan this stuff. You can't fake spontaneity. If you truly don't know what's going to happen next, neither will the audience. If you map it all out prior we'll see it coming. So, don't get fazed by fails, they are almost always useful investigations, so long as you don't beat yourself up about them.

In a class situation if you're timid, or play it safe, how are you ever going to learn? I've watched scenes in class that were just awful. Then there was a moment where the work shifted. We glimpsed gold. A voice coach said to me once: 'if you're going to say it wrong, then at least say it *loud*.' Act loud too, so we can see the 'mistake.' Your talent lives in that mistake. Let us see it.

In the same spirit, when you're working, include impulses that come up in the playing. Your instincts are seldom wrong - experience will hone your judgement as to how to express them. Nuanced choices often have more power than big gestures, especially for the screen. Let the audience do some work and make them guess where the impulse was leading you. But if you try something and it doesn't work, who cares? There's always another take, or the next night. With experience, as your technique is honed, your fails will become better. Accidents will become the best thing about your work. You'll grow your resilience, that quality that almost defines actors - the ability to get right back on the horse after a bum note, scene, day or season. Working at the margins will become second nature.

PART 4

LIVING

All the world's a stage and most of us are desperately unrehearsed.
Sean O'Casey

CHAPTER EIGHTEEN
TELLING TALES – THE IMPORTANCE OF STORIES
Pathei mathos.
Aeschylus, in 'Agamemnon.'

STORY

I sometimes ask actors in my Studio to share a short, 3-minute story. Just before they start I tell them that 'the best stories are true.' This is storytelling in its simplest form. But these are some of the most hilarious and heart-rending moments that we ever see in class. The best stories are always personal; about the storyteller themselves.

When actors tell stories they aren't usually of their own invention. Actors bring to life another's truth by making it their own. We're here to entertain, for sure, but also to enlighten. Some kinds of insight can't be learnt any other way - or at least not with the same impact. We directly commune with our fellow citizens, communicating ideas, thoughts and feelings that can be read and taught - but have a more powerful revelation as a shared experience.

But all humans are storytellers. We love telling stories and we love hearing them, whether we're catching up on the weekend's gossip on our tea break, or calling our partner to moan about the boss. We'll blob at home or go to the theatre or an exhibition, or the opera - all to hear stories. Stories are not going away any time soon. In all their forms, from women's magazines to podcasts, they are our guide books to living, helping us navigate our world, consoling us, distracting us and arming us with wisdom. Stories live in the very core of our being, embedded, as we'll see, in our very DNA, and inherent in how we perceive, interpret, survive and thrive in the world.

BEING HUMAN

In his recent book, *Selfie*, Will Storr pulls together multiple strands of research, much of it new, to summarise what really makes us tick. What makes us human is a pile of inherited and socialised traits that we have far less control over than we'd like to admit.

We share a common ancestor, and more than 98% of our DNA, with chimpanzees, and our behaviours mirror theirs in many respects. We hide our feelings to get our way, hold long-term grudges and have a strong sense of fairness. We punish the selfish, are biased towards our own, and are suspicious of outsiders. Violence is rife within and between different groups of both species, and the conflict is usually driven by an obsession with status and hierarchy. Chimps and humans are the *only* species that make war on our own. But victors – the ruling Alphas - in human and ape societies both typically display the qualities we value in a leader such as the Prime Minister of New Zealand Jacinda Ardern: a combination of strength, wisdom and caring.

After we were apes we became us: for most of the last 100,000 years Homo sapiens lived as hunter-gatherers in small tribes. This gave us a preoccupation with reputation: a good one meant we could rise up the totem pole of the tribe; a bad enough one could mean exile and death. Reputation was bound up in our love of gossip; as much as 90% of human conversation is still made up of it. Gossip was and is the way to figure out who you can trust, who's a good guy and who isn't, and what success looks like. Gossip policed the tribe, producing outrage against individuals who had broken tribal codes. We see this tendency alive today in the waves of social media condemnation that crash down upon the heads of moral transgressors. Our tribal ancestors, just like us, were reputationally driven to get along AND get ahead – urges that are in contradiction.

So far, so good. But in the same way that a fish at birth knows how to swim, our animal and tribal inheritances have instilled in us innate tendencies that are *already in place when we're born*. We know this from experiments with babies. One such experiment (described in Storr's book) involves a puppet show where a ball is trying to climb a hill. A helpful square is behind the ball, pushing it up, but a nasty triangle attempts to shove the ball back down. When six-month-old babies watch the show and are then offered the shapes to play with, almost all of them reach for the selflessly helpful square. This tells us that the value of being 'good' for us *at birth* really means *selfless*. And sure enough, toddlers expect sharing and police fairness. As adults, says Will Storr, 'we celebrate and reward those who are willing to make some sort of sacrifice for the benefit of others…'[96]

---

96 Will Storr, *Selfie*.

The bigger, more complex higher brain of the Homo Sapien, the cerebrum, helps give us the ability to reflect on and interpret our actions. Our consciousness distinguishes us from most of the animal kingdom. But our immediate responses to the world are often, in fact, generated unconsciously. The feedback we receive from the outside world passes through our ANS, or autonomic nervous system: a motley nerve network, some of it ancient in origin, some with more modern wiring, that runs throughout our bodies, connecting our brain, spinal cord, and sensory organs (like eyes and ears).[97] The ANS constantly clocks our external environment for cues of safety or danger without involving the thinking parts of the brain. Everything from butterflies in our stomach and an elevated heart rate, to barely perceiving a flash in our peripheral vision, are signs of the ANS at work. It works fast, as we saw in the previous chapter, with its primitive focus on our survival. Neuroception precedes perception, so that long before you become consciously aware that something is not quite right, your body has already reacted. After that your mind kicks in and tries to figure out why you feel the way you feel. Then it tells you a story about it: 'The mind narrates what the nervous system knows,' says psychologist Deb Dana. 'Story follows state.'[98]

Practically this means that we all have a ceaseless internal monologue that narrates our day to day lives, trying to make sense of our involuntary unconscious responses, as well as our voluntary, conscious ones. This is the voice in our head that praises us, but also beats us up. Neuroscientists call it the 'left brain interpreter;' an inbuilt survival mechanism gabbling in our heads. And we have surprisingly little control over it. If you don't believe me, close your eyes, relax, and think about NOTHING for one minute…

How did that go? I'll bet you were bombarded with thoughts. This incessant inner chatter is the writer of the story of your life, scribbling away one step behind your actions and reactions. It's not a reliable author. Sometimes you are correct in identifying what has just happened, but sometimes you are not. The stories we make up to explain events, presented to us as fact, are often untrue. Our inner story-teller acts on incomplete information, inventing stories because it wants to make us feel like we're in charge. The guesses our brain makes might be right but just as easily might be wrong. We're a lot like Riley from the movie *Inside out* – manipulated and controlled by elemental internal forces we're not even aware of. Our ceaseless inner monologue about

---

[97] The ANS is a term coined by Professor of Psychiatry Stephen Porges. For more see his book, *Polyvagal Theory*.
[98] Deb Dana, *The Polyvagal Theory in Therapy*

what's going on turns the chaos of our lives into a tidy narrative. So, a serial killer could justify himself as an avenging angel, as Kevin Spacey's character, John Doe, did in the film *Seven*. But this is just a comforting story for Doe. It's just as likely that he's not in charge, that he is in fact at the mercy of dark internal impulses – much as, sadly, Spacey was revealed to be himself when he was outed as a sexual predator.

THE PURPOSE & FORMS OF STORY

Let's bring this all back to culture: the creation of it and our role as actors in it. Our culture is made up of art, religion, race, TV, the gossip we overhear, the books we read, and so on. As we strive to get along and get ahead, who any of us becomes is the result of our ape and tribal legacies. They mutate to fit the structure of what our culture tells us we should look like, behave, and want. We internalise culture's ideas as if they were laws inscribed in eternal marble tablets. But cultural beliefs change over time, society to society, and they are often based on mistruths.[99]

So, it mystifies some people why someone like President Trump can be plain wrong so often and still be popular. It's because his *story* is so appealing. If it's a good story, it doesn't matter if it's wrong. Stories, our species' cultural stock and trade, are more important than pretty much anything, and certainly more important than facts. At a social level, as well as inside our heads, it's not the truth we humans want from the tales we tell. Quite simply, stories are about survival.

In a TV interview in 2019 the (then Senator) Joe Biden was asked about how he had coped with the death of his son some years earlier. He creatively mangled a quote from the philosopher Immanuel Kant, saying there were three aspects to happiness: 'something to do, someone to love, and something to look forward to.' His reply highlights the need we all have to make some sense of our lives. A big part of that is the notion of progress. The life story we make up about ourselves typically depicts us as a hero on a quest replete with obstacles, reversals and happy breaks. Our tribal brains demonise our enemies and cast our friends as the good guys. We like to feel we are moving ever onward as we make our lives, and perhaps the world, better.

This heroic story is a cultural invention of the Ancient Greeks. They came

---

[99] For example, Sigmund Freud's Oedipal idea influenced generations of therapists. But it was wrong. Nelson Mandela's famous inauguration speech, of which he never wrote or said a word, continues to inspire and console. The inspirational poem *Desiderata* has comforted millions. Almost every copy of it carries the claim that the original was found in Old Saint Paul's Church in Baltimore, dated 1692. But it was written by Max Ehrmann in 1927.

up with the idea of each of us being the sole author of our destiny. Their mythical heroes, such as Jason or Odysseus, were upright types in pursuit of lofty ends, reinforcing the idea that with courage and sheer will, we can overcome. Today, with films as contextually different as *Unforgiven* or *A Wrinkle in Time*, we're telling and are told this same story.

Other cultures though, such as those of China, India or Japan, have stories more concerned with teamwork and harmony. People are not seen as solely responsible for their fate. The classic 1950 Japanese film *Rashomon*, for example, examines the same incident from four points of view, without having to decide which version truly happened. Things happen to people rather than people making them happen.

What unites both story types though is that they're both about how to deal with change. In the West we seek to defeat the forces of change while in the East the hero or heroine seeks a way of bringing them into a new harmony. Both versions help us understand and cope with a frightening, ever-mutating world. Stories tell us we can be in control, distracting us from the chaos, chance and unfairness everywhere, and the horrid truth that at the end of it all, we're just going to die.

If I cry along with my daughter in a Pixar movie it's because we are both equally affected by the power of a classic story, the basic structure of which might have been laid eons ago. When the hero sacrifices themselves, in movies such as *Shane*, *Titanic*, and *Avengers: Endgame*, we are deeply affected. Isn't this, Storr asks us, just the story of that mean old triangle and the helping square? Here selfishness = the bad guy; and selflessness = the hero. Other films, like *Maze-runner* or *Gladiator*, show us a world regenerated from below. This is an idea again with origins in our ape past, where the old leadership is toppled; in ape societies, via violent revolution, and via our more mundane modern version of election cycles. Stories, and their moral world, live in our DNA from a time before we were even human.

It's chilling to think how strong a hold our ancient origins still have on us, and how deep our attachment to stories is. The failure, post the GFC and bank failures of 2008, of a story to arise that could bind society together again with a new shared narrative, has opened the planet up to populism, authoritarianism and extremity. Stories aren't some social nice-to-have; some optional add-on to civilisation. We need stories, and storytellers, to live.

KNOW YOURSELF

In our western tradition of storytelling, the hero or heroine overcomes immense psychological and actual obstacles to achieve success and happiness. The trap in this kind of story is the assumption that we have a perfectible self: we can do *anything* if we just set our minds to it. We are certainly surrounded by stories and images of perfection and can spend years dieting, working out, or reading self-help books; trying in different ways to become some ideal.

But a personality test that psychologists have been honing in recent decades challenges the much loved western idea of a perfectible self. It's called OCEAN, and it tests against five traits: Openness, Conscientiousness, Extroversion, Agreeableness and Neuroticism.[100] All personality tests should be approached with caution. But this test's validity, by at least one unsavoury but reliable measure, was demonstrated when it was used by Cambridge Analytica to target Facebook users with tailored political advertising in the 2016 Trump, Brexit, and other political campaigns.[101]

You can do the OCEAN personality test to find out what mix of attributes make up your personality at https://bigfive-test.com. But it's important to understand first that being high or low in any trait is not a negative. It just is. For example, if you're high neurotic that'll make you touchy, but you'll also be highly sensitive, which won't hurt your acting. If you're disagreeable, indeed, it's true, you won't be good at defusing arguments. But you'll also be less likely to obediently follow immoral orders.

For *our* purposes, the interesting take out of the OCEAN test is that people who do the test at different points of their lives don't change their answers much. They get much the same results 5, 10, or 20 years apart.

This suggests that our basic personalities may not be that changeable, let alone perfectible. Richard Dawkins described evolution as a blind watchmaker.[102] We've been thrown together like Friday cars: hastily assembled clumps of biology, with a veneer of culture and civilisation sprayed on. We're improvable – but we're still us.

The truth; that we can get to know ourselves better, that we can make little improvements over time, isn't such a good story. But once you recover from the shock of it, something is comforting about rebuffing perfectibility. 'Know thyself,' says the ancient Delphic maxim.[103] If you know who you are, you can put your energy into managing your personality, rather than pretending to be

---

100 To find out more about this test read *Personality* by Professor Daniel Nettle.
101 "'I made Steve Bannon's psychological warfare tool': meet the data war whistleblower," by Carole Cadwalladr, *The Guardian*, 18 March, 2018. See also the doco *The Great Hack*.
102 His book has the same name: *The Blind Watchmaker*.
103 This was the first of the three maxims inscribed in the forecourt of the Temple of Apollo at Delphi, the second being 'nothing to excess' and third 'surety brings ruin.'

someone else. We're not defined by our traits - unless we deny them.

As an example: it's the foundation of our professionalism to be on time, and if you want to be an actor you're going to have to be punctual. If you're low in conscientiousness, this may be a battle. But it's still worth the effort. Don't however think you can become the kind of person who can get up at 4 am, do pilates, clean the house, learn a foreign language, all before rocking up to set.

The idea of perfectibility can become a stick that we beat ourselves with. If beating yourself up helped your acting, believe me; I'd advocate it. However: it doesn't. British actor Christopher Eccleston has said that there's a kind of arrogance in self-hate.[104] How often have you finished a scene in class or on set and then thought of the five things that went wrong? When we do this we are not 'owning' our work. We are holding it up to some ideal against which we will reliably be found wanting. There's nothing wrong with high standards, but that's not the same as perpetually falling short of some imagined greatness. A greater potential may well exist in us. But right here, right now, this is as good as we can be.

Find the space in your work to pause and tell yourself everything you liked about what you just did - before tearing it to pieces. This is the quiet genius of Dean Carey's 'best thing/ ready for' system, whether you use it in your 1B4, or in your scene work. The 'best thing' is tough, because it forces you to own up to the fact that in this moment, this truly is your best. That's a place you can learn and grow from. The 'ready for' is kind because it takes a criticism, but forces you or the observer to make the effort of turning it into a suggestion.

We can, and must, learn new things. My high school motto was 'per Angusta ad Augusta,' which means (roughly) that through hard trials comes great achievement. This old motto puts me in mind of another story we inherited from the Ancient Greeks. In 'Agamemnon,' the 5th Century BC play of the writer Aeschylus, the chorus tells us: 'pathei mathos.' This translates as 'one learns through suffering.' The sense here is that some things can't be taught; they have to be experienced, and at some cost. In Greek tragedies after great hardships, the hero (if he doesn't die) learns something meaningful of himself and his place in the world. As an actor in service to your fellow human beings, and as a human being on your own life's journey, that would be an ideal worth living for. Preferably minus the dying bit...

---

104 Gareth McLean interviewing Christopher Eccleston, 'I gave Doctor Who a hit show and then they put me on a blacklist,' *The Guardian*, 11 March 2018.

CHAPTER NINETEEN
A LIFE IN ACTING

I'd rather regret the things I've done than regret the things I haven't done.
Lucille Ball

TAKING THE LEAP

Actors - unless born into the profession – begin their careers in happy ignorance of what the life entails. The most important decisions we will ever make – to get married, choose a profession, or buy a house – are often instinctual leaps in the dark, defiant acts of faith in the face of imperfect information. Michael Caine began acting classes in high school because he was no good at sport and noticed that those classes were inhabited mostly by girls. Ian McKellen, as he confided to Richard Eyre, figured acting was his best chance of meeting boys. The lure of fame, money, popularity, the chance to pretend to be someone we like more than ourselves; any of these reasons may initially compel us to act.

At first, we may be worried about our choice, dissatisfaction being the rocket fuel of art. But then, on stage in a school show, or in an early acting class, we stumble over the revelation that this acting game can be more satisfying than anything we've ever done. We are living spontaneously in the moment and yet are also somehow in command at the same time. What a potent feeling, that when we're pretending to be someone else we feel more ourselves than at any other time!

This is the moment of our calling – for acting is more than a job, it is a vocation. It's a vocation because of the extraordinary demands the job will make of you, the main one being that an actor is defined by their readiness, regardless of their day job, family life, and other obligations, to commit fully to every acting opportunity that comes their way.

Inevitably we fall in love with performing before we have any idea what the life actually demands of us, namely an eclectic range of skills: an artist's sensibility combined with a disciplined work ethic, a gambler's disregard for life chances; and a little dose of arrogance. As actor and teacher Stella Adler put it, 'actors must have the soul of a rose and the hide of a rhinoceros.'

The decision to become an actor is not always an easy one. It can involve acknowledging a need within us that flies in the face of social expectations as well as our current abilities. You can expect everything from blank stares to utter horror when you announce your wish to family or friends that you wish to be an actor. Our personalities, with all our ugly bits, can feel like disqualifications. But in acting our contradictions are assets, if only we can learn to live with them.

It feels risky to commit but there is an even greater risk if you don't, because then you'll never know how it might have played out. Can you live with that? Jim Carrey's father, a stand-up comic and musician, took up accountancy and gave up the artistic life to raise his family, only to be made redundant. 'You can fail at what you don't want,' says Carrey, 'so you might as well take a chance on doing what you love.'[105]

Think of yourself as an artistic entrepreneur, backing yourself as you invest time in your craft with no guarantee of future return. That's the gamble you have to take. Commitment precedes result. But a commitment to *anything* is always rewarded with *something*. That something may not always resemble what you were going for. Be open to any accidental opportunities that come along. Doors may not open if you have too narrow a definition of what it means to be an actor. You might miss out on working in a film crew, or travel, or helping a friend mount a show – all activities with the potential to enrich your life and feed your acting.

If you commit, say, for ten years - not just to acting but to a creative life - if you dig in and really apply yourself, I'll wager that you'll at the end of that decade have achieved something you can be proud of; if not the ability to make a living out of acting, likely some other unpredictable, but tangible, outcome.

So give it a go. If it doesn't work out, it will have led to an opportunity that suits you better, and you won't care. Take the leap.

And then get ready for resistance.

KEEP MARCHING

Creativity is the process of moving from just an idea in your head, to something real and tangible. The result might be an opening night, a book,

---

[105] Jim Carrey 2014 Commencement Speech at the *Maharishi School of Management*.

or a new business. Immensely fulfilling, the act of creation is also inherently risky; making the temperaments of the artist and the entrepreneur not so dissimilar. So, we find that James Joyce, the writer of *Ulysses,* launched Ireland's first cinema. At one time he also held the Guinness franchise for France. Joyce's business and writing activities each involved following a hunch with tremendous hard work to an uncertain outcome, with the public being the ultimate arbiter of success or failure.

If you are passionate about your creation and invested in it at a deep level, you have something to lose. Fear is a given. In his wonderful book *The War of Art,* Steven Pressfield argues that your greatest fear lies exactly where your talent lives. So, sometimes, the decision to follow your passion can unleash a ghoulish parade of personal demons.

Pressfield calls this phenomenon 'resistance.' Resistance is whatever version of self-sabotage peculiar to you that can appear when you take positive creative action. Fear and nerves are resistance. Getting sick or depressed or anxious is resistance. Procrastination is resistance. Even drinking, picking fights with your partner, drug-taking and other forms of self-medicating can be forms of resistance, says Pressfield. It's a survival instinct at work – an inner voice, the 'Ego' (if we use the thinker Jung's terminology, as Pressfield does), saying 'don't rock the boat, don't do anything too risky! STOP!'

Our Ego is important, no question: it makes sure we do all the practical stuff like paying the rent and providing for our dependents. But when it comes to nurturing what Jung called the 'Self' – our creative being and personal needs – the Ego can rebel against what it perceives as a threat to its survival. Pressfield believes that this rebellion, this resistance, can be overcome through persistence and hard work: you can win the war of art. You just have to get out of your own way.

In our creative lives we are constantly striving to strike a balance between the important but competing demands of the Ego and the Self. We must find a way to be creative and follow our dreams that doesn't leave us penniless and bitter. A sane home life will be supportive of your artistry far more than domestic chaos. The entrepreneur, aviator and philanthropist Dick Smith always told would-be inventors not to mortgage the house on their ideas. He'd encourage them to tinker in their garages on weekends until they had secured a commercial patent. On the other hand, if you always prioritize only life's urgent and important tasks, such as paying bills and raising the kids, you risk stifling your creative life. Fulfilment lives in striking a balance.

Steven Pressfield's big idea is that horrid internal and external obstacles are likely to present, *especially* if we are on the right path. If we're doing what we love but things keep going wrong, with practical, creative and emotional bombs exploding all around us, it may well mean that nothing's fundamentally wrong. We just need to hang in there. We must be able to tolerate a degree of discomfort. If you can't, then you'll never do the hard things, you'll never really commit, you'll never finish anything and you'll never realise your potential. You'll be defeated at the first hurdle, every time.

Now and then we need to change course. Other times we need to sort our head out. But, often in this game of life, and acting, we just need to sit in horrid feelings, ignore the doubting voice screaming in our head, and keep marching. The artistic path, the one tailored just to you, will only reveal itself as you walk it, embracing all the contradictions and uncertainties you encounter, without trying to make sense of them. Beneath these uncomfortable feelings is your lived truth, one that can only be uncovered through action.

In 1817 the poet John Keats, just 22, and only three years from his death, realized what went to make what he called a 'great man of achievement in literature' (female literary greats were clearly a little thin on the ground at the time). What made someone a Shakespeare, Keats thought, was negative capability: 'when a man is capable of being in uncertainties, mysteries, doubts, without any irritable reaching after fact and reason.' Negative capability means - in Oliver Burkeman's interpretation - being able to sit in unpleasant thoughts, feelings, and situations, without feeling compelled to do anything about it. The ability to do this Burkeman rates as a 'minor superpower.'[106]

Growth, artistic or otherwise, cannot occur if we continually evade taking action because it's not always fun. Sure, that conversation with a difficult colleague, or decision to move to another agent, or getting up at dawn to write, or going to the gym, is something that a part of you is dreading. But if you can push through that dread then, 'the rewards come so quickly,' says Burkeman, 'in terms of what you'll accomplish, that it soon becomes the more appealing way to live' - more appealing than procrastinating, or venting on Facebook, or avoidance.

I read a study of Swedish entrepreneurs some years ago. The research concluded that the successful ones didn't sit around commissioning marketing research, trying to figure out what people wanted. They jumped in a car with a new widget and set out to convince the market that it was needed. Real world feedback came straight back in, they were able to tweak

---

106 'Oliver Burkeman's last column: the eight secrets to a (fairly) fulfilled life,' *The Guardian*, 4 September, 2020

the design of said widget, or the advertising, and get back in the fight. They had no grand plan, just a hunch. They made it up on the hoof. So did writers such as Charles Dickens, for most of his novels, which were serialized in monthly form. He made it up as he went too. It would take almost two years for each book to be completed. The plot turns and endings were influenced by reader responses.

There's a magic that comes just from taking the first step. Screw ups and feedback follow. As you self-correct the next steps, at first unknown, become obvious. Your anxiety, your emotional ups and downs, begin to fall in with the ups and downs of your creative work. Things start to fall into place, and ideas come to you unbidden, like little rewards. Inspiration can appear. It's like the Gods have started to take an interest in you, helpfully nudging you along.

The Noble prize winner Daniel Kahneman contends that we all have an experiencing self in the here and now *and* a remembering self. We tend to be happier when we're older and I believe that's in part because happiness derives from the store of memories of our remembering self. If things are tough at the time they don't necessarily become negative memories, but rather rich experiences to ruminate about later. Memory really is a fond deceiver.

But if you're going to have a store of enriching memories you're going to have to get out there and experience life. If you're acting that's an excellent start. You'll open yourself up for triumph, failure, great times, and dark times.

In the mighty lyrics of 'Tubthumping' by *Chumbawamba*: 'I get knocked down, but I get up again, you're never gonna keep me down.' When you get knocked down, get up, dust yourself off, and get back in the arena. That's where you belong. There, alongside your comrades, there's no shame in failure. You are not what happens to you if you learn from it.

DRAMA SCHOOL

At some point you may wonder – should I attend a drama school? Thanks to the 'user pays' changes made to the Tertiary education sector since the 1980's, education has become good business. The number of drama schools has grown, as has the debt students can amass to attend. Some schools are of dubious quality but all are anxious to attract students and the government funding they bring. The lesser schools can fail to connect their actors with the wider industry at large, because those that teach are out of touch, or the school is not rated by industry insiders. Over the decades the better ones swing in and out of fashion as teachers change, but they churn out graduates regardless, who join the many already enrolled in acting agencies that inhabit the major cities of Australia, New Zealand and the world.

Drama schools have long been the traditional path to a career, even if not the guarantee of one. Their creative advantage remains. They are a place where, in private, you can dedicate yourself for years to practising your craft. In a job that promises more than occasional stretches of unemployment, that's a formative experience, and an important one. You will bond with your fellow students and make friendships for life. If you can afford it, if you're young and have some growing up to do, a school may be just the thing. But only consider the best schools. If you apply and aren't successful don't waste your money on a second rate one. Wait and try again. In the meantime just get on with it.

'Everywhere I go,' wrote Irish writer Flannery O'Connor, 'I'm asked if I think University stifles writers. My opinion is that they don't stifle enough of them. There's many a best-seller that could have been prevented by a good teacher.' Similarly, drama schools don't work for everyone. *Fleabag* creator Phoebe Waller-Bridge found herself unemployed for several years after graduating *RADA* in London. 'I went to *Rada* thinking I was quite a good actor,' she said, 'and came out thinking I was appalling.'

Not enough schools drill their students sufficiently in screen, audition and self-testing technique. Working with the same narrow cadre of eighteen students and regular teachers for three years can be creatively stifling. Some graduates emerge diluted of their flavour; perhaps their specialness has been sacrificed at the altar of obedience. I worked recently with a young and successful graduate of a top Australian drama school. He described the experience as one where the students ended up all trying to please the staff. This can be happening even without the encouragement of the teachers.

Actors must be professional; that is, compliant to the practical needs of the job. But they also need to be creatively wild; connected to their inner artistic voice. No two actors' approach to a role will ever be the same. Pleasing others is just about the opposite of what is needed in a career. Obedience is sometimes the first trait any drama graduate must unlearn.

Of course many drama school attendees don't have this experience. Some skip cheerfully out of their degrees straight into a decade of employment. Others stumble out slightly shell shocked and overloaded with information. That's okay. Delay can be the way you learn. But, however you learn, your uniqueness must be nurtured. The one thing in a global market-place that will make you stand out and get you work, is *you*. Everyone else is taken.

A Life In Acting

Employment opportunities are now global, without a doubt - but rather more depends on luck in a career than we'd care to admit. New Zealand actor Frankie Adams was in her early 20's when she was cast in the international Sci-Fi series *The Expanse*. This was from a self-test in New Zealand which casting director Liz Mullane had sent her. At that stage Frankie had only a handful of acting credits on her CV, including *Shortland Street*. New Zealand actor Thomasin McKenzie, was catapulted to stardom at the age of 17, into Hollywood. This was on the back of one self-test, put down in her home in Wellington for the 2018 independent movie, *Leave no Trace*.

I caught up with Miranda after she'd been travelling around the planet with her daughter for the best part of a year while Thomasin made films and picked up awards. Hers, of course, was no overnight success. Thomasin had been acting since she was a child. Her dad Stuart McKenzie is a writer/director and Miranda is an actress. But Miranda is wise enough to acknowledge the part that luck had also played in her story. Miranda's experience as Head of Acting at New Zealand's Drama School, *Toi Whakaari* meant that she'd witnessed plenty of Kiwi actors of Thomasin's promise who had never had the opportunity to realise it.

We live now in a rapidly changing world where we need to be nimble, and much of our profession is best learnt on the job. Frankie Adams or Thomasin McKenzie never went near a drama school but both had done a lengthy stint in that incubator for New Zealand talent, the TV Drama *Shortland Street*. Early on in my career, on the set of the TV series *Hercules*, I was surprised to discover that only a handful of my fellow cast members had ever done an acting class, let alone been to a drama school.[107] The star of the show, Kevin Sorbo, was an ex-American Gridiron player. Scotsman Eddie Campbell was ex-British army. John Sumner worked in direct marketing before taking up acting without any training. Tim Raby had done a few acting classes; Willa O'Neil none at all. For many actors drama school has been the making of them. But there are no guarantees. Do what feels right for you.

Once out of drama school – or not, as the case may be - say to yourself: 'I'll give this five years.' Or ten. Or whatever. But commit to that. That means taking whatever action you can take now, from a position of woeful ignorance, and learning from the inevitable mistakes you make as you go along. Said Johnny Depp: 'Just keep moving forward and don't give a shit about what anybody thinks. Do what you have to do, for you.'

---

[107] Another shock was earning more money, just in that one episode, than I had in the previous four months of professional theatre. This was not necessarily the best lesson for a starting actor!

It is living the artistic life that will pull a career together for you. As important as attending a drama school is how busy you make yourself when you leave one. Work begets work.

AGENTS

When you're starting out, the relationship you have with your agent is important because you, as yet, have no reputation, and they do. But that's just the start of your relationship building. Through them you meet casting directors, who you want on your side so they go out to bat for you. Later the producers, writers and directors you work with become important. It's repeat business with these collaborators that will get you a career.

But it all starts, and returns back, to your agent. It's hard in your early days when you're just so grateful to even have one, to understand that your agent is not your employer – in fact you employ and pay them to find you work.

To find one, visit all the websites of agents in your town. Look at their actors, and if they are ones you recognise, or they have significant CV's, then that's an agent you should consider.

Not all agents are created equal. A better agent will get more drama briefs from casting directors. And a casting director will listen to them more readily if they are trying to get someone into the audition room. When meeting prospective agents you want to choose one you like, and whose values seem aligned with yours. That's important. They represent you. They stand in for you when you're not there.

Once you're signed to an agent, don't be a stranger. Stay in touch with your booker, brief them on recent achievements they may not know of, invite them to any shows you are in. Call once a month to remind them of your existence. Stay on their radar.

Many actors switch agents at some point, and some fairly regularly. They might be moving up a notch to a better one, or looking for a better personal match. There's often a boost to your acting from taking this kind of positive action; in part from being newly recognised and appreciated by the new agency, in part from your own determination to make the new relationship work. But switching agents may not immediately affect your place in the industry. If you don't like the briefs - or lack of them - that your current agent can get you, that may not instantly change when you switch.

No agent is perfect. But there are benefits in longevity of relationship too. You don't have to reinvent the relationship wheel again and again. They know your strengths and your weaknesses, and vice versa.

YOUR CREATIVE FAMILY

Early on in our careers we can sometimes feel like wanderers in a kind of creative no-man's land. The most important work we do – our prep – is on our own. On the job we will rarely get told what is good in our work, and never what is wrong. We find ourselves reaching out to our fellow actors, running lines, filming scenes, trying out monologues – and listening to their input. We must do this: acting has always been a collegial activity.

Until the invention of cinema, actors tended to be members of close-knit creative communities: theatre troupes clustered around the colourful personalities of the day. From before the time of Shakespeare, until the rise of television these impresarios reigned the entertainment airwaves, touring small towns and setting up permanent shop in the bigger ones. They picked and produced plays that had the meatiest roles for themselves, shamelessly cutting text and blocking stage action to showcase themselves.

There were drawbacks to this theatrical cult of personality: the actor/managers of past times were often vain, ego-ridden tyrants. But they had to be good or their companies went under. Acting was an eccentric, outlandish, even despised profession. One tended to be born into the profession and live a fringe existence, like gypsies or circus performers. Performers were tolerated but also distrusted, at times even feared. Starting young, actors learnt by observation, taking the smaller and chorus roles, then over time growing into bigger ones. To this extent they were fostered artistically, their strengths exploited, their weaknesses well known in the tribal world of the theatre.[108]

Then, just over a hundred years ago, in 1912, Constantin Stanislavski started to teach more than just voice and movement at an acting school in Moscow. His new subject was called 'acting technique.'

Stanislavski was not born into acting. He was a wealthy theatre outsider who was obsessed with it. Until his time actors learnt almost entirely on the job. But because technique learnt unconsciously cannot be easily passed on, when people from outside the tribe started to join, a teachable technique was needed. Stanislavski was just the chap to provide it. Coming to the profession relatively late - his family's discouragement meant that he appeared only as an amateur until he was thirty three - Stanislavski was denied the traditional career route, of learning acting via osmosis from an early age. Instead he cobbled his craft together by experiment, trial, and error.

---

108 On a much smaller scale this system survives today in the British tradition of 'Rep' theatre.

In time the results became 'the Stanislavski system' - a technique which allowed acting to be taught outside the relatively closed world of the theatre that had existed till that time. In 1930's America, after a visit from Stanislavski's company, and where theatre was in a rut, his system was seized on eagerly. His New York converts diverged, each holding up a torch for their supporters to follow. Teachers such as Lee Strasberg, Stella Adler, Elia Kazan (also a director) and Sandy Meisner guided their students into a new and undoubtedly exciting style of naturalistic acting that ideally suited the emerging medium of 'talkies' – modern film.

The different competing approaches to acting that arose from this period offered actors a set technique and a working structure. A new brace of teachers and schools spring up each subsequent generation in the turbid soil of California, fertilised by big dreams and big promises. But until a century ago these techniques, these teachers, almost all of today's drama schools, and most of the industry of actor training, simply didn't exist - at least not as we would have recognised them.[109] Back then, actors had teachers. They were the public: a crowd that jeered or clapped their efforts. This was training in real-time, in what worked - and what didn't. Actors directed themselves, much the same way Charlie Chaplin did in his films. It was only as technical demands grew – exponentially once TV and film came on the scene – that the director became more important.

From the 1920's, film, and then from the 1950s, television, supplanted the function of popular entertainment once held by the Music Hall tradition, and compromised the popularity of theatre. Before World War I pretty much any sizeable town in the western world had a resident full-time professional troupe of actors. Most of those theatres are now gone. There are still a lot of actors on agents' books, but most are unemployed at any time. We have a much bigger audience watching fewer actors on screens – and increasingly that's likely to be on a hand-held device.

Film stars once held an exalted status. As Joseph Campbell observed, they had the quality of Gods; that ability to be in more than one place at once. But these stars have had their cachet eroded by being so accessible. Instead of waiting months for their next cinema appearance we can binge-watch them on TV anytime. The merging of TV and film talent in the new on-demand world of pay TV has led to a thrilling renaissance for television. The best scripts for actors used to be in theatre, but now that's contestable.

---

109 It's true that a handful of drama schools existed throughout the western world before 1912. However for the most part they imparted a technique that we today would consider extremely 'stagey.'

A Life In Acting

TV scenes were, for a time, scripted so short they made you dizzy to watch. But in Season 2 of the TV series *Fleabag*, over a 23-minute episode, Kristin Scott-Thomas took up 5 minutes of it just with *one* monologue.

We live in an ever-changing world, with new viewing platforms, cheap filming technology and a global glut of screen production. The actor needs different skills to survive, and thrive. Long gone is the old training ground that was family-based theatre. Employment can validate us, but may not always sustain us creatively. A whole industry of acting teachers, coaches and drama schools fills the vacuum of collaboration actors have always needed. Halle Berry thanked her agent when she won an Oscar for her performance in *The Monster's Ball*. In 2018 Nicole Kidman mentioned her 'creative family' at both the Emmy's and the Golden Globes when she won best actress awards.[110]

It's lonely work sometimes, this acting caper. Work to make it less so. *Your creative family is anyone who backs you when you're up and backs you when you're down. They're on the sidelines cheering for you, no matter what.* Just as a hundred years ago, you can't do this on your own.

SPIN CITY

There are many working professional actors in Australasia, but not many matinee names. A good reputation will get you steady employ, but big roles don't necessarily lead to bigger roles. You can build a body of work, but not necessarily a market power. We manufacture minor celebrities but we do not make acting 'stars.' That can only happen in the rarefied and pressure cooker place called Hollywood.

Hollywood has for almost a century been the global epicentre of film making, much the way renaissance Italy or nineteenth-century Paris was for visual artists. LA has hoovered up talent from all over the planet since the First World War. Its continuing dominance is in part thanks to Hollywood's willingness to co-opt the particular, the specific, the quirky, and then re-introduce it into mainstream global culture.

Our Antipodean obsession with Hollywood was not always so. Until the 1970's most Kiwi self-exporting thespian talents, such as *Royal Shakespeare Company* actor Lisa Harrow, or Martin Shaw, who went on get his break in the TV series *The Professionals*, were more likely to head to England.[111] But

---

110 Kiwi coach Miranda Harcourt was among the names Kidman mentioned, much to her delight.
111 This was because, until *Toi Whakaari* the NZ drama school opened its doors in 1970, there were government grants to be had to UK drama schools.

equally a great many Australasian actors and directors have made the jump to LA-based careers in recent decades. Most made the heroic decision at some point to not just wait for lady luck. They got on a plane and took the plunge. There were no guarantees that it'd work out and they deserve every bit of their success.

Now a move to LA isn't the only path that actors can take. There's the option to return to New Zealand or Australia after a stint there, which needn't be a bad thing if it keeps your lifestyle and family life intact. As French novelist, Gustave Flaubert said: 'Be regular and orderly in your life, so that you can be violent and original in your work.'

Film and TV is now made all over the world. An initial visit or ten to LA might be necessary, and perhaps an ongoing presence there. But many – Bret McKenzie and Jemaine Clement among them - would argue that you don't have to live in the States because Hollywood is not really a physical place. It is a casting niche where you are considered by LA casting directors for roles in main release US feature films and TV, no matter where you are geographically in the world. The way to get on this international casting list, to achieve a 'name' that has some pulling power that impresses producers, is to somehow get known to those casting directors.

International recognition may come through a local production, such as *Once were Warriors* for Cliff Curtis and Tem Morrison, or *Shine* for Geoffrey Rush. Or Hollywood can come to you. You might land a big role in a prominent overseas production that happens to be shooting here – this happened in 2019 to teenager Erana James, the star of the film *The Changeover*, who was cast as one of the leads in the US TV series *The Wilds*, which filmed in New Zealand. Finally, once you have built up enough of a CV that you will rise above the heaving multitude of aspiring actors, you could make a hard landing in LA without *too* much of a calling card, sleep on a friend's sofa, and do the rounds of agents and managers.

I've only ever made the one trip to LA so can be considered in no sense an expert. Some friends briefed me ahead of meetings and the best advice I got was that LA was a 'yes' town. No-one ever says 'no' to your face. Managers or producers might lavish you with praise even as they disappear behind a smoke-screen of PA's, forever taking messages that are never returned. Every meeting in LA becomes a successful one because no one wants to be the person who blew off the next Heath Ledger.

Los Angeles is flat and featureless. Car fumes tend to collect in the basin locked in by the Hollywood hills. You can forget that it is built atop a desert:

the air is dry, and rehydration essential. The streets are grid-locked by day and almost deserted by night. The place is so spread out that much of the social life occurs in peoples' houses. The city is less a group of communities than a collection of self-sustaining cliques. The people are typically American: friendly and hospitable. It's a town that can feel hard to break into but holds a powerful allure. Orson Welles said: 'I sat down in an armchair in Los Angeles when I was 23, and when I got up I was 61.'

Tinseltown promotes itself as the land of dreams and so attracts more than its fair share of the naïve and the crazy - as well as the truly talented. The tricky part is telling the difference. The number of people doing or making anything is tiny. Most are putting their energy into chasing the next big actor, script or film. This is a competitive town. With classes, tests, meetings and auditions, you'll work harder than you ever have: being an unemployed actor in LA is a full time job.

LASTING THE DISTANCE

In *Siddhartha*, the imagined story of the Buddha (who was born Prince Siddhartha Gotama), Hermann Hesse writes: 'I can think. I can wait. I can fast.' This was Siddhartha's answer to the question of what a holy man, ignorant in the ways of commerce, could bring to the job of being a merchant. In the film version, Siddhartha goes on to say: 'if a man can live on nothing, he doesn't have to work. He can wait for another job.'

There are no overnight success stories. Even once you are good, it takes time for people to notice that. To help you last the distance, take a leaf out of Siddhartha's book. Take a vow of modern-day poverty and you'll be able to devote more time to what you love and less in that low paid casual job.

Living on the bread line can be hard when we're endlessly bombarded with the message that if we buy more stuff we'll be happy. You may be watching your friends with real jobs 'getting ahead.' Materialism is a luxury that any serious apprentice cannot afford. Do you need a full-time job to pay for all the stuff you think you need, but which is only leaving you evenings and weekends to pursue your passion? Why not do what you want to do?

Acting is a long game. Wanting to become a 'star' or go to Hollywood might get you off the start line with a strong start. But a sprint is hard to sustain over any distance. Your glittering dream of what your acting career will look like may smash to bits against the reality of what it actually is right now.[112]

---

112 Read John Keats for some 200 year old wisdom on this topic in Appendix 1.

CHOOSE A MOTIVATION TO SUSTAIN YOU OVER TIME

Bryan Cranston's decision to become an actor was negatively influenced by the example of his Dad, a man who was in thrall to stardom and consequently turned down multiple career opportunities along the way. Because he never got his 'big break' he regarded his life as a failure. In his early 20's Cranston Jnr. was in college studying to eventually become a police officer. He realised that he would rather do something he loved, and might become good at (acting), than something he was good at but didn't love (being a cop). All he ever wanted was to be a working actor.

Steve Carrell started just wanting to make a living too. I'm not even sure this goal is all that modest: acting is so competitive that just earning a buck out of it is a significant achievement. But it is realistic.

Michael Caine wanted to see his own (East London) class portrayed truthfully on screen – he had seen too many upper-class actors playing inauthentic characters and accents.[113]

Another motivation to consider is to follow my advice and make your goal in acting about embracing the learning. That way you'll always get better and in the end that will translate into employment. But the learning goal is really about staying alive, curious and fascinated with process – not outcome. Along the way you'll create great characters and productions. You'll assemble a growing band of collaborators. And you might surprise yourself, even if only modestly. Two years out of my one year of drama training I was, to my amazement, making a living out of acting. Sure, it was only a pittance. But even so I was thrilled to be able to write my profession as 'actor' on airport departure cards.

Within your long term motivation sits the signposts of achievement: getting an agent, getting paid work, self-producing your own show, getting your first casting – and so it goes. Goals that envision these achievements have a power, no doubt. It's invigorating to plot out where you want to be in 10 or 15 years, then practically figure out what you would actually need to do in the next 1, 3, or 5 years to get there, and finally to achieve those outcomes. Goals are an invitation for a feedback loop to start. They get you off the couch and doing something. But as the information comes in don't be a slave to your goals. Change them if the timeline is wrong, or a goal no longer feels right for you.

James Pratt is a talented actor who was a year ahead of me in my Diploma

---

[113] All these examples happen to be male but I'm sure similar rationales have held for actresses too.

of Drama at *Auckland University*. On graduation he scored a juicy guest role in the BBC TV series *Soldier Soldier*. We were all jealous. He did a great job. But he didn't enjoy it. He decided to turn his energy to creating his own work and has carved out a satisfying niche for himself as a writer, actor, deviser and director doing just that in Australia and around the world.

I've worked with a bunch of well-known international actors over the years. Scratch them a bit and every one had a nemesis, a competitor who was a nose ahead of them in the acting race. They all had their regrets. At the top of every mountain, there's just another mountain. Otherwise why did Sir Edmund Hilary not just pack it in and retire after conquering Everest, instead of then leading a motorised expedition (the first) to the South Pole?

The real success in reaching a goal can be what has to positively change in you to make it there. But the prize itself can feel anti-climactic. Life is not a 'to-do' list, a bunch of achievements to tick off. It's full of random events and unanticipated meanderings that defy explanation. Enjoying the trip makes achieving any goal more likely, and makes the final destination less important anyway.

If you're earning minimum wage then that's more time spent away from acting. But our chaotic freelancer routine and natural entrepreneurial bent lend themselves naturally to running a sideline business. Chances are you have a side hustle going on right now, which may or may not relate to acting. It might be voice-over work or teaching or a hobby. Or there might be something you're interested in but have never got around to doing.

Think about how you can grow that side hustle, or turn that passion to a dollar. Don't put all your smarts just into acting. Think creatively about how you can turn your talents to supporting yourself to stay in the game.

THE 15% RULE

I didn't start acting till my late 20s, and never attended Drama School. When I landed my first big role in the Australian TV series *A Difficult Woman*, I wanted to run away before they figured out they had cast the wrong guy. It was only in my early 50s that I began to feel some sense of truly belonging in the profession.

I didn't know till recently, but there's a name for this fear of being found out to be phony: Imposter Syndrome. It is far more common that we might think, through all professions, and for actors in all stages of their careers.

In New Zealand's recent history Todd Miller suffered from Imposter syndrome as he battled his way through his 53 horrendous days as leader of the political opposition in 2020. More surprisingly Ashley Bloomfield, New Zealand's Director-General of health, almost a folk hero thanks to his assured handling of the Covid Pandemic in the same year, also confessed to suffer from the same condition. Through New Zealand's Covid crisis he suffered sleeplessness and anxiety ahead of every single 1pm stand up to the media. 'I had many mornings,' he admitted later, 'where, especially early in the pandemic, I would get up and think 'gosh; can I really do this?'[114]

What got him through was what he called the 15% rule. This is the idea that we are probably only responsible for about 15% of the things that happen to us. The rest is out of our control. Bloomfield's rule suggests that whether we like it or not, we are all making it up as we go along, muddling through, doing our best - improvising life.

By this thinking it's then entirely understandable that you might feel like an imposter on occasion - particularly when under stress. Unless, that is, you are deluding yourself that you are in control of everything all the time. But if you're suffering from Imposter syndrome it might be because you realise how helpless you actually are. The solution is to concentrate on that small slither, the 15% of what happens to us, that is in our control, and work on that.

This 15% is what Steven Pressfield, in his book *The War of Art*, calls our 'territory': the artistic patch that's unique to you. A focus on territory, he says, is smarter than focussing on hierarchy, which will have you wondering what your place is on the career ladder, always looking up or down, always feeling either vain or bitter. You can waste years on that ladder.

When Leonardo DiCaprio won his Golden Globe for *The Revenent* in 2016, he was careful to thank his parents. Growing up in east Los Angeles, they drove him to auditions every day after school. If he'd had parents who couldn't have been bothered doing that, would he have won his first Oscar nomination, aged just 19, for *What's eating Gilbert Grape?* Of course, DiCaprio did the auditions, and did them well. That was his 15%. But his parents driving this talented young man, year on year, through LA traffic? That is out of any teenagers control. I think it was pretty wise of DiCaprio to thank them.

The 15% rule allows us to let go of everything else, the 85% that really can drive us crazy: the unfairness, the nepotism, the bad luck, the failed shows, the recalls that lead nowhere, the TV pilots we make that are not picked up – the list goes on. Focus on your 15%, stop worrying - and take control.

---

[114] 'Can I really do this?' New Zealand's Ashley Bloomfield reveals self-doubts at height of Covid; Eleanor Ainge Roy, *The Guardian*, 24 September 2020

A Life In Acting

TAKING CONTROL

The 15% rule has no scientific basis. But research *has* shown that job satisfaction stems from a sense of control, creativity, and sociability (income is not high on the list).[115] Acting scores well by these measures. We work in a supremely creative job that's also highly sociable. We do however lack control over getting work, and what kind of work it will be. The perennial underemployment will test you at times. But you earn your place in the profession as much by sticking out tough times as by your successes. The key to a long career, says British actor David Suchet, is resilience – learning to live through disappointment and failure without becoming bitter. Resilience – and with it, longevity - result when we take control of our lives and our creative destiny.

This is not the same as settling; that is, as passively accepting the judgement of those that supposedly know all: agents, casting directors or producers. 'Take care to get what you like or you will be forced to like what you get,' said George Bernard Shaw. With creative partner Vicky Jones, the unemployed Phoebe Waller-Bridge founded a theatre company. She started writing a series of short plays, including the ten-page script that would become the hit TV series *Fleabag*.

In that spirit here are some ideas to help you, an artistic entrepreneur, take command of your creative destiny. These strategies are your 15%.

Remember you get to choose what work you do, so it's not a given that you must accept every job you are offered. All you have is you: what you stand for (and can stand) and the stories that excite you. Your creativity flows from who you are and authenticity is your brand. It's the reason you will get work, as well as why sometimes you won't. Think of yourself not as solely an actor, but as a human being who happens to act. If your entire definition of who you are revolves only around acting, what does that make you when you're not doing it? Take this further and get engaged with life outside the industry. For all we revere Stanislavski, his life was so narrowed by his obsession with acting that at times he was a pain in the ass to know.[116] Find a passion and interest that *isn't* to do with the profession. It could just be something you love to do as a hobby. Helen Clark took up tramping. Being Prime Minister of New Zealand wasn't enough. She needed some balance in her life.

---

115 These and some of the following insights reported by Mary Holm in 'Why money can't buy you happiness,' *NZ Herald*, 24 Nov, 2018.
116 See *Dear Writer, Dear Actress: the love letters of Anton Chekhov and Olga Knipper,* Selected, edited and translated by Jean Benedetti, Methuen, 1996.

If your talent goes unrecognised for too long where you are, don't submissively accept the judgement of the ruling theatrical clique in your town. Move to a new city where you will be the new kid on the block; all shiny and interesting. If it all gets too hard, take a break; for a month, or five years. You'll return with a new maturity in your acting.

Another way of taking control is to work on your craft. The better you get, the easier you make your agent's job, and the more work you'll get. Choose a teacher who nurtures you; if he's one of those 'break you down and build you up again' types, leave. As well as a regular acting class think about starting your own scene group, which has the advantage of being free.[117] Acting classes or self-run scene groups both have the virtue, at the very least, of allowing you to work on quality material regularly. You might be getting auditions for TVC's and three-line drama roles. But what if a test for a juicy part in *Lord of the Rings* randomly lands with a thump in your inbox?

As well you should think about doing some kind of regular workout of voice and accent. Aim to do a little and often, setting your sights on achievable bite-size chunks of improvement you know you can manage every day. Accent mastery will broaden your casting possibilities. Just a few visits to the relevant coach, a good App and some exercises, can get your voice and accent work started. Anything that helps you inhabit your body with more fluency, such as dance or a martial art, is useful. Fitness is also part of your readiness - it is much easier to put on weight for a role than the opposite!

Mastery of something, like learning an accent well, is not a mystery. You have to do the hard yards. It's *time* doing the craft that makes you better. But you do have to figure out how to *enjoy* doing the time. If you don't, if your daily acting practise isn't much fun, you won't keep it up. It takes 30 to 60 days to establish a new habit. The website *Futureme.org* allows you to send a letter to your future self, congratulating you on reaching your habit-changing goal for... anything: giving up milk in your coffee, getting up an hour earlier to write, or cutting down on your alcohol consumption. Try it.

Some mornings you're going to wake up and the LAST thing you feel like doing is a voice work out, or going to the gym. Working on your craft in an artistic isolation tank can be hard to sustain. In between jobs we face the problem that growth in technique tends to only stick when it is mated to need. Otherwise it can feel a bit like ritual; it doesn't sink in.

Craft practice will make it more likely you get work, but creating your

---

117 See Appendix 2 for some guidelines on how to run your own group.

own work guarantees it. Why wouldn't you? There are no rules. The truth is actors have always multi-tasked. Disregard the nay-sayers who tell you that actors can't direct. Or produce. Or write. Tell that to Clint Eastwood, Reese Witherspoon, Nicole Kidman, George Clooney, Kenneth Branagh, or the aforementioned Waller-Bridge - and to their many Antipodean equivalents. We are not only actors; we are story-tellers. We really do have the power to help people find their way out of the dark. Our stories can shine a light on society's hidden nooks and crannies. Just the courage it takes to conquer our fear and perform, the transformative act of becoming a character, can inspire.

Creating work is grist to the mill of your acting too. You'll always do great work with your own creative family, where you feel relaxed and know the material well. You'll be busy, and if you have to tear yourself away from that self-funded short film to do an audition the stakes won't be so high, you'll be more relaxed, and you'll do better. When you get the gig you'll have to figure out how to juggle it along with everything else. You can rest when you're dead.

Start by getting engaged in your creative community: meeting people, helping out and collaborating. A career in entertainment lives at the intersection of Art and Commerce. You can be the most talented person living, but if people never see what you can do, you'll die without having moved an audience with your artistry. Like everything it starts local. So, leap into the performance milieu in your town. Fringe theatres like *The Basement* in Auckland, *Bats* in Wellington, and *The Old Fitz* in Sydney are where careers begin. Australian playwright and screenwriter David Williamson's first plays were shown at *La Mama Theatre* in 1960's Melbourne, which then had just a 120 seat capacity. New Zealand Film director Toa Fraser's first shows were staged at *The Basement Theatre* (then called the *Silo*) in the late 1990s. Watch local work and figure out your tastes and preferences and who you want to work with. Start a theatre company. Do stand-up comedy. Write a one-person show, and tour it. Devise new plays; stage existing ones. You'll need to read a hundred to find one that you like – so get started! In the theatre, directors tend to hire people they know, so get along to opening and closing nights. You don't have to chew everyone's ear off in the half time foyer – it's enough just to be seen.

When I produced and directed the stage play *Milo's Wake*, I decided to take the play to where people already congregated. Rather than pulling a crowd, I took the show to a crowd – in community halls and pubs, all over New Zealand. That would still work today. But 15 years on there are new audiences, and new platforms to reach them on. I expend a great deal of my parenting energy trying to keep my children off screens and social media. But they know far better than me how a new generation of viewers are watching content. The young actors behind *Candlewasters*, who make short films and web-series, have, from the get-go, used social media in clever and innovative ways to build a loyal following. Check them out at http://www.thecandlewasters.com/

Next, google these guys: *Viva la Dirt League*. At the time of writing, after about five years of hard work, Adam King, Alan Morrison and Rowan Bettjeman's Youtube channel, which specializes in parody built around three weekly sketch show formats, now has 2 million subscribers. Their strengths? Well, they're talented. Ably assisted by actress Britt Scott Clark (an, a-hem, ex-student of mine) they make content, unashamedly, about what they know. And, like all true kings of comedy, they are unafraid to take the mickey out of themselves. Ultimately, you can't wait for recognition or money or even an audience. One way or another you have to get out there and do it and hope that those things will follow. There's many ways to reach an audience and showcase your talent.

Believe it or not, the like-minded individuals that you band together with now will, with you, end up running the industry. Where else do you think the future actors, producers, writers and directors are going to come from? They don't drop, fully formed and aged 40, ready to helm a feature film. They are sitting next to you in acting class or on stage on opening night: raw, harried, and unsure of their ultimate place in our industry, just as you are.

Pablo Picasso defined art as whatever an artist and his dealer say *is* art. If you can sell it, it's art, and if you can figure out how to reach an audience with it, the money will follow. But money, beyond satisfying your basic needs, shouldn't be your principal concern. Then you're a hack, creating what you think the public wants. There's a credo in Danish Public television (that has seen global success with a succession of hit shows of Nordic Crime noir): they don't make the shows the public want, they make the shows the public don't realise they want yet. If you tune into your muse by following your eclectic whims and fancies you'll create what your heart tells you. In the end it's the personal and peculiar that engages the biggest audience. With his blockbuster movies Taika Waititi has now brought a particular band width of Kiwi sensibility, one might say even an East Coast (Maori?) way of satirically viewing the world, into the global mainstream – to huge acclaim. As James Joyce said: 'In the particular is contained the universal.'

A Life In Acting

Taika Waititi was an actor, then an artist, then a director. There was no grand plan; he was following his creative nose, and it was sniffing a path to greatness. But he was listening to his heart, not chasing a dollar.

So, as well as theatre, get busy with a self-made web series. Put a team together for the next 48-hour film festival. Make a short film. Make a film! The results are often raw, but such work has the advantage of connecting your voice and vision directly with an audience. You'll learn renewed respect for the multiple competencies that go up to make a modern day production crew, because you'll be taking on those roles - as a producer, or Assistant Camera, or running the Unit table - whatever is necessary to organise, shoot and post-produce your story. Then you can commune directly with an audience, cutting out the middlemen - teachers, critics, and sometimes even directors - and learn from the best: the public.

The ultimate risk-takers by virtue of our choice of profession, actors are natural entrepreneurs. Why not emulate the gall of the impresarios of the past and do your own creative thing? Initiating your own work is the best insurance policy.

The best way to survive the industry...

... is to become it.

CHAPTER TWENTY
EXERCISES, GAMES AND GROUP WORK

You must get rid of all the rubbish! By that I mean you have to constantly pare away all unnecessary colouring and tension and the paraphernalia which you feel you need to convince an audience and which, in fact, gets in the way of direct communication. I am sure that one of the actor's greatest concerns is the fear of not feeling enough and, therefore, of not being interesting enough. The greater the emotion in the part the more he tries to convince the audience of his feeling and so ceases to be specific. You know that this often occurs but it is difficult to trust yourself. You must believe you have a right to be there.

The late Cicely Berry, OBE

INTRODUCTION

There are exercises peppered throughout this book specific to Line patterning, Objectives, Repetition, Intimacy, Sub-text, Opposites and Character. The additional exercises in this chapter can be used to work on a performance or the actor themselves, across teaching, rehearsal and working situations. Many can be used by actors working solo. There are also warm-ups, and exercises for working various actor muscles such as imagination or connection. There's an eclectic array here, gathered under no single umbrella or system. Here are the exercises that I happen to use most often in my teaching because they are the ones that get the best results. They come from teachers such as Eric Morris, Ken Rea and - particularly - Cicely Berry. Some I've mangled via repeated use in class almost beyond recognition to fit my purposes. Students and teachers to the *Actors Lab Studio* have contributed one or three as well.

If conducted with the right spirit and good judgement, physical and vocal based work can be remarkably effective. The actor is working with their whole body so they very quickly get out of their heads and into the intelligence of their full imagination. Unexpected discoveries are made that tend to stick as they are remembered physically, organically. As well, physical work builds ensemble. The process when forming a group for any new enterprise is called,

Exercises, Games And Group Work

in corporate circles, 'Forming, Storming and Norming.' The middle word is a giveaway that some conflict is inevitable. Group games and exercises help channel tension into creative energy, pulling everyone into the orbit of exciting shared experiences that build up team spirit and make excellence the norm.

BREAKING THE ICE
The following two exercises are easy to learn and are a fun way to kick off any process of work or rehearsal.

1. Bang
'Bang' is an ice breaker that also forces people to learn the names of the others in the group and brings out our competitive spirit. There's a value in fighting to win, and there's a value in handling losing.

Someone starts by calling (loudly and clearly) the name of a person in the circle (this first person can't call out their own name, or the name of someone next to them). The person whose name is called must duck and the people on each side of her must point at each other and yell 'BANG!' Whoever is slowest dies and leaves the circle. OR, if the person whose name was called is too slow to duck, they take the imaginary bullet and die.

The person who dies leaves the circle and calls out the next name.

At all times point at the person you are trying to kill, not the person who is ducking.

Once you get down to the last two you can do a 'mooooo off' (first to laugh dies) or a duel to find the ultimate winner.

A variant is someone in the middle making eye contact and calling names.

2. Sound and Movement
An exercise from Ken Rea, an acting teacher at *Guild Hall* in England.[118] From the circle the first actor ventures into the middle and makes a sound with an action. It can be anything, so long as it is a noise with a repeatable movement. Don't think about it too much. Just start making different shapes and sounds. Once the person has created their masterpiece they then turn to someone else in the circle and show them how to do it. When satisfied they stand back in the circle and this chosen person goes into the centre continuing to do the (copied) sound and movement on their own for a bit. Then they stop and come up with their own unique sound and movement, which they in turn share – and so on until all have participated, including

---

118 Ken Rea, *The Outstanding Actor*

(ideally) the teacher or director.

This is a surprisingly challenging exercise. Note the following:
- Don't fudge the three stages of copy, create & share.
- While waiting, watch - don't think of what you'll do when it's your 'turn.' Focus on what is going on in front of you.
- The sound you make cannot have any meaning or sense. It can't be a word for example.
- Do try and embody the physicality, vocality *and* spirit of the person you copy as specifically as you can.

GELLING A GROUP

Games like *Synchro clap* and *Zap*, as well as being very silly, are simple to learn and hard to master. So, it's good to introduce them when you know you'll be able to work on them regularly – i.e. every day for a week, or weekly for a month. They can be a litmus test of the collective focus, as well as incredibly frustrating at the early stages, as the 'ball' gets dropped again and again. Repeated over time, as mastery develops, so does a childlike sense of pride and *esprit de corps*.

As well as helping gel a group these games test and teach readiness. We need to turn up ready to work – switched on. If the actor isn't 'on'/ ready/ connected to themselves – in the second circle, as Patsy Rodenburg would say – the warm-up game will reveal it, which is useful for the actor. Sometimes we think we're ready but we're not, because we're not connected to our 'stuff' - what we are feeling or carrying into the work.

These games are useful in any working environment to get everyone up on their feet, working their whole bodies, before boredom can get a hold. Learning is enhanced in rehearsals or class by getting everyone up to move at least every hour or so.

1. Synchro-Clap

Everybody stands in a circle.

Stage 1: One-way traffic

Someone starts by turning to the person to their left, making eye contact, and then initiating a single clap. The other person claps at the same time, and now they have the clap. They turn to their left, make eye contact, and clap at the same time as that next person, and so on.

At the start just focus on getting a nice steady rhythm going. Make sure people are making eye contact and a nice clear clapping motion to help the person they are passing it to. Make sure the person receiving is ready to clap

Exercises, Games And Group Work

(i.e. hands out in front and separated).

The clap can go from a slower to a faster rhythm, and back again, but keeping a rhythm will save you.

Do remember to breathe. It can be easy to hold your breath as you wait to receive or give a 'clap.'

Once your group has their heads around this layer in the following stages:

Stage 2: Reversing direction
The person who just received the clap holds eye contact with the person who sent it and returns the clap. As usual, both players clap at the same time. Now the clap is going in the opposite direction - until someone changes it again.

Stage 3: Across the circle
Rather than just going left or right, you can pass the clap across the circle. Eye contact becomes critical, and wherever you are you need to be watching for who has the clap - *and have your hands up and ready to clap*. As with reversing direction, you can return the clap to the person who gave it to you by simply retaining eye contact and clapping again.

Stage 4: While moving
The game continues but everyone moves about the room, randomly walking to fill the space. Now eye contact and focus become *really* important. It can be fun to send the clap to someone quite close or make eye contact across the room.

2. Zap

Zap only
Someone starts by turning to the person to their left, making eye contact, clapping at them and simultaneously saying 'Zap!' That person then passes it on.

Adding in
The next command is 'Boing!' This changes the direction of the zap, passing it back so it continues back around in the opposite direction. Come up with a blocking action for this.

Next to add in is 'Bounce!' – the person puts a triangle shape over their head with their arms and the 'zap' bounces over their head AND the head of the person next to them. The person after that then passes on the 'zap.'

Next is 'Zoom!' Zoom throws across the circle. The person who says 'zoom' points to who they want to have the zap, both arms outstretched. The receiver then looks in the direction they wish to continue to play and the zap moves on.

Note:
You can't boing a boing, you can't zoom a zoom, you can't boing a zoom or zoom a boing - you can only zap a zoom and zap a boing!
Crikey!

ACTING & How To Survive It

WARM-UPS
Simple warm-ups for the mind, body and voice.

1. 10 Minute Shake-Off To Music
To music actors enter the space one by one, moving against the beat and slowly taking in the space and people around. Actors then peel off one by one.

2. Dancing On Your Own
To music, in the following ways, dance on your own...
- With the worst possible sense of rhythm (not too hard for some of us...)
- As a terrible dancer – but who thinks they are best.
- With incurable shyness
- Like your feet are made of concrete
- Spending the least amount of time touching the floor as you can as if the floor is scorching hot
- Like you're a gorilla/meercat/camel/ etc...
- However you wanna dance!

3. Acting Gym
This is a group physical movement exercise to music where each actor has a minute to come up with a movement with a start/middle/end relevant to the character they are playing. It can be one fluid movement or several: a symbolic expression of their character's journey (a bit like the Psychological gesture mentioned in Chapter 2, but to music). Then get some loud party music going and each actor gets up in front of the group and shows their jam, which the whole group then repeats 3 or 4 times over. Everyone gets a turn.

4. Vocal Warm-Up
- Actors pair up, give their partner a body massage and the 'massagee' gets to warm up their vocal chords on a 'hum' to an 'ah' sound.
- As a group, run some exercises to warm up the dexterity of the lips, the tongue and the jaw (get googling!)

5. Movement Warm-Ups (with Text)
The following are vocal exercises, so let the exercise affect your voice:
- Play tag running the story or scene. Other actors can play and help one or other actor. Keep the dialogue moving – no unwarranted pauses!
- In the space organise a simple football or throwing game. Or just get the two actors running a scene to throw a ball to each other as they run the lines.

6. Vowels, Consonants – And a great vocal work out
Before language there were only vowels, noise really: shouts, grunts or cries that were meant as warnings or welcomes or lamentations. With words came consonants, which broke up the vowel sounds, giving them sense. Consonants

are all we need to comprehend meaning. Texts on our mobile phones used to contain no vowels, but we *gt th msg*. In fact the first written language that we know of, Sanskrit, contains only consonants.[119]

While the spoken word is composed of both emotion *and* meaning, in our literal age we actors sometimes we get caught up only with the meaning. We play emotion *around* but not *in* the words. We miss the emotional, perhaps primeval, parts of speech. And as well as just information, consonants provide a structure and energy to the words. So, there's a value, especially for a long speech or monologue, in sounding out both the vowels and consonants in turn.

Do this for a speech, starting with sounding out just the consonants. It'll help you explore the energy in the speech, as well as diction, and hence the clear communication of the meaning of the words. Then sound out the vowels, remembering that the job of the vowel is to carry the emotion of the words.

You can hold the text in front of you if you have to, but there's a value also in remembering each word, each syllable, sounding out each LETTER, giving it it's vocal due. Much like the Cicely Berry exercise 'Attending to the word,' sounding out gets you working at a micro, specific detail.[120] Just the sounds you are making are connecting you with the power that resides in each word.

You can say your speech through honing the specificity further with a final exercise. Go through your monologue or scene and highlight as follows: circle the verbs, underline the nouns and pronouns, then square the adjectives. As you speak the words for every adjective, jump; and explore the feeling of that specific adjective as you do – sad will feel differently than old, for example. For any noun or pronoun – any object, name or person - place it precisely in the space, and point to it as you say the word. Finally, do a movement, say an upper-body roll, describing with your body what every verb is doing.

STIMULATING IMAGINATION

It's often said of artists, including actors, that they can be flakey or absent-minded, not so good at balancing their cheque-books, and so on. But it's also true that a bit of flakiness is necessary to the work. The way our imagination works is that once we've identified some creative problem consciously, our unconscious can make random and unanticipated connections to solve it. Sometimes we have to get our conscious thinking out of the way to allow

---

119 Consequently we know what it means, but not how it sounded.
120 You can find the 'Attending to the word' in Berry's book *The Actor and the Text:* each word is sounded out in turn, to explore its energy and meaning, independently of the sense of the whole sentence.

this to happen.

The following exercises offer explorations into our unconscious creativity, stimulating our sense of play, and giving voice to a wild artistic self we may only be scantly aware of. They can also bring the passions and peculiarities of each individual to the fore. We are taken out of the every day and encouraged to think differently about the world. We get a sense of everyone's hidden strengths and complexity, and our imaginative horizons are broadened.

1. Talent OR Show & Tell

Just like at a second rate Beauty pageant, in a few (and definitely no more than three) minutes, everyone gets up and demonstrates or talks about a talent they have that isn't acting (for a bigger group you may want to spread this work over several sessions).

Sharing a 'Talent' the actors often reveal a side of themselves we never would have guessed at. This can be talking about something that interests the speaker – a passion or hobby, anything from collecting graphic novels to travel. But in class we've also had everything from dancing, dazzling musicianship and home baking (my personal favourite…). We've heard beautiful recitals, talks about kite-running in Pakistan and walking the length of New Zealand for charity. We've watched martial arts demonstrations, seen exhibitions of pottery and painting – and much more.

Extraordinary!

Sometimes the idea of sharing a 'Talent' sounds somewhat daunting, so an alternative title can be 'Show and Tell.'

2. The 3-minute story

Everyone gets up and – impromptu and unprepared – tells a 3-minute story.

Before doing this, lay down the ground rules: The story must have a beginning, a middle, and an end; be three minutes or less; be personal and be true. Finally, the story must hold the attention of the listeners.

This exercise can be a real eye-opener into a fresh, hitherto unknown other side of the people in the group: revealing of who they are, and perhaps what they are holding back in their acting. The 3-minute story connects us with our storytelling function and reminds us that acting is not a free pass – if people get bored, they'll change the channel: we have to be truthful AND intriguing. To reinforce this in my classes if I see anyone watching who is drifting off, I'll stop the story.

A variation of this is *Pitching* – an actor gets up and makes a 90-second pitch of any original film, TV, podcast or web idea. At the end the group can figure out the one-sentence pitch (or *log-line*, as it is known) together.

3. Free association – Solo or pair
The root of imagination is 'image.' And the activity of imagining is making of associations.
Judith Weston

As Weston reminds us, the world of free associations is the world of the unconscious. Her free association exercise encourages a stream of consciousness that is not just having a chat. You must let the words go to anywhere in your head. Don't be afraid to go to the ridiculous, the surprising, or the dark, places. Then your stream of consciousness may be revelatory – illuminating something surprising perhaps even to yourself.

On your own or in a pair, start with one word (usually given by the teacher or director). Then say the first word or reaction that comes into your head. Keep going, putting words to the pictures presenting in your head, describing what you see: making associations. Keep following that train of thought, fearlessly striking off down random back alleys of your unconscious. If you get stuck, repeat the original word.

There are no rules for this exercise, no right or wrong. Keep talking. Surprise yourself!

Here are some initial words to get you going; you can come up with some of your own: *Rain. Family. Grass. Sun. Blackboard. Summer. Brother. Lockdown. Gun. Snow. Blood. Sick. Dog. Home. Circus. Vomit. Fingernail. Scar. Sacrifice. Ice. Mother. Rainbow. Flood.*

CONNECTION & INTIMACY EXERCISES

Acting is, after all is said and done, just you, making a connection with the other human being in front of you. Sometimes though, without knowing it, we can do a kind of ersatz connection. It feels like the real thing but in fact we're at emotional arms distance. It's hard to trust our prep but to allow it to serve you we must really focus on the person in front of us. They are the new variable, the piece of the jigsaw you didn't have when you prepared alone. If you tune in and react to what they give you, they'll keep you present.

The ability to establish warmth and intimacy is a hallmark, I believe, of all great actors. Danny Huston and James Nesbit are just two actors I have worked with who had this quality in spades. But the ability to be intimate on demand is an aptitude all actors possess and is a muscle that can be grown. These exercises reinforce connection and intimacy, encouraging you to relate to and *with* each other rather than *at* each other. They're great warm-ups to encourage closeness prior to playing a scene.

1. Intimate share – verbal - in a pair

Unless we are willing to reveal our pain, our loneliness, our humiliation, we are not really revealing anything of ourselves.
Judith Weston

In this global marketplace, that's awash with opportunities yet so easy to get lost in, you're only going to get work for who you are. Unique, quirky old *you* is your fundamental point of difference: there is no one in the world like it. In performance you must bring your full self to the work. To do this you'll need to be honest about how you're feeling moment to moment; to be non-judgmental about the flow of emotions in your work. Initially there can be reluctance around this. We've all had a lifetime of being socialised to hide things about ourselves we feel we should be ashamed off – our negative feelings, or our exuberance, or sadness, or anger. The problem is that in our day to day lives if we suppress one of our emotions, we can end up suppressing them all. We can't pick and choose our feelings and try to present only what we perceive to be the positive ones. All our emotions run in a river, in a flow, all together. Allowing ourselves to feel the difficult feelings allows a flow from those to the next.

For some actors it can be that if certain feelings or behaviours are taboo in their lives, that can carry over to their acting. This exercise chips away at our root fear of exposure and ridicule if we reveal our true feelings; inviting us to visit all our emotional nooks and crannies, including the dark and scary ones.

Split up into pairs. *Do this exercise as yourself, not in character.* Your partner starts by asking you: 'tell me everything you need to tell me about how you feel right now.' They then become the world's best NON-VERBAL listener as you answer in an honest stream of consciousness, moment to moment, what you are thinking and feeling, for three-four minutes. Then you swap and repeat.

This exercise doubles as a warm-up, so you may share any fears you have that may interfere with the work ahead. Always bring your words back to how you feel ('I feel XYZ'). If you get stuck observe and comment on the other actor, or the room, and share how that makes you feel. You might start telling a story, but if an emotion intrudes do share it. Use the exercise to reveal how you are feeling moment to moment. Your difficult feelings may want to hide, but we must be able to express them. If you do, you may be pleasantly surprised, moving through some negative feelings into other feelings – you'll have a *flow* of feelings.

Like the exercise *Free Association* this isn't about expressing negative feelings per se, just the freedom, uncensored, to express *anything*, understanding that the shitty feelings are safe, necessary for the work, and flow on anyway often to become something else.

It's important that you take some risks and are unafraid to share feelings you worry might invite ridicule – but of course won't. But do remember: your privacy is sacred. Don't share anything you don't want to. We don't want confessions - we want to hear about your feelings *right now*.

This Intimate Share exercise establishes a strong shared bond between the actors ahead of the work. Now that you have shared all your secret fears, instead of putting energy into hiding them, they can be available to your acting.

2. One Word

Another way to grow intimacy in a group.

Pair up. Actor 'A' starts by saying one word about the other actor that they know to be true (make it true but avoid being nasty). Actor 'B' replies with one word, also about themselves, that contrasts with that word, or contradicts it, or is its opposite – but is also true. Actor 'B' then says one word about actor 'A' that they know to be true. And so it goes.

3. Mirroring

This is a warm-up to hone your focus and get paying attention to your scene partner. Get into pairs. Everyone stands in two lines, facing each other, about a metre apart. One is the leader, the other, the 'mirror.' The leader begins to make simple gestures or movements. The 'mirror' duplicates the leader's movements exactly – just as a mirror would. So, if the leader raises his right hand, the 'mirror' should raise his left, just as your reflection in an actual mirror would.

If the leader moves carefully we won't be able to tell who is the leader and who is the follower. Use smooth, continuous movements: abrupt movements almost always catch the 'mirror' out. Maintain eye contact at all times. After a while call 'change.' At this point the leader and follower swap: make it as seamless as you can. I then like to say 'no leader.' Boy, does that get interesting.

Look after your scene partner. If you go too slow, it'll be boring for them. Too fast and you'll lose them.

Again, do this exercise as yourself, not in character.

4. Physical Intimacy - Pair

For actors playing two people who have known each other for some time, the most helpful thing they can do before playing a scene is to touch each other: just hold hands! It's hard to play someone you are supposedly intimate with if you've never touched them. Many great actors I've worked with were instinctively warm, tactile, touchy-feely types, quick with a handshake, a hand on the shoulder or a hug. It isn't always easy to stroll up to a stranger and embrace them, and it's a gesture that of course can be misconstrued, so take care! In class or rehearsal it's up to the director or teacher to lay down the ground rules: that there is plenty of trust, it's clear that the exercises are all about the work and that no one will be made to do something against their wishes.

So, *in character:*

- Dance to the song from your first date or wedding. This can be one of those slow dance, party type post-Midnight shuffles, with no dancing prowess required. Get the actors to come up with the song and if they want to the story around it.
- Get the actors used to each other physically by making up a couch, as if they were watching TV, and asking them to drape themselves over each other; get comfortable with each other. They can run some of their scenes that way, or do improv's around them. Put a podcast on that they can listen to that as they chat, taking appropriate pauses to listen, and so on. Encourage them to physicalise.

These exercises will create a physical ease of each actor for the other. They'll be able to form shapes and find each other physically in the playing much easier.

5. The Hands

Mike Leigh uses this exercise as part of his process, principally to introduce a new character towards the end of a rehearsal process, creating backstory between two characters. I've seen Rob Marchand (a Character-Based Improvisation proponent) use it to repeat and drum in a past experience – say of being bullied at school, or having been a sex worker.

Quickly discuss with the actors the detail around a specific encounter – typically it's the first time they met, or hooked up, or fell in love. Figure out where it is, what time of day or night, who else is there. Then work out what *happens* in the encounter – what's the beginning, middle and end? Once the basic scenario is agreed to, get the actors to sit as close as they can without actually physically touching. Then get them to place their hands close to each other, palms down, and fingertips *almost* touching. From now on they may *only* look at their own hands or their partner's hands. Remind them that they are playing this game in character. Then get them to initiate the meeting in their minds by touching. Then the actors act out, non-verbally, only interacting with their hands, the encounter. It ends when they break off contact.

While not infallible, this exercise can have a spooky quality of making an imaginary backstory real in the actors' minds.

6. For Physical Attraction

When you give someone your full attention, when you are genuinely fascinated by them – this looks like love or physical attraction. If you are playing that you are in love with someone, or strongly attracted to them, that means you are fascinated by them, by everything they do. You find everything about them super interesting.

In character, standing opposite them, give the other actor/ character your full physical attention. Scan their face and body and eyes as you would for Emotional Connection (see *Stage one: Close Observation* below). Or do it through a scene. Paying attention to them in this way looks just like that in a scene – like love. Remember, you are in character, looking at their *character*.

See what is beautiful in them *physically*. In what is quirky or odd or unsymmetrical there may be found the one thing that you find especially fascinating about them. You may become especially fascinated with their lips, or eyes, or adam's apple. In the film *The English Patient*, it was a part of Kirsten's Scott Thomas' neck that Ralph Fiennes' character named as 'The Almasy Bosphorus.'

If running a scene pay close attention to everything they say and do. Get interested in them. In acting, it boils down to this – you and me, in character, here and now. Really looking. Really listening.

Then see what is beautiful about them *emotionally* – see if you can perceive their hidden strengths, what they have endured and survived, their hopes and fears. Can you perceive their emotional scars? We are attracted not necessarily to people who are like us, but to people that have shared our backstories. So, was their childhood also chaotic, or sad, quiet, or full of laughter – as yours might have been?

7. Emotional Connection - Pair

In class I'll run the following connection exercises sequentially, moving to deeper and deeper intimacy. You can do this exercise in character to develop intimacy with the *character* of the person in front of you, not the actor. Again this is all done non-verbally.

Stage one: Close observation

Again have a good look at the person standing opposite you. If in a professional environment, sneak the odd glance at them in the make-up bus, or while you're working with them in rehearsal, or chatting over coffee (but don't make them uncomfortable). You're just looking for all the things you have never noticed about them before: blemishes, eye colour and shape, mannerisms, traits, quirks of voice, the story their body tells – and so on. It's all part of getting more and more familiar with someone in the same way you would if you'd known them for a long time. Just being looked at can be rather confronting – but this self-consciousness is usually quickly dealt with by making the other person, not your discomfort, the focus of your attention. And being watched is, in any case, something we actors all need to get used to, right?

So now: *really* examine their face. Study each other's faces and take in the physical details, imperfections, flaws and asymmetries. Look for anything new, one thing you have never noticed before. Then ask a series of increasingly intimate questions of the other person's face. Looking at the lines, are they caused by laughter, or by frowning? Are there bags under the eyes? How much light is in that eye - how much warmth do you see there? Do they look happy? Pensive? REALLY look and interrogate what you see (the answers will be pure guesswork, and the other actor needn't ever know what you're thinking). Look for the story this character's face tells of the life they may have lived, of the events of their day. You can make up stories in your imagination about what you see on their face too – the blemish that tells a story that only you know.

Stage two: Eye tennis

Now start to communicate with each other - but without gestures, words, touch or mime. Just use your eyes. Don't try too hard, just let the connection deepen. Start to have a conversation with your eyes about how each of you is feeling, to and fro. Let the responses develop easily as a sort of emotional collaboration.

Stage three: Telepathy

As above, only now look into each other's eyes and guess as to where you think the other actor is at emotionally right now. Then give them what you think they need right now *with your eyes.*

In fact, telepathy is a version of the Repeat game, just using the eyes. It's fundamentally good for actors to do for their screen acting, which is about behaviour but is subtle, especially in close up. So that for screen acting it's all happening in the eyes. Work to affect a change *in the other actors' eyes.*[121]

---

121 Audrey Hepburn is reputed to have said: 'for beautiful eyes, see the good in people.'

Exercises, Games And Group Work

Remember to breathe through this exercise. It's not a staring competition.

Then: end this sequence by giving your fellow actor a big hug. NOT a Nana hug, but what Miranda Harcourt calls a 'honey sandwich' – stuck together like two pieces of white bread with honey. And hold the hug, so it can move beyond self-consciousness. As you hug, give your partner *everything you think they need right now*. Hug for at least a minute, release and come out of character.

As a quick footnote to this, do watch once you come to work any tendency to overdo eye contact. You may end up looking like a possum startled by car headlights... stay human!

8. Intimate Share - Physical - Pair

This is an isolation exercise where the actors get as intimate as they can just by touch.

Again, try this exercise as yourself, but then another time 'in character,' especially if that fits your rehearsal process better. Being in character adds a layer of protection allowing you, conversely, to go deeper into the work.

Sit as close as you can without actually physically touching.

Roll up the sleeves of your right arms, so that as much of your right arm is bare, from your fingertip to your shoulder.

Place the palms of your right hands together.

Close your eyes. Then, starting gradually and gently, in three or four minutes, get to know the other person solely through touch, seeking to get as close to them emotionally as you possibly can. You may only touch them from the tip of the fingertips of their right hand to their right shoulder. This isolation makes the actors safe.

The best way to get to know the other person is to be open yourself, so make yourself available emotionally. Don't be afraid to be vulnerable. With the physical exploration, don't lead, or force things. Surrender. Just let it happen.

If a certain feeling starts to emerge let that happen too.

After a few minutes whoever is convening the exercise should say: 'in about a minute you should be back where you started, palms touching. In your own way and in your own time, find yourself back in that starting position.'

Once there keep the physical contact, keep the energy pulsing between you – and keep your eyes closed. When prompted to open your eyes notice the change in the other actor's eyes: they'll be connected to you, their feelings, and ready to work.

9. Connection for a Scene or Monologue

A good exercise to encourage an intimate connection in a scene quickly and simply is just to hold hands through the scene, gazing into each other's eyes (never mind the actual blocking for this run). Squeeze the other actor's hands if you don't believe what they are saying and they must repeat. Do this in a supportive manner – you're helping the other actor to work at a deeper, more truthful level.

GELLING A CAST

In a New Zealand Film Commission workshop I attended some time ago we were told that the two most common failures in short films were poor sound quality and poor acting. In TV and film there can still be a lack of time and care given over to the actual performances – the only thing really that the audience will care about in the end.

Budget allowing it's not all that hard to turn around. Rob Marchand told me a story once about how he was brought into the popular Australian TV drama *All Saints* as a show doctor. Ratings were sliding, and Rob discovered the cause: poor performances by guest actors. This wasn't too surprising. In a long-running TV show the core cast is generally confident and strongly embedded in their characters. The show stands or falls on the guest roles. These actors have to get up to speed in minutes. If the crew and cast are relaxed and welcoming it's a help. But it can still be a daunting task.

Rob's medicine for the show was to establish a new procedure where guest actors were well looked after. They got a script meeting with the director well ahead of filming, and rehearsals. They got a day on set, paid, where they got to meet the cast and observe how the filming went. These and other changes turned the show around. As an ongoing guest on the show I myself enjoyed the benefit of these changes. And yet this kind of practice is not the norm.

1. Place

So often the first time an actor will inhabit their character's lounge or office will be when they walk on set to block, or for the tech rehearsal (if a play). But actors get so much from making a space their own. Get access to locations in advance. Make the space your own – sleep there if you want to. Viggo Mortensen reportedly took this approach during the filming of *The Lord of the Rings*. If you've read Lisa Chappell's contribution to Chapter 14 you'll see she used a similar approach in preparing for her role in *McLeod's Daughters*.

If rehearsing a play get actors into the performance space as early and as much as possible, so they can understand how the relationship to the audience will play out. Be irreverent with the space – have the actors run the play all over the auditorium, losing their fear of all those empty seats, learning where the audience will be and how they will relate to the story of

Exercises, Games And Group Work

the play. Get props and costumes into the rehearsal early on too of course, again so an easy familiarity can be developed with them.

2. Shared tasks

Give your actors tasks or activities to do together. Relate them if you can to the kind of things they would do in the film or play. Or they can be random, like a trash treasure hunt game.

These 'treasures' can find their way on to the set too, as can other objects the actors create or find that makes the space real to them. Get your cast hanging out, having adventures, forming bonds of shared experience. If there is a specific skill the actors need to master, like gun handling or making cocktails, get them all learning it together, rather than at home alone.

The time spent working together on these tasks leads to a genuine familiarity between the actors.

3. Fast-Tracking Intimacy: Dr Arthur Aron's 36 Questions Exercise - And Bungy Jumping!

There was a tradition I tripped over when I was living in Moscow. If you are about to embark on a new project with a stranger the two of you would, on your first night, bond over a bottle of vodka. After imbibing enough spirit, so the theory went, inhibitions are dissolved and confidences shared.

Fortunately, there's another way to bond that spares you the hangover: Psychologist Dr Aron's 36 questions. His 1997 study looked at whether intimacy can be better created between two strangers by having them ask specific and personal questions, versus just having them an unstructured chat.

Having done the exercise I can testify that, counter-intuitively, the 36 scripted questions work much better at creating closeness than the simple chat. The questions gradually increase in intimacy until the two people taking part are sharing some of the most sacred details of their lives. It's the best 45-minute short cut around to get close to anyone. The differences between you melt away until all you can recognise is your common humanity.

So, if you're gelling a group and don't have much time you could start with Dr Aron's questions. You can find them with a google search.

You could also take a leaf out of Miranda Harcourt's playbook and get your actors to share some heightened experience, such as a Bungy jump, white water rafting, or ballooning.[122]

---

[122] Dr Aron's experiment went viral in 2014 after Mandy Len Catron wrote about it in The *New York Times*, although I first heard about it from Miranda Harcourt. Without much time to rehearse, Miranda had Timothy Spall and Erana James share a bungy jump as a bonding exercise going in to the filming of *The Changeover*.

SCENE, STORY & CHARACTER EXPLORATIONS

All these exercises are for working with and exploring text. Some erode obstacles to the actor's ability to play a scene; all deepen understanding of the material.

1. Improvisations to Explore the Change/ Travel/ Value

In an improvisation there are no lines to remember and so even if the actors know the beats they have to hit, the scene is unplanned and rolls out spontaneously. So, an improvised scene has the essential quality of real-life: although we know what we'd like to happen we can't be sure of exactly how it will run. When we run the scripted scene after an improv it is injected with this freshness, reminding us that our acting at its best has this unplanned, unforced quality: as if for the first time.

When running improvs remember TWO rules for them, which are also great principles to remember for your acting. The first is *no denial*. This means that if the other actor suddenly says you're in a bedroom, then *you're in a bedroom*, end of. This is just as it should be for your acting, where you must imagine the facts given to you in the script to be true. Second, *say yes* to everything that happens, with no obligation to be interesting or good – just go there without attempting to manipulate the results.

The following improvisations aim to freshen up the dialogue and explore the actors' understanding of the architecture of the scene. Start by reading the scene. Then do your improv. Then do the scene again to feel the discoveries in the work/ with the lines. Permit yourself to work anywhere in the space. Interfere with each other physically and forget about the 'blocking' of the scene. When you come back to do the scene that energy, that urge or instinct to move, will be present in your body.

Simple Improvisation

The actors in the scene agree on the story's main beats – the beginning middle and end – and identify the turning point/ decision. If there is an emotional shift in the scene there can be some discussion about that. Then the actors run the scene as an improvisation without worrying about getting the dialogue right or the story beats in the right order. The actors will discover how much they understand about the bones of the scene.

Imaginary Foreign Language/ Gibberish

If the actors are a bit 'stuck in their heads' this exercise helps them understand the scene intuitively by removing the obligation to make sense of it.

As above but the actors do the scene substituting an agreed imaginary foreign language, or gibberish, instead of the words. If doing an imaginary language it can be helpful to agree on the 'type' of language – a Germanic or Chinese accent, etc. But any noise coming out of your mouth is fine, so long as it doesn't make any sense.

Monkey

As for the above improvisations, except the actors do the scene as monkeys, with no dialogue, only noise and movement. Primal behaviour forces actors out of their heads and into their bodies to explore the nuts and bolts of the relationship, the shape of the scene, and sometimes unexpected things, like backstory.

To Music

Not strictly an improv, as we are working from the text. But a good way again to highlight the contours of the scene. Run the scene AS SCRIPTED, only over really loud music, as if you were at a party.

Variations of the above

A variant for any of the above improvs can be to use any of them to play out a different, invented scene, which can be used to explore or clarify the moment before, or some aspect of backstory or relationship between the characters. The actors should again create elements of the story in advance and agree on the premise that begins it: for example, one character has just broken a valuable object of the other.

2. Exploring Opposites

An Eric Morris exercise, this helps if an actor is leaning toward playing a character black and white or two-dimensional. Say if your character is constantly spewing hate and bad feeling, go for the opposite choice for a scene, or an act - or if it is a play then a run of the entire play. The actor will be able to discover layers and nuance in the work. So, if playing a villain, doing a run for that character for love and reaching out may also uncover insights as to why the character turned out the way she did. The feelings of hatred may start to arise organically as, despite the character's warm and fuzzy choices, she is still rejected or reviled.

Again, you can do the same for a 'nice,' loving character, and so explore the possibility of any fury or hate that may exist underneath.

3. Exploring Sub-Text: Simultaneous Monologue

A variation on a Mark Travis exercise, this also explores the competition in a scene.

Ask the actors, in character, about their back story, as it relates to the character in front of them. Get the actor to state their objective – what they want from their scene partner, then get both actors to start simultaneous sub-textual monologues.

This exercise is NOT like the repeat game. The actors shouldn't listen to the other character - they should make THEM listen! Demand of them what you want. Don't implore – stick it to them.

4. Outrageous Exaggerations

Eric Morris again: the aim here is to free up any work that is being choked to death by the actor's sense of obligation to the material. Here that responsibility takes a back seat to the actor making outrageous choices, exaggerating all of her behaviour – vocally, physically, verbally, whatever. Once the actor feels freer and more impulsive, she can return to using choices more aligned with the scene or monologue.

5. To Explore Conflict or Heightened Emotion

Fuck you

An exercise for two actors that I first observed working at a Screen workshop with the inimitable Miranda Harcourt, this is a variant of the children's game red hands.

The actors extend their hands forward so that they are almost touching. Each actor takes it, in turn, to slap the other actor's hands, saying 'Fuck you!' as they do. It's not about winning the game by successfully pulling your hands away, it's about getting increasingly cross! Do maybe three slaps each, because that's about all your hands will stand! Then run the scene.

Issue Clash

The actors hold each other's shoulders. One will say 'come into my life,' followed by the other saying 'get out of my life.' Keep repeating until the convener calls cut. Which line each actor is given depends on what suits the scene or the purposes of the director. The actors can move around, pull and push, all the time keeping their hands on the shoulders of the actor opposite them. As they repeat the phrase they should allow themselves to explore the violence in the words and with that their entire vocal and emotional palate – whatever they might need to play the scene later. Very quickly the words become unimportant, and the charge between the actors, the relationship, takes over. Go straight into the scene at the end.

Sense Memory

To explore emotion in any speech or monologue the actor can do a sense memory type exercise, eyes closed, where they recall something that makes them feel a certain way. Possibly the actor/ teacher can side coach them to make the memory as sensorially vivid as possible. This might be purely imaginative – excrement smeared on a wall may make them feel disgust, even if they have never actually seen that. Once the actor has painted their picture sensorially (either of an actual past event or an imagined one) they can quietly connect with their character's intention and then, with their eyes still closed, start talking the text, initially whispering; off voice. When they are ready they open their eyes, carry on and slowly start to share.

WORKING ON THE ACTOR

These two exercises work on any unconscious mannerism or bad habit that the actor has slipped in to, or to tweak at some aspect of their acting. This is to be approached with caution. We don't want to make a mountain out of a molehill, and often just pointing out the issue is half the fix.

1. Bad Habit/ Essential Quality

There's a lovely scene in the movie *The Sixth Sense* between Dr Crowe, (Bruce Willis), and Cole, (Haley Joel Osment), where Dr Crowe makes a series of guesses about Cole. If he gets a guess right Cole steps forwards; wrong and Cole steps back a step. If he gets enough guesses correct Cole will come in, sit down and engage in a therapy session. But Cole ends up stepping out of the room and going.

Sometimes actors don't realise how they are coming across, even when the teacher or director tells them. Their acting can feel outrageous to them but we're unable to see much happening at all. Or it can be the other way around – they don't realise how big they are playing.

Inspired by that scene in *Sixth Sense*, Bad Habit/ Essential Quality is a way of using a similar pressure, a peer pressure, to help the actor work on an aspect of the scene, or their acting.

Before you run the scene isolate an essential quality that you want one actor to focus on in the scene. This is that actor's 'ready 'for' – what they want to go for in this run of the scene. This could be about correcting a bad habit, like fidgeting, or focusing on vocal clarity, connection, or some other quality the scene needs they are struggling with, such as being vulnerable. When the scene starts the second actor, as well as playing, steps forward or backward, giving real-time feedback on how the other actor is going on their 'ready for.'

It needs to be stressed that this other actor is a helper, not a critic. They are there to give moment to moment feedback on how the actor is going on their point of focus. This will help them calibrate for themselves next time.

Another way – gentler and perhaps, therefore, more effective - is to play the scene holding hands. Whenever the actor wants more of the 'ready for' quality they squeeze the other actor's hands.

2. Choice/ More

Again, it's hard sometimes for the actor to appreciate how their choices are playing. The choices may be spot on, but not discernible. If I'm not seeing the actor's choice on a particular line, I may say, 'more' – meaning let me see the choice more clearly, more specifically. Or to make them aware of the many choices/ ways to attack a line, I'll say, 'choice' – meaning to give me *another*, different choice.

CICELY BERRY & FURTHER EXPLORATIONS

I was honoured to have worked on two occasions with the late Cicely Berry, voice coach for the *Royal Shakespeare Company*. The first was in a one week Shakespeare masterclass, the second a masterclass production (that is, with rehearsals open to the public) of a play, *The John Wayne Principle.* On the latter occasion Ciss (as she liked to be called) was the voice coach and Bob Benedetti the director.

Many of the exercises that follow in this section are Cicely's, or inspired by her. I'd like to provide some context for the exercises by describing, briefly, her working style.

I learnt from Ciss a profound appreciation of how important voice work is for the actor. This is not just because we may have to work through issues with our vocal instrument, but because voice work can be such a non-intellectual, counter-intuitive, and therefore fruitful way to open up the work. But Ciss' voice work almost always sprang from a physical and imaginative place. Her exercises get you up on your feet and out of your head, making discoveries while not knowing what you are looking for. She hardly ever actually looked at us actors when we performed. Instead, she would gaze down at her feet and listen. Above all Ciss had a great ear. And it's all you need: if the actor's voice is alive, then their acting comes to life and everything else falls into place. I've found in my own practice that there is nothing like half mask work and Cicely's exercises, together, to pull this vitality, this *aliveness,* into the performances.

Ciss loved the earthiness, the *violence* in language; that is, everything the words did to have a direct effect on us that lived in them beyond their literal meaning. She told us that acting in Shakespeare's day was a matter of life and death: in the *good olde days* of the *Globe Theatre,* circa 1600, actors were only ever given their own lines and the last three words of their cue. All scripts were handwritten and there just wasn't time to write out the whole play for the actors. So, if you didn't know your cues, if you didn't *listen* for them and missed one, you really would *die* on stage. Act Shakespeare, Ciss advised us, as if someone could sink a dagger between your shoulder-blades at any moment.

She also reminded us that Shakespeare would have studied rhetoric at his Grammar school. Certainly, the classical rules and principles of rhetoric can be found in his writing. A key one was forward momentum. To illustrate this lost art-form (sound-bytes convince nowadays, not lengthy argument) Ciss told us that Michael Foot, once the leader of the British Labour party, was never interrupted when he spoke in the House of Commons. Why? Because he employed that rhetorical trick of never drawing breath at the end of a thought. Shakespeare does this too. How can you interrupt when the speaker crams all the vital information into the second half of the sentence, then without drawing breath plunges on to the next one? In theatre the result is to keep the listener keyed in, hanging out for the next auditory tidbit.

While Ciss worked mostly with Shakespeare's texts her observations and exercises seemed to work just as well on scripts of any genre. She taught us to trust our intellect, but cultivate our instinct. That principle has fed my work ever since.

I count myself lucky to have seen these exercises on the floor in person and done many of them with Ciss. You can watch them too: just get searching on Youtube. And you can find them described much better in any of her excellent books. I don't think she would have wanted anyone to be too reverential about them. For Ciss it was always about what helped the work here and now and never the rigid application of an exact system. So, use your intuition too as to which exercise to use – and feel free mash it all up with your own shtick. I do!

Here are some quick guidelines in the use of these exercises:
- There's a knack to figuring out what may move the work forward at any time. After a while, your intuition will tell you which to use and when. Most exercises will reveal *something* of value.
- When an exercise doesn't work blame the exercise, not the actor. You just picked the wrong one. Shrug and move onto another idea.
- There's sometimes value in keeping from one actor what other actors might be about to do, such as heckling, because then the actor, walking into the exercise, will be surprised. Events lived and discovered in the moment tend to stick to the work once it comes to performance.
- Remind actors whenever embarking on any physical exercise especially that they must at all times keep themselves, each other, and the room safe. To

preserve the atmosphere of trust and support actors need to also protect their privacy. They should only divulge personal information about themselves that they feel comfortable sharing.
• These are voice exercises, so when doing any exercise the actor should allow what they are *doing* – panting, pulling, jumping, ducking - to affect how the words come out. The actor should be *on voice*: letting the exercise affect their voices. Amongst all the cries or trampling of feet if you have to yell to be heard, then yell. Don't pause: let the discoveries stick to the words.
• Sometimes I'll call a monologue a story, as I think that's a more useful way for us actors/ storytellers to think of them.
• A circle is sometimes recommended for these exercises, but generally don't be scared to move, walk, run, jump - and enjoy!
• The categories below are pretty arbitrary - the exercises often work on multiple fronts at once.
• A typical working sequence for these exercises is to run each section/ scene or monologue normally, then do it with an exercise, on text, and then run the scene again. Ciss stressed how important it was to do this third run to bed in the work. We want the discoveries to have a useful impact on the work, and the way to see what has stuck is to do that third run without the exercise. Cicely used to say, 'good actors remember.' This seems to be especially true when the learning is remembered in our bodies, in our muscle memory.

TO EXPLORE RELATIONSHIPS & STATUS
1. Group Scenes
Try the following for a scene or a monologue with many listeners:
• Sit at a long table with more chairs than characters. As the scene plays actors should change chairs at each change of thought, moving toward or away from other characters as they wish, one chair at a time. You can move regardless of whoever is speaking.
• Play out the scene in the space. Again, whenever any actor gets an urge to, they should move to any other character or to another part of the space.
• To explore status have your 'ruling' character walking fast around a prescribed circle – supplicants have to follow, speaking into her ear, getting her to sign documents etc.

2. Competition
A great exercise to explore a sense of play and competitive behaviour in any scene amongst the characters is the *Tick to Win* exercise in Chapter 3: *Acting Boot Camp I*.

3. Activities: to highlight relationship

Doing something in a scene or monologue grounds and earths the words, helping the actor discover a more life-like rhythm. So, using the whole space set up an activity in which both actors in a scene are involved, like moving furniture, or tidying up: do be precise about what you want to achieve, and make it important. Speak the dialogue as you do it.

In the masterclass I attended Ciss gave Barry Otto the task of tidying up; specifically to neatly stack up a dozen books scattered on the floor as he spoke. The effect was that the words come out in an easy, flowing cadence, interrupted by the physical actions – much as words are broken up by thought.

Variations:
- Relate the activities – if X wants a reaction from Y then only Y does the activity. In this case the activity can be something as simple as Y copying out a passage from a book. X can interfere with Y's activity if she wants. Then, if you want – swap.
- Make the activity between two characters – for instance, X tries to make Y comfortable. Y can resist or go with it, whatever seems appropriate.
- Rather more simple, but still helpful in getting the actors out of a pattern in their speech, is a simple game of noughts and crosses.

It's important that, while they can pause doing it – and when they do this will be telling – the actors shouldn't give up on the activity until they have to.

TO FIND THE VARIATIONS IN PITCH, VARIETY & THOUGHT

1. Two Chairs

A very simple exercise, but one that is surprisingly useful for highlighting changes of thought, and helping the actor discover the inner state of the character. The actor sits on one of two chairs, sitting side by side, and starts the speech. On every change of thought or phrase the actor changes chairs, quickly sitting on the other chair. DON'T PAUSE.

Two chairs is good for speeches where the character is figuring something out with a speech/ story – like Benedict in his 'This can be no trick,' soliloquy. Finally, *Two Chairs* can help bring the words to life if they lack variation or vitality.

2. Change direction

As an actor tells a story she moves to a new space in the room with each new thought – as if moving to where all the different thoughts are placed in her brain. Move with some degree of urgency. This will reveal the shape of the character's thought processes and also manifest the inner state of the character – agitated, excited, calm - in the actor's body. The exercise makes you engage with each new thought physically and forcefully. One idea should impel you (literally) forward into the next.

EXPLORING IMAGERY/ IDEAS
1. Back to back
Two actors play a scene sitting on the floor with backs touching. The other actor repeats words that strike them as interesting while the actor is speaking - about one word a line. The rest of the group could sit around and repeat the odd keyword that hits them too.

These repetitions help each actor understand the keywords that trigger their responses, but also gets them inside their character's head. With Shakespeare's words particularly the imagery a character chooses tells us where they live psychologically.

2. Mime
While speaking the actor mimes the speech, describing every phase physically as if performing to an audience that doesn't understand English. Don't be too literal - this is not pantomime - and *only* mime the images. You can speak the words yourself as you do it, or as another does the speech. A great way to explore the imagery of the speech, if you focus in on just the images described.

RESISTANCE & RELATIONSHIP
These exercises dig in to relationship dynamics and also help the actors find the meat and muscularity in the language, helping them find their voices.

1. Resistance - Physical
For a situation where one of the characters might want to keep a distance from the other, even if just emotionally. One of the actors (say X) wants to get face to face with the other (Y) but Y runs away, presents obstacles, hides etc. X can also be blocked by some other actors, helping Y to get away. The actors should use physical interposing only and keep it all safe of course. Y should feel free to tease or taunt X, even vocally if that helps.

Variations:
- Several actors physically block in X with items of furniture, chairs etc.
- Y hides an object from X, who tries to find it while Y watches.
- One person speaking a story/ monologue has to get from one side of the room to the other by the time she finishes, with everyone else trying to stop her. Don't be rough, enjoy the roughness in the language – as Ciss would say.

2. Resistance - Verbal

The actor should never assume the attention of the audience or his fellow actor is a given – they have to work for it! So as the actor shares their story the group (instructed prior secretly) can talk loudly so the speaker finds it difficult to be heard – the group can shout across the room at each other for example. At a certain point they can stop and allow the speaker to finish.

Variations:

- Heckling: As the actor speaks their story or scene the other actors heckle or boo him in some way, maybe whispering criticism at him, maybe jostling him at the same time. *This challenges the actor to define his thoughts.* Stand around a person in a circle if you wish, repeating words, hissing them, challenging him. OR the actors can question what he speaks, questioning his motives, in their own words.
- Snubbing/ ignoring: as the actor speaks the group talk among themselves and pay no attention to him or her. The actor can have the instruction to connect with people in the room who will walk away and not make eye contact.

This exercise can reinforce a sense of loneliness or emphasise the character's lack of connection with others.

3. Resistance – Heightened Emotion

Physically hold back the two players – lovers, fighters - from touching each other as they fight to get to each other, all the while on text. The actors restraining the players can also repeat any words to do with pulling/ drawing/ outside force. At a certain point the actors can release them and the energy of that exchange can remain in the dialogue.

EXPLORING SUB-TEXT/ OPPOSITES

1. The Harpies

Get two or three actors ('The Harpies') to position themselves around the actor who is delivering their monologue and repeat any words in a whisper from the speech that are riffs on an agreed theme. It might be violence, or time, or regret in a speech from *Macbeth*, or sex for Parolles in *All's Well that Ends Well*. The actor should hear these words and allow them to affect her performance as if her conscience were speaking to her.

2. Repetition

For a monologue/ story or scene have someone stand behind each actor softly repeating everything they say and do, but by listening, a split second behind. This is useful for finding the layers/ associations/ sub-text in the scene. The actors need to be open to be affected.

DISCOVERING THE WORDS

Sometimes the words lose their freshness; they start to sound second-hand, somehow reported. Rather than being discovered in the saying, they are being recited. These exercises address this tendency.

1. Drawing a Picture

Drawing some kind of picture while you do the scene/ story can make the words freshly minted again. I saw Ciss do this in a scene from *Othello* between Olivia Pigeot and Lucy Cornell, playing Desdemona and Emilia. We know that Desdemona is surely soon to be killed by Othello. Regrettably, so do the actors, and all too often this premonition pervades the scene, weighing it down. So, Ciss got Lucy and Olivia to sit back to back, and focus on drawing what they could see in front of them on sketchpads. Suddenly we could hear the almost banal domesticity of the words. We saw two friends sharing a recognisably human moment - and playing it in a simple and unaffected way. The full impact of impending doom hit us ten times harder than if the actors had 'acted' that feeling themselves.

Here are some guidelines:

- If you focus on drawing something specific and precise then the words will be specific and precise.
- If the text is fussy and precise draw a complex pattern of some kind, something you can see in the room.
- If the text is meditative draw from memory: your first school or house. This will help activate your inner world.
- If the text is active, of now, draw what is right in front of you: what you can see outside the window or the other side of the room.

Variations:

- For a scene just get each actor to look out the window without drawing, each character concentrating on what they see as they speak.
- Get the actor or actors to go into separate rooms and have to talk through a wall or doorway, raising their voices to be heard. Add in an activity to give the delivery an even more everyday feel.
- Get the actor to say the speech as if they were dictating a letter, weighing the phrases, rushing along to the next idea, and so on.

2. Direct Address - Solo

Another exercise for discovering the words is to put the actor in the centre of a standing circle (or a semi-circle of seated actors) and get them to say each phrase of their monologue to a different person each time. This is direct address, so make sure you follow through with the one phrase/ thought (and preferably breath) just to one person in the circle before you move on – don't break up the thoughts. Also dn't let the actor methodically move around the circle – this can lead to a deadening vocal rhythm - they should choose the right person for the next phrase intuitively.

The actors in the circle or semi-circle can be like the thoughts in the characters head, having to be discovered in the moment for the actor to conceive of the words. So the actor will get a sense of the inner state of their character (short sentences, abrupt changes, or long flowing thoughts) and also the sense of discovering the words, of making them up as they go along.

3. Discovering the words - Group

For a long speech give each person a phrase (the distance between two major punctuation marks) and get them to speak out the speech, phrase by phrase, person by person. The effect may be of an urgent and unpredictable argument between a dozen different voices; an illustration of how a character in Shakespeare's world uses language to solve problems, needing to speak to think, with each thought made possible only by the preceding one.

EXPLORING INSANITY
1. Playing 'Affects'

Not a Berry exercise, but an effective way to explore insanity, is to figure out your character's particular brand – manic depression, borderline personality disorder, schizophrenia, and so on. Then research the actual outward symptoms of that – or 'affects,' to use their medical term. Don't worry too much, initially, about the character's inner mental and emotional state. Just play those symptoms. What you will find, say if you go down the road of schizophrenia - hearing voices, seeing things, believing them to be real, and so in – is that after a while you will start to feel what that's like. This is particularly true if you are working on an improv with another actor: how they respond to your behaviour also adds another layer of understanding.

2. I am not mad

For another way in… have a read of Constance's heart-rending monologue from *King John*, Act III, Scene 4 when she's grieving the death of her son ('Thou art not holy to belie me so; I am not mad…'). Constance is denying she's mad, explaining that her response is humanly exactly what it should be, given her dire circumstances. While running the speech I've seen Ciss have an actor move to different spaces in the room, repeating all the while 'I am not mad!' – in all the ways that show her levels of madness, demonstrating all the ways she is not mad, exploring all the ways she fears she might be…

The same idea can be used to help establish a play against any character who is distressed and perhaps questioning their sanity. Running the scene the actor can just repeat at any time those four awful words: 'I am not mad.'

FINAL RIFFS

Ciss was a great one for making Jazz analogies, encouraging actors to play 'off the beat,' and so on. So here are a few final riffs...

1. Making Given Circumstances, Internal Landscapes, or Themes Real

As the actor speaks she builds a monument representing something of importance to their character – a loved one, an idea, a belief, or an object. The monument can be built of anything at hand in the room: clothes, bags, people, chairs, whatever. This can get even more interesting for a scene. The two actors can build two contrasting or competing monuments.

Australian actor Sandy Gore did this exercise during a masterclass I attended with Cicely Berry. She was playing Cleopatra extolling the dead Antony's virtues, beginning with, 'I dreamt there was an Emperor Antony,' and ending with the anguished, 'think you there was, or might be, such a man as this I dreamt of?'

2. Listening/ Reacting/ Specificity

Three words

Put the two actors doing a scene back to back on the floor, speaking their dialogue through – but before they say any of their lines, they must repeat the last three words of their cue line, so that what they say comes out of the other character's words. The speaker will hear something fresh, and their own words then come out as a more concrete and specific response to the other character. Plus the actors learn their cues!

Variations:

- Again sit back to back on the floor, speaking the dialogue through – the actor who is listening repeats roughly one word per line that is being spoken… the speaker should take account of this then carry on.
- Turn the lights off and whisper the other to each other. This forces the actor to listen and their words are a direct response to what they have heard.
- Again sitting back to back the actors speak the scene. The actors watching have to close their eyes. The actors become aware of those hearing, and this informs their choices, again tending to make them more specific.

3. The Sentry Exercise

This exercise allows an exploration of any existing elements of danger, intrigue, or place. Examples of where this might be useful vary. You might be working on a scene where the characters are meeting in a public space like a

Exercises, Games And Group Work

café because one of them is fearful of the other, or they are being secretive, or they live in a political world – such as in Shakespeare's *Richard III* – where danger lurks around every corner.

Create a set space, box-shaped, where the actors can work. Place one or two sentries around this. The sentries will move randomly and if at any time, they enter the acting area, the actors must pause and wait for them to leave. During the pause they must keep the energy of the scene alive.

The exercise makes real the sense of danger, highlights the need to communicate, adds a sense of urgency, and the need to find the right word to alight on.

4. Sharing the Story & Building Ensemble

Milo's Wake, the play I directed in 2005, was rich in storytelling, packed with lots of monologues recounting past events. Most of these yarns were known to all or most of the characters, who typically would make interjections and contributions. Most of the monologues were the title character's – Milo. Even though he dominated the play in terms of words spoken, the other three characters were on stage with him all the time. I wanted the play to be an ensemble piece, which the entire cast should 'own,' by being engaged and invested in all of these stories. Cicely's exercises proved very helpful in creating that.

Reading from our hard copies of the play, the cast (four actors, later joined by three musicians) would speak the story around, punctuation to punctuation. We'd do this standing in a circle with a sense of momentum and excitement about the act of storytelling itself, moving from one person to the next.

Then we'd pass the speech around, this time with one person speaking at a time, in any order, for any length – any actor could just grab the story and run with it. This brought a sense of competition for ownership of the story alive, imbuing it with energy, and a sense that the language itself was not well behaved.

Other Variations:
- Sing the story around – don't be afraid of humour; commit to the sound
- Shout it – moving around
- Finish this sequence with a very quiet read, or whisper, *preferably in the dark*, ensuring *that every syllable is heard*… now with the actual person who is playing the speech saying it.

APPENDIX 1
ON FAME – TWO POEMS

Fame I
Fame, like a wayward girl, will still be coy
To those who woo her with too slavish knees,
But makes surrender to some thoughtless boy,
And dotes the more upon the heart at ease;
She is Gipsey, will not speak to those
Who have not learnt to be content without her;
A Jilt, whose ear was never whispered close,
Who thinks they scandal her who talk about her –
A very Gipsey is she, Nilus-born,
Sister-in-law to jealous Potiphar.
Ye lovesick bards! repay her scorn for scorn;
Ye artists lovelorn! madmen that ye are,
Make your best bow to her and bid adieu –
Then, if she likes it, she will follow you.

Fame II
How fever'd is that Man who cannot look
Upon his mortal days with temperate blood
Who vexes all the leaves of his Life's book
And robs his fair name of its maidenhood.
It is as if the rose should pluck herself
Or the ripe plum finger its misty bloom,
As if a clear Lake meddling with itself
Should cloud its clearness with a muddy gloom.
But the rose leaves herself upon the Briar
For winds to kiss and grateful Bees to feed,
And the ripe plum still wears its dim attire,
The undisturbed Lake has crystal space—
Why then should man, teasing the world for grace
Spoil his salvation by a fierce miscreed?

John Keats (1795-1821)

APPENDIX 2
SCENE GROUP GUIDELINES

Here are some guidelines for running your own scene group, the fruits of my own experience of running and participating in scene groups over many years. These are offers, not laws set in stone; guidelines for you to evolve from.

1. Start with a firm commitment from participants to run one full term

There is no set group size, and advantages and disadvantages to both small and larger groups. If doing camera work smaller groups are better – especially if you're doing playback. There's less time watching and more time on your feet in smaller groups. On the other hand, if you get too many no shows then your group may not be able to function. I would say a minimum of 6 and a maximum of 12.

2. Stick to short terms

A four to six-session term is a suggested initial length for people to commit to. It allows everyone to work with everyone else in the group about once. People are ready for a break after six weeks. People usually start dropping off after three to four weeks with work commitments etc. Have a good break, then talk about availability, new people, when and where to start again. Meet weekly – or fortnightly. Meeting fortnightly has advantages: more time for busy people to prepare, less people dropping out. But it does lengthen out the term.

3. Everyone should have one monologue up their sleeves

If your partner does not turn up - *no dramas*. Pull out your monologue and do it. This way you always get to work every week. And it's good to practice your monologues. Alternatively, get someone to read your scene against you. That's good audition practice.

4. Spread the load

Often it is one person who steps up and makes a scene group happen. You owe a lot to this person. They are only ever an administrative leader however: your *uber-organiser/ convener*. Scene Groups are creative democracies. There are no 'leaders'. You might consider having a different convener every term to spread the load. The convener is someone who makes sure everyone has a partner each week, chases up absentees, collates and hands out contact details. This doesn't mean that everyone else takes no responsibility, but it is useful to have one central point of contact. You may want to pay the convener a little for their time or, if there is a venue rental, let them off paying that.

5. Get money upfront for rent for your space – or…
And all up the cost should still be only $10 max per person per session. **Make any fees all payable in advance at the first session.** This gives people an incentive to attend regularly and makes collecting money easy.
An alternative to meeting in physical space is to film work at home. You can then share it with your group and meet on Zoom to discuss.

6. Choosing People
Try and find actors that challenge you a bit, that will lift everyone's game. Ideally, new participants start in at the beginning of each term. They should be nominated then decided on by the group before they start. Do not just invite people along: run it past the group first. Unless you have a good reason for excluding someone, let them in. If participants feel their suggestions are being consistently ignored they will leave and start their own group (which might be what you want, but that is another story…).

7. Working Structure
Start with the scene alignment structure that you may have learnt in one of my workshops, which I, in turn, learnt from Dean Carey: best thing, ready for, or, alternatively, 'what did you like/ get out of it,' 'what do you want to go for this time.' This structure is simple, democratic, participatory, road-tested and seems to utilise the combined insight of the whole group in the most efficient manner. Do evolve how you work over time if you feel the need: we should always be flexible to new approaches and suggestions. I do recommend however that you stick to the following basic principles:

- Keep comments brief: this is always more helpful for the actors, as it minimises the time between 'takes.'
- Do not to allow negativity or conflict to creep in, under any guise. It will kill creativity. *Appraise the work not the worker.*
- In your 'best things' be positive but honest.

Sometimes it's more useful for the actor to make a specific note on a detail rather than lavish generalised praise.

- Keep the atmosphere workmanlike and focused.
- No one should ever dominate.

8. Be cautious about…
Keep chatter to a minimum in the class – arrange to have a beer after the odd session to allow for broader discussion.

Be careful about non-participants – directors, spectators, friends – attending, except occasionally. The space needs to be safe and secure to be challenging and effective.

Scene Group Guidelines

9. Scene lengths tend to sneak up in size

Which is fine, but have a rule of two runs for long scenes, three for shorter ones. Otherwise you may run short on time. Similarly if you have a lot of participants/ scenes/ monologues you should consider running everything just twice. It kind of focusses us to do a better first run, doesn't it?

10. Find your own scenes

At the end of each session pair up with someone different for the next one. It is the responsibility of each pair to find a scene for the next week. There is no point joining a scene group unless you are prepared to commit to reading a lot of plays, films and TV episodes in your ongoing search for good and challenging scenes. Get into the habit of visiting your local library, internet sites (Drew's Script-O-Rama, the BBC provides scripts, and there are others – have a look around) and bookstores, building up your store of potential scenes/ monologues. There is an enormous personal benefit in this. As actors we need to be informed about what work has preceded us and is going on around us. Choose a scene quickly so you have more time to learn the lines before the next session.

Don't work with someone twice in a term unless you've already worked with everyone else.

11. Be self-reliant

Each scene group relies on the maturity of its members. It is not the convener's job to run around after participants, helping them find scenes etc. Nor is it your scene partner's job to find your scene.

Learn your lines thoroughly and meet with your scene partner to run them if you wish. If you have to skip a session contact your scene partner directly so they can prepare their monologue.

12. Why don't ya…?

Do a cold sight-reading session or an improv night or a warm-up for 15 minutes after start time or start on time even if everyone isn't there or do a poetry reading/ party piece or a musical/ play reading night or bring some of your own writing to work on or a bottle of wine. Dance a bit. Start at 6.30 or 7pm to avoid traffic.

13. Be patient

Scene groups are your growth laboratory. They build craft, confidence and flexibility *over time*. Commit to regular attendance and you will start to notice a significant improvement in these areas.

APPENDIX 3
SCENES

MEMENTO
INT. NATALIE'S LIVING ROOM – DAY
Leonard is sitting on the coffee table, relaxed, looking at his Polaroids. Natalie (without bruises) BURSTS in through the front door, scared.

LEONARD
What's wrong?
NATALIE
Somebody's come. Already.
LEONARD
Who?
NATALIE
Calls himself Dodd.
LEONARD
What does he want?
NATALIE
Wants to know what happened to Jimmy. And his money. He thinks I have it. He thinks I took it.
LEONARD
Did you?
NATALIE
No!
LEONARD
What's this all about?
Natalie looks at him bitterly.
NATALIE
You don't know, do you? You're blissfully ignorant, aren't you?
LEONARD
I have this condition –
NATALIE
I know about your fucking condition, Leonard! I probably know more about it than you do! You don't have a fucking clue about anything else!
LEONARD
What happened?

NATALIE
What happened is that Jimmy went to meet a guy called Teddy. He took a lot of money with him and he didn't come back. Jimmy's partners think I set him up. I don't know whether you know this Teddy or how well –

Leonard is getting frustrated.

LEONARD
Neither do I.
NATALIE
Don't protect him.
LEONARD
I'm not.
NATALIE
Help me.
LEONARD
How?
NATALIE
Get rid of Dodd for me.
LEONARD
What?
NATALIE
Kill him. I'll pay you.
LEONARD
What do you think I am?! I'm not gonna kill someone for money.
NATALIE
What then? Love? What would you kill for? For your wife, right?
LEONARD
That's different.
NATALIE
Not to me! I wasn't fucking married to her!
LEONARD
Don't talk about my wife.
NATALIE
I can talk about whoever the fuck I want! You won't even remember what I say! I can tell you that your wife was a fucking whore and we can still be friends!

Leonard stands up.

LEONARD
Calm down.
NATALIE
That's easy for you to say! You can't get scared, you don't remember how, you fucking idiot!
LEONARD
Just take it easy, this isn't my fault.
NATALIE
Maybe it is! How the fuck would you know?! You don't know a fucking thing! You can't get scared, can you get angry?!

Leonard steps towards her.

LEONARD
Yes.
NATALIE
You pathetic piece of shit. I can say whatever the fuck I want and you won't have a clue, you fucking retard.
LEONARD
Shut the fuck up!

Natalie gets right in his face, grinning.

NATALIE
I'm gonna use you, you stupid fuck. I'm telling you now because I'll enjoy it more if I know that you could stop me if you weren't a freak.

Leonard grabs his Polaroids and finds one of Natalie. He reaches into his pocket for a pen, but cannot find one.

NATALIE (cont'd)
Lost your pen? That's too bad, freak. Otherwise you could've written yourself a little note about how much Natalie hates your retarded guts.

Leonard moves around the room searching for a pen. Natalie follows him, speaking into his ear.

NATALIE (cont'd)
No pens here, I'm afraid. You're never going to know that I called you a retard, and your wife a whore.

Leonard turns to face her, barely controlling his anger.

LEONARD
Don't say another fucking word!
NATALIE
About your whore of a wife?

Leonard slaps Natalie. She smiles, then speaks softly.

NATALIE (cont'd)
I read about your problem. You know what one of the causes of short term memory loss is?

Leonard fumes.

NATALIE (cont'd)
Venereal disease. Maybe your cunt of a wife sucked one too many diseased cocks and turned you into a retard.

Leonard turns away, body tensed, ready to snap. Natalie reaches out to gently brush the hair above his ear with her fingers.

NATALIE (cont'd)
You sad freak, you won't remember any of what I've said, and we'll be best friends, or even lovers.

Leonard spins around, BACKHANDING Natalie on the cheek. He PUNCHES her in the mouth then pushes her to the floor. He stands over her, furious with himself as much as her.

© AMBI DISTRIBUTION

MUNICH

Carl, Avner and Robert enter the apartment.

CARL
We followed him today from his doctor to his hotel.
AVNER
He's here for eye treatments.
STEVE
Salameh? You saw him? You followed him?
AVNER
Yes.
STEVE
Salameh?
CARL
Wearing sunglasses in the rain.
STEVE
Why didn't you shoot him?!
AVNER
He had bodyguards. Civilians.
STEVE
Were they armed? Then they're not civilians. I'd have done it! If you'd ever give me have a chance to to actually shoot someone, I'm the only one who actually wants to shoot these guys!
ROBERT
You can take my place the next time out.
CARL
Maybe that's why we never let you do it. Your enthusiasm.
AVNER
Only our target gets hurt.
ROBERT
Since when?
STEVE
Yeah, why start worrying now?
CARL
Do you have any idea how many laws we've broken?
HANS
Well, I forge the documents that get you in and over and across and

around those laws so I have some idea, yes.
CARL
Do you know how many treaties we've violated?
HANS
And still I manage to get a night's sleep, every night. It's time to stop your hand-wringing, it's counter-productive.
STEVE
Why don't you make a list of every single law, Carl, or, or...
CARL
Including, incidentally, the laws of the State of Israel, which has no death penalty.
STEVE
I'll tell you what your problem is, habibi: These guys we're killing are dressed in expensive suits, this is London and not some ugly Arab village, and that disorients you.
CARL
I'm not disoriented, I'm keeping my sanity by occasionally reminding myself that in spite of the work I do...
ROBERT
I'm going to vote that we adjourn our little minyan for the evening.
STEVE
But it's the same old war we're fighting, over the same old scrap of desert.
CARL
Remembering I'm still at least in principle a human being ...
HANS
Remembering that you're human is one thing, broadcasting it so relentlessly is something else.
HANS
(to Avner)
Are you going to call a halt to this? I'd recommend it.
CARL
A thing which I've noticed ... Some people surrender all too willingly.
ROBERT
Let's find a pub. Who besides me needs a drink?
STEVE
We've brought our war to Kensington and, and Copenhagen and it's not like these European anti-Semites don't deserve that!
Until we we learn to act like them we'll never defeat them.

CARL
We act like them, all the time. You think they invented bloodshed? How do you think we got control of the land? By being nice?

STEVE
I think we have a double-agent in our midst. Pull down his pants, see if he's circumcised.

Carl suddenly goes for Steve. Avner and Robert get in between Steve and Carl, who keep struggling to get at one another.

AVNER
Stop it! Goddamn it, stop it! Both of you! just ... Just tired and...

ROBERT
Please, please, calm down, calm down. Everyone's just... Just tired and --

HANS
Nonsense, nonsense, infantile undisciplined distraction and nonsense.

CARL (to Steve) My *son* died in '67 you foul mouthed sonofabitch! Everything you can ask I've done for Israel.

HANS (to Carl)
Get a grip on yourself! Ask for a reassignment if this is so distasteful!

CARL
Isn't it distasteful for you?!

STEVE
No. And know what? The only blood that matters to me is Jewish blood. What's your problem?
(to Avner)
Nice job leading, by the way.

Steve leaves the room, slamming the door as he leaves.

AVNER
We'll kill the bodyguards if they're armed.

CARL
They're armed.

AVNER
Then we'll kill them.

© UNIVERSAL PICTURES

IN BETWEEN LIVES

INT. TOM HACKETT'S HOUSE - BRIAN'S BEDROOM - NIGHT

Tom, now carrying a cocktail and a small can of Ensure with a straw, enters a small guest room that has been outfitted with a hospital bed and a large Barcalounger. In the chair sits Brian Sinclair, British, 78, staring straight ahead.

TOM
You scared off the nurse, Bri.
BRIAN
She was a nasty bitch. Who are you?
TOM
It's me. Tom.
BRIAN
You're not Tom. You're an old man.
TOM
We're both old now. It goes like that.
BRIAN
Speak for yourself, grandpa.
TOM
Here. Drink this.

Tom hands him the Ensure. Grabs a photo album off the table.

BRIAN
I dont' want that. Where's my dinner?
TOM
You threw it at the nurse, you troublemaker.

Brian laughs, takes it as a compliment. Then he sees the book in Hackett's hand and snatches it away.

BRIAN
I'll show you my Tommy.

As he opens the book we see photos of young Tom Hackett, with the very dashing Brian. Laughing on the dock of a ship. At dinner in Paris. Celebrating Christmas in their living room, and standing beside Tom is a teenage Cassie, laughing. Her face is open in a way we've never seen. But Brian only has eyes for young Tom...

BRIAN
Isn't he handsome? I really robbed the cradle, didn't I? What a magnificent lay.
TOM
Good to know.
(points to Cassie's photo)
Hey, remember this little waif? I saw her today. She's all grown up.
BRIAN
(nods vaguely, then)
Tom arrested her for... something.
TOM
Drinking underage. She was running the streets...
BRIAN
We practically adopted her.
TOM
That's right, we did.

Their eyes meet, and for a moment Tom thinks they've made a connection, but then Brian looks around, sad and afraid...

BRIAN
When can I go back home?

... and it's gone. Tom gestures to the Ensure.

TOM
You are home babe. One sip. Come on...

Off Tom, as Brian takes an obligatory sip...

© NBC

WHEN A MAN LOVES A WOMAN
Michael and Alices Apartment. Michael enters.

MICHAEL
You ok?
ALICE
Never better.
MICHAEL
What happened? Something at AA?
ALICE
Ah... I'll be ok. It's just a bad day.
MICHAEL
Do you want to tell me what's wrong? Something I can do?
ALICE
Ah, thank you. No.
MICHAEL
Can't fix it unless we know the problem.
ALICE
How was your meeting?
MICHAEL
First time — I'll get used to it. There was a lot of people there feeling sorry for themselves. It's like an alcoholic has ruined their lives and they'd rather be a victim that try to fix it.
ALICE
Fix it, huh?
MICHAEL
What did I do now, Alice?
ALICE
Nothing, Michael.
MICHAEL
I'm talking about some losers at my meeting. You're taking it personally.
ALICE
The trouble with these losers at your meeting is that they're not perfect, like some people. They're married to alcoholics who are about to knock the walls, and they don't know what the fuck to do, so you might be a little tolerant and give them the benefit of your expertise in problem solving.
MICHAEL
Good meeting, huh? Did you drop acid or something?

ALICE
Like I said, I'm having a really bad day and I don't mean to take it out on you.
MICHAEL
What is it? Do you want a drink really bad?
ALICE
That wouldn't distinguish it from any other day, Michael.
MICHAEL
One of your friends fall off the wagon?
ALICE
Nothing happened. Nothing has to happen for me to have a bad day. That's the thrilling part of all this. It just comes and hits like a goddamned freight train.
MICHAEL
OK. When's the next freight train coming through? Can I get a schedule? I could plan around these things so you could… smoke.
ALICE
Maybe… you shouldn't have to Michael. One of the women at my meeting is going to a halfway house because she's… she's not making it in her home environment.
MICHAEL
What?! You're actually thinking about this?
ALICE
Don't jump to conclusions.
MICHAEL
What? Excuse me for taking my life personally, Alice. What is wrong with our home? Nothing. You said it was something? What is it, huh? Is it the couch? Is it the rug? Or is it possibly, Alice, me? Is it me?
ALICE
It's not your problem.
MICHAEL
No, it's not my problem. It's just my fucking fault. Everything is my fault. My wife is not making it in her home environment. Why is that exactly?
ALICE
(crying) It's not your problem. I am not your problem to solve. It was so much fun in the old days, wasn't it? I'd get drunk, I'd pass out and you'd put me together. That was the best, huh? That made you feel good. And that's what hurts.

He pulls her close but she breaks away violently.

Scenes

ALICE
Fuck that! Fuck making it better, Michael. It's not getting better. I don't know how to make it better and I swear to God you don't either.

MICHAEL
Maybe.

ALICE
Every time you say that, every time you look at me like that I want to come right out of my skin. You've made me feel like a stupid, worthless, weak animal. I don't know how to try anymore.

MICHAEL
I'm not giving up. Sticking together — isn't that what we should be trying for?

ALICE
No, Michael. We're supposed to try to be real, and when you feel alone, you're not together and that is real. And when you don't know, you just don't know. I think I can love you again if you could for once just say 'I don't know'.

MICHAEL
I don't know. It didn't work, did it? I'll go back and pack some stuff.

ALICE
Michael, I didn't ask you to do that.

MICHAEL
No, Alice?

ALICE
No.

MICHAEL
No?

ALICE
No.

MICHAEL
Come on, let's be real. You're clean. You stay hopeless and confused. Keep polishing those skills and I'll take the heat because I have some needs of my own. When I touch someone, I like it better when their skin doesn't crawl, when -

ALICE
- that's not what -

MICHAEL
- my wife hurts and I need to say, 'What's wrong, honey? Something I can do?' And I love you, so fuck me.

© DISNEY

THE LIMEY

EXT. BEACH. NIGHT.
A rocky cove. Valentine looks back up the way he came, Wilson. A dark figure. Coming into focus. Walking inexorably this way. Valentine painfully rights himself. A small bone protrudes from his broken ankle. He FIRES at Wilson, gun in one hand, other hand gripping his wrist to try and steady it. Doing his best to aim. But the SHOTS miss their mark.
Wilson - Steadily coming.
Valentine - Out of bullets now. Gun CLICKING crazily on empty. He simply drops it. Wilson Now stands before him. The two of them both breathing hard.

WILSON
Tell me.

This is not what Valentine expected.

VALENTINE
What.
WILSON
Tell me.
VALENTINE
Tell you ...
WILSON
About Jenny.
(closer)
Tell me about Jenny.
(closer)
About the deal. Whatever fucking deal you had to kill my daughter for when she found out about it, you bastard.

Wilson drops to the ground too, in a passionate fury, starts strangling Valentine.

WILSON
Tell me. Tell me about it, you fucking bastard.

Easing up just enough for Valentine to sputter out a response.

VALENTINE
She could've had the deal! I would've handed it to her if she wanted. I would have given her everything.
WILSON
Why then. Why did you do it!

They're locked in a kind of embrace. Sprayed by the waves crashing into the rocks. Sweating and gasping and exhausted and hurt and furious.

VALENTINE
She didn't want to share it, she wanted to stop it. To stop me. She said she'd turn me in.

Wilson - Shock of recognition on his face. At those words.

VALENTINE
She said, "You go ahead with this, I'll turn you in, Terry."

Wilson sits back. Panting. Totally spent. The two of them. Both on the ground now. Whatever energy they had left drained -- Valentine from his confession, Wilson from hearing it. Valentine shaking, sobbing. Still not realizing the pathetic folly of his actions.

VALENTINE
She was serious. She would have done it. She had the phone in her hand. She was going to do it.

Wilson - knows that the girl he loved ... loved Valentine, too. Having heard the truth, the last vestige of revenge has vanished. He gets up and walks away. Leaving the quivering shell of Valentine behind.

© LIONSGATE ENTERTAINMENT

RECOMMENDATIONS FOR FURTHER LEARNING

Continuous learning means keeping an eye on what you may need to pull up in your work. When I started acting there was little around in the way of professional development in New Zealand outside of the (then) two major drama schools, and acting books. Thankfully that has changed! There are now visiting teachers, brilliant masterclasses, online resources, good local teachers, and more. Here are some ideas of how you can further your learning:

- Become a member of your union, Equity (fees start at about the cost of one coffee a week). They have a regular e-newsletter that includes information about upcoming workshops. You'll pay a special equity price for some of them, but most are free.
- Chip in with some friends and buy the all-round pass to Masterclass.com - they have classes on just about everything; acting, directing, writing etc.
- There are websites where you can find TV scripts and screenplays – the *BBC Writersroom* is amazing. The BBC also have online workshops from time to time. Reading scripts is hugely worthwhile. And you can use the scenes you find in your own scene group (see Appendix 3).
- *Britain's National Theatre*, *The Met* and Britain's *Globe Theatre* all film their shows and these are readily available online. Save yourself the price of a plane trip and still catch the best of international performance. It's inspiring stuff.
- Classes are a great place to meet people and find your peer group. So, many actors from my classes end up getting together and creating work themselves – everything from Improv to web series. There's now a good choice of weekly classes in Auckland – and in places like Sydney, Melbourne, LA and London there's an embarrassment of training opportunities.
- Watch content: go to the theatre/ binge-watch content or watch the 'Making Of's' documentaries on Netflix, then discuss with friends.
- Attend any weekend workshops of visiting master teachers, and others that may help your employment prospects: professional development programs and workshops, Equity Casting Hothouses etc.
- Work body, voice and accent practice into your weekly routine. Classes are important but in the end progress comes down to your personal regular practice.

USEFUL BOOKS AND RESOURCES

Much of what I teach, understand, and have included in this book is owed to the following books and resources.

For Technique

Audition, Michael Shurtleff

This book is almost half a century old, but it's packed with the wisdom of Shurtleff's decades of experience working at the highest levels of Broadway and Hollywood. A brilliant study of both auditions and acting. Shurtleff's key ideas, such as role-playing and the importance of humour and discoveries, are peppered through this book.

Different Every Night, Mike Alfreds

Alfreds' book will take you a year to read and then you'll have to start all over again because you've forgotten half of it. It's the summation of the man's life's work (although I recently discovered he's written yet another; a horrifying thought). He has great exercises for understanding actions and circumstances. There's lots of good stuff on Character too.

Tricks, tools and good advice

A Practical Handbook for the Actor, Melissa Bruder

This book is the bible of the Atlantic Theatre Company and Acting school. The company and school were founded by William H Macy and David Mamet; noted Alumni include Rose Byrne. Mamet *seems* to pick up on just one aspect of acting, actions, and argue that they are, pretty much, ALL the actor needs. In the handbook Bruder calls intentions 'actions' - as per the Stella Adler terminology popular in the States. So, be clear about what you're reading. I teach a version of Bruder and Mamet's technique, calling what they describe *Scene Actions*.

Michael Caine Teaches Acting In Film, (1987), Youtube

Acting in Film (book)

Caine is very good for film acting and like Bryan Cranston (see below) instructive on professionalism and how to live as an actor ('be sane in your home so you can be crazy in your work', as Cranston puts it).

On being Human

If the story of what makes us human interests you, read Will Storr's book *Selfie* (which informs much of the *Telling Tales* chapter) and anything by Yuval Noah Harari – particularly *21 Questions for the 21st Century* and *Sapiens: A brief history of Humankind*.

ACTING & How To Survive It

Emotion

If you'd like to delve deeper into Eric Morris' work in irreverence, inclusion and unblocking emotion, he has written about eight books, four of which I've read. Of those I found *Irreverent Acting* and *Freeing the Actor* the most helpful.

Accents

For standard American:
Achieving the Standard American Accent, The Corff Voice Studio.
For Standard English:
How to do Standard English Accents, Edda Sharpe and Jan Haydn Rowles.
All other English accents:
How to do Accents, Edda Sharpe and Jan Haydn Rowles.

Living

A life in Parts, Bryan Cranston

Actor's biographies can be inspiring; if nothing else you'll see your own doubts and dilemmas reflected reassuringly back at you, plus a happy ending. Bryan Cranston's is an antidote to the insularity of some approaches to acting. He refreshingly tells us that his craft is cobbled together from his imagination, personal experience, talent and research - ALL. He's the consummate professional jobbing actor.

The War of Art, Steven Pressfield

This is a small paperback – you can read it in an afternoon – but if it lands on your coffee table at the right time of your life, it can have a profound effect. Pressfield is a terrific personal coach at helping you wrestle with your personal blocks and inhibitions. Highly recommended.

The Head Game

Anything by Oliver Burkeman is a bracing antidote to the present day virus of positive thinking. In *Range*, David Epstein, the patron Saint of late bloomers, uses recent research to argue that late specialisation and early sampling are important to creative thinking and high achievement, especially in wicked (not kind) learning environments – which acting undoubtedly is.

On Failure

F Word, David Harewood,
In this documentary, British actor David Harewood explores the rejection and setbacks of the acting profession and how important failure has been in the careers of him and his actor friends, such as Damian Lewis. Harewood believes actors need to recognise failure's creative usefulness.

Chasing Great, Feature Documentary on Richie McCaw
Watch and look out for Richie McCaw's mighty 1B4 notebook.

Inspiration

True and False, David Mamet
Mamet's is a lively and confronting read. He manages to be somehow cynical *and* inspirational at the same time.

The Film Director's Intuition: Script Analysis and Rehearsal Techniques (2003) and Directing Actors (2019), Judith Weston
These two books very nearly dissuaded me writing this one, as I knew they could not be surpassed. Here are the insights of a great mind who has also been in the game of acting, a portal through which every great teacher of acting must pass. There's a sprinkle of magic in Weston's writing, an ability to comprehend and communicate the unseen. Written for directors, there's a great deal for the actor to pick out.

Respect for Acting, Uta Hagen
Hagen was greatly respected in New York as an actor and teacher in her time, and once you have figured out your spine of craft – what works for you – she's great to go to for left field ideas, exercises and quotes.

Online Masterclasses
Check out Masterclass.com. Everyone from Jodie Foster to Dustin Hoffman now has an online masterclass. Highly recommended.

The Empty Space, Peter Brook
An oldie but a goodie – a cry from the artistic wilderness calling for authenticity and honesty in theatre.

Dear Writer, Dear Actress: The Love Letters of Anton Chekhov And Olga Knipper, Methuen 1996, edited by Jean Benedetti – all the letters, about 400 each, of this remarkable and touching correspondence that reminds us how creative differences are normal, and how doubt and crisis tend to accompany any meaningful creative effort.

Life in Stages S1 Ep4: Bill Nighy, Andrew Lincoln and Chiwetel Ejiofor in conversation at the NT
Bill Nighy quotes are peppered throughout this book, and they are all from this interview with him - https://www.youtube.com/watch?v=SOSlo4AqvVs. It's part of the wonderful National Theatre series of discussions between actors. Subscribe to the National Theatre on YouTube to see them all.

The Actor & the Text; Text in Action, Cicely Berry
Cicely has written many books; these are just two that happen to adorn my library at home. At the heart of Cicely's work is setting the voice and the actor free from inhibitions she sees as being the result of the conditioning of a warped society.

SELF-TAPE SOFTWARE GUIDE

Below is some info and links (current at the time of writing) to different freeware programs that you can use for editing and compression.

Editing

iMovie: Free editing software for Mac or iOS (available in the app store)
https://www.youtube.com/watch?v=aRLT9L_L1Pw

Da Vinci Resolve 16: Free editing software for Windows/ Mac
https://www.blackmagicdesign.com/nz/products/davinciresolve/
Full tutorial: https://www.youtube.com/watch?v=52vK5mzl1jQ

Compression

HandBrake: https://handbrake.fr/downloads.php - downloadable software that compresses MP4, AVI or MOV easily.

PS2PDF: https://www.ps2pdf.com/compress-mp4 - online software for MP4 or MOV files.

ACKNOWLEDGMENTS

Good teachers give a puff into our rigging that keeps us sailing for quite some time. It's who they are that stays with us, as much as what we've learnt from them. So first and foremost I'd like to thank Dean Carey and the late Cicely Berry, two formative teachers of mine, for their example and inspiration.

Miranda Harcourt's influences have leached into my own teaching practice over the years.: I've worked with her, observed her coaching, and acted with two of her children. So it's no surprise that much of her wisdom has ended up in these pages. Thank you Cicely, Miranda and Dean too for your support at different times when I was taking my first steps into teaching.

I've worked with Rob Marchand on several occasions, and on his watch first felt the transformational possibilities of character work. I heard about Key-wording from casting director Tom McSweeney, and a workshop with Dave Newman gleaned many useful insights for the *Self-Tests* chapter.

I've been inspired by many of the acting books I've read. Mike Alfreds' *Different Every Night* informed much of the *Character* chapters. Judith Weston's books were also most helpful, particularly for *The Head Game* section of this book.

Steve Logan, the first-ever reader of this book, was a great cheerleader; Tim Carlsen you were a rigourous and insightful reader as well. This book is a lot better thanks to the two of you. Thanks as well to Lisette Prendé for her help navigating the rocky roads of writing and publishing - just your adage, 'write a shitty first draft!' was invaluable. Emma Campbell proof read the work at two different stages of progress and picked up a scandalous quantity of errors. Mark Mitchinson suggested I write a book about acting in the first place - please blame him if you don't like it!

Gratitude is also owed to all the crew, actors and directors who have put up with me over the years, and who I have learnt so much from. Big ups to those actors who kindly shared their process of work: Lisa, Tammy, Neil, Emmett, Joel, Bronwyn and Jennifer. And a huge thank you to Alikki Vernon and David Moore, who hosted me in pre-pandemic Melbourne in 2019, while I filmed the Network 10 show *Playing for Keeps*, and wrote the first draft of this book. What a long time ago that feels!

Last and never least: fulsome thanks are due to my wife, Nic; first for putting up with me at all. But then, to add insult to injury, she also designed and edited the book. Nic: we did it!

ABOUT THE AUTHOR

Peter Feeney's professional acting career began in 1994 after an Honours degree in Politics and History from *Melbourne University*, graduate study in Moscow and a Diploma of Drama from *Auckland University*. Since then his square jaw has been a familiar screen presence, on both sides of the Tasman, in Australian, Kiwi, US and UK TV and film roles.

Feeney has made a virtue of the necessity to diversify in order to sustain a creative life in a small country. On the other side of the camera, he's been a casting director (including for the TV series *The Amazing Extraordinary Friends*, in which he also acted). Since 2001 he has taught acting; from 2004 at his boutique acting school in Auckland, *The Actors Lab Studio*. Feeney has also turned his hand to theatre acting and directing. His New Zealand adaptation of Australian play *Milo's Wake* was a hit for its Auckland and nationwide seasons in 2005 and 2006. His one-man show *A Night with Beau Tyler* (an adaptation of his Memphis Meltdown persona that ran in a series of television commercials) toured New Zealand in 2008 and 2009. Peter is currently writing and developing various projects, including filming a television adaptation of his acclaimed coming of age novel *Blind Bitter Happiness*.

Peter is represented by Kathryn Rawlings in New Zealand and Lisa Mann Creative Management in Australia. He lives with his wife and three children in Castor Bay, New Zealand.

To buy more copies of 'Acting and How to Survive It', or to find out more about Actors Lab studio, visit www.actorslab.co.nz.

www.ingramcontent.com/pod-product-compliance
Lightning Source LLC
Chambersburg PA
CBHW051351290426
44108CB00015B/1966